FootprintAfrica

Egypt
Nile Valley & R

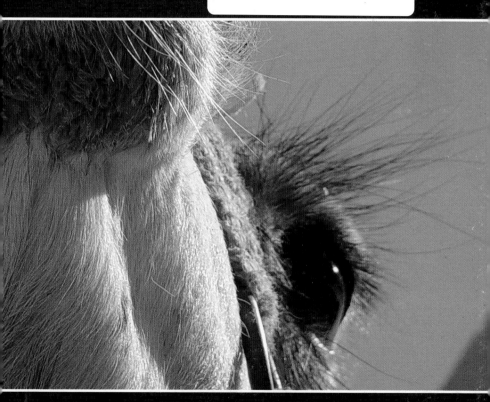

Kelly Pipes

Introducing
the region

About
the region

Cairo

Luxor

Aswan,
Abu Simbel &
Lake Nasser

The Red Sea

Practicalities

Contents

About the author

Kelly Pipes is a British writer and editor who has single-mindedly dedicated her career to the travel industry and genre. Various assignments for guidebook publishers and holiday companies have sent her all over, from glitzy launches of gargantuan cruise ships to stalking vintage trams on a wet weekend in Portugal. More at home practising yoga or swimming in the ocean than transport spotting, she perfected her scuba skills as well as the downward-facing dog whilst working on this book in Dahab. Yoga-diving is next on her agenda.

Acknowledgements

Firstly, a huge thank you to Vanessa Betts, author of Footprint's Egypt Handbook, the sound foundation upon which this book was compiled. Thanks and love to the following people: Dan Crack for his constant support and for teaching me to play backgammon and most importantly how to win! Dan, Fleur Stanford and Ryan Mowat: dive buddies extraordinaire; also Jane Ackroyd. Desert Divers' guides and instructors for their patience and passion. Cheers to Liam for the calming Bedouin tea, Jimmy Mohamed and Father-in-law Mohammed Ali, 'Barracuda' for decanting his herbal stomach cure, and my favourite taxi driver in Hurghada. Appreciation and thanks must also go to Mara, Aladin Al-Sahaby, Karin Coolen, Tanis and Said Khedr, Farag Soliman, Mohamed Salah Keylany, Noha, Robin Woods, Tamar, Wouter van Gent, the James and Mac Diving Center, Andrew Heiss and Shaimaa, for their input into this guidebook and help along the way.

And finally, thanks and respect to the Footprint team for bringing this guide to fruition, you know who you all are, especially Alan, Angus and Kassia, and to the authors of *Diving the World* for your facts and concise copy.

About the book

The guide is divided into four sections: Introducing the region; About the region; Around the region and Practicalities.

Introducing the region comprises: **At a glance** (which explains how the region fits together); **Best of Egypt Red Sea & Nile Valley** (top 20 highlights); **Month by month** (a guide to pros and cons of visiting at certain times of year); and **Screen & page** (a list of suggested books and films).

About the region comprises: **History**; **Art & architecture**; **Egypt Red Sea & Nile Valley today** (which presents different aspects of life in the region today); **Nature & environment**; **Festivals & events**; **Sleeping** (an overview of accommodation options); **Eating & drinking** (an overview of the region's cuisine, as well as advice on eating out); **Entertainment** (an overview of the region's cultural credentials, explaining what entertainment is on offer); **Shopping** (the region's specialities and recommendations for the best buys); and **Activities & tours**.

Around the city/region is then broken down into four areas, each with its own chapter. Here you'll find all the main sights and at the end of each chapter is a listings section with all the best sleeping, eating & drinking, entertainment, shopping and activities & tours options plus a brief overview of public transport.

Sleeping price codes
€€€€ over €142 (US$200, E£1610) per night for a double room in high season
€€€ €71-141 (US$100-200, E£805-1610)
€€ €35-70 (US$50-100, E£402-805)
€ under €35 (US$50, E£402)

Eating & drinking price codes
€€€ over €21 (US$30, E£241) per person for a 2-course meal with a drink, including service and cover charge
€€ €14-21 (US$20-30, E£160-241)
€ under €14 (US$20, E£160)

Picture credits

Mosque of Abu El-Haggag, Luxor Temple.

Contents

Dunes of the Great Sand Sea.

Introducing the region

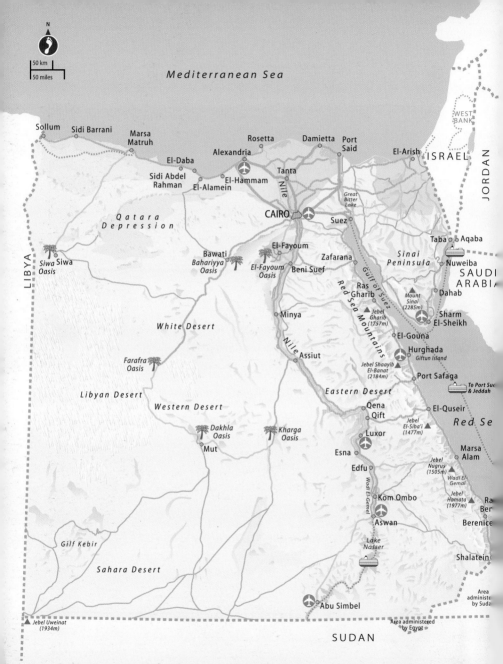

Introduction

Egypt will astound you. The ancient rulers, rituals and ruins that captivated you as a curious child stand open for exploration. At every turn there are sights and sounds that previously only ever lived in your imagination; camels feeding at the side of dusty rural tracks, the call to prayer from a dozen minarets clashing outside your window and clouds of sheesha smoke rising above backgammon boards. Likewise, Egypt's natural wonders – epic desert terrain to multicoloured marine life – will leave you breathless.

Many things will, however, catch first-time visitors off guard, including the carefree passage of 'Egyptian time,' the unceremonious melding of grandiose ancient relics with disorderly everyday life, and the tenacious market traders who leave you guessing how you and your cash came to be parted. It can be a frenetic or ultimately laid-back country, depending on where exactly you happen to be. One day everywhere is as claustrophobic as the epicentre of Cairo's Khan El-Khalili market, the next as liberating as standing alone beneath a blanket of stars in the Sinai Desert. These things and more make this a genuinely affecting destination, rich with experiences that both bewitch and bewilder. Egypt's complexities are so dense and multifaceted that they could take you a lifetime to unravel, driving you to delve a little deeper every time, *insha'allah* (God willing), that you return.

At a glance

A whistle-stop tour of Egypt Nile Valley & Red Sea

Pulsating Cairo, the apex of metropolitan madness, is the first stop for the majority of sightseers who come to experience legendary ancient sites and gilded treasures. Along the Nile Valley, pharaonic monuments reign supreme. Abydos and Dendara defy all logic with their perfect engraving and reliefs, while Luxor, the Karnak Temple and the Valley of the Kings have been mesmerizing travellers for millennia. Cruise to Aswan, passing through emerald green landscapes that clash with apricot sands, down to Nubia. Then strike off across the Eastern Desert for the coast, switching freshwater sailing for salt-water diving among the thriving coral gardens of the Red Sea.

Cairo

Few capital cities leave as deep an impression on first-time visitors as Cairo. This metropolis stands at the crossroads of Asia, Africa and Europe, the largest city in the Middle East and Africa. The Nile runs like a vein through the centre and on either bank the extraordinary remains of civilizations past intermingle with the dwellings and lives of modern Egyptians. Wonder and awe are visitors' standard reactions as they stand dwarfed by the monumental Pyramids of Giza. Then, face to face with unfathomably ancient treasures at the Egyptian Museum, most could stand and stare at King Tut's burial mask long after closing time. Add to this the crazy culture shock of present-day Cairo that hits you the first time you encounter the horn-honking, swarming traffic. Not to mention

Decorative shop front in Islamic Cairo.

the cacophony of an estimated 16-million-strong population going about their daily business, criss-crossing between the car bumpers. But nowhere in the city seethes with as much life as Islamic Cairo, packed with mausoleums, mosques and markets – the most famous being the maze of the Khan El-Khalili. Beyond this are mega malls, diverse restaurants and varied nightlife to suit everyone – whether a revolving restaurant, all-night *ahwas* (coffee shops) or belly-dancing shows are your thing.

The lowdown

Money matters
Depending on standards of comfort and cleanliness that you are prepared to accept for accommodation, food and travel, it is still possible to survive on as little as E£55-85 per person per day. However, prices for everything are constantly rising. Also bear in mind additional costs including a 12% tax on to bills in sit-down restaurants plus a 10% tip, and *baksheesh* (a modest tip) that is expected in return for a variety of small services.

Opening hours and etiquette
Museums generally close for Friday prayers at noon, around 1200-1400. Do not enter mosques during a service and take photographs only after asking or when clearly permissible. Shoes must be removed when visiting mosques and other religious buildings and women should cover their heads. Men should never enter the area designated solely for women.

Discounts
Full-time students with an International Student Identity Card (ISIC) receive substantial discounts (up to 50%) on many forms of transport (air, sea, rail) and at most ancient sights and museums. Before you leave for Egypt, contact ISIC (isic.org) for details. In Cairo, cards can be obtained from Egyptian Student Travel Services (ESTS), 23 Sharia Al-Manial, Roda, T02-2531 0330, estsegypt.com. Bring a photograph and E£93.

Tourist information
The provision of tourist information is variable. Offices in bigger cities do tend to be quite well equipped but where they fall short, hoteliers and other travellers are often better sources of reliable travel information.

Alf Leila German bakery, Dahab.

Introducing the region

Luxor

Second only to the Pyramids as Egypt's most visited attraction, this ancient capital is among the world's oldest tourist destinations. Located in the hotter, drier reaches of Upper Egypt, Luxor has an overwhelming number of well-preserved sandstone temples and elaborate tombs. Many

Top: Karnak Temple, East Bank, Luxor.
Above: The Nile at Luxor.

deem it the world's greatest open-air museum and even the most avid of Egyptologists are selective about what they hope to see in one visit. Splitting your time equally between the city's East and West Bank is a wise move. Karnak Temple on the East, is a vast and beautifully preserved complex built over a span of more than 1000 years, and a highlight of any trip if you time your visit right. Close by is Luxor Temple, once a refuge for every great religion that thrived in ancient Egypt, it rises gracefully alongside the Nile. Crossing to the West Bank takes you into what the ancient Egyptians knew as The City of the Dead, where the dramatic desert landscape is spotted by magnificent mortuary temples and the tombs of Kings, Queens and Nobles. Broaden your Luxor experience away from the cool yet crowded corridors of the burial chambers with an exploration of the West Bank villages or a gentle sunset felucca ride.

Aswan, Abu Simbel & Lake Nasser

The Nile Valley between Aswan and Luxor may be home to some of the world's most stunning monuments, but in this region it is the Nile that is the luminary and the central vein. For 228 km, the ancient river languidly meanders past the stripes of crops with ibis paddling in their watery furrows, ancient sandstone quarries, donkey's turning wooden waterwheels and sheep among the sugar cane. The further south you venture, the more

Feluccas in a Nubian village.

apparent the melding of Africa and Arabia becomes. Aswan, the provincial capital, is populated largely by Nubians, a taller and darker-skinned people with a unique language and tradition. Endless time can be lost exploring nearby islands, wandering amid Nubian villages and reclining on feluccas. After the Pyramids and the Sphinx, Abu Simbel, adorned with four enormous colossi of Ramsis II, is the defining image of Egypt. Just 40 km north of the Sudanese border, the temple was erected as testimony to the Pharaoh's might for anyone who dared approach from the south. Three millennia later, the monument's sheer size still inspires awe.

The Red Sea

Beyond the mountains of the Eastern Desert, the diving is supreme. The Red Sea coast stretches from Suez down towards Hurghada, encompassing the enclaves around Ain Soukna and becoming increasingly beautiful as it extends south. With no rivers flowing into the sea to disrupt the translucent waters, the coral reefs blossom undisturbed and shelter a thriving expanse of brilliantly coloured fish and marine life. Hurghada attracts the bulk of tourists to who come to party and scores of scuba-divers are drawn here to experience the profusion of underwater delights. The plush and extensive resort of nearby El-Gouna, built on a succession of islands, often feels more like Europe than it does Egypt. Some 80 km south of Hurghada is the small, sleepy port town El-Quseir, a peaceful little place with narrow pastel-toned streets and accommodation that suits backpackers. The name 'Quseir' means 'short' as this was the starting point both of the shortest sea-route to Mecca and the shortest way to the Nile Valley, five days away overland by camel. Located in a small inlet sheltered by a coral reef, the modern road inland from El-Quseir to Qift, just south of Qena, follows an ancient pharaonic route that is lined with forts. Further south is the tiny fishing village of Marsa Alam. Its small harbour is nestled in a beautiful area where swathes of untouched coastline are dotted with appealing and environmentally aware campsites and guesthouses.

Church at St Catherine's Monastery, Sinai.

Across the waters of the Gulf of Suez is Sinai, a triangular wedge of earth home to just 340,000 people. Trekkers and pilgrims journey from afar to scramble up the splendid face of Mount Sinai with a reverence that is matched by that of the convergent divers and snorkellers who gather on the coastal regions. Ras Mohammed National Park, at the peninsula's southern tip, is a remarkable sanctuary to every species of life that thrives in the Red Sea, while Sharm El-Sheikh's 60-km of rainbow-coloured reef, dramatic drop offs and breathtaking formations are unparalleled anywhere else in the diving world. Dahab, to the north of Sharm, is a place where time dissolves into tea, smoke and the ever-changing colours of the surrounding mountains. It also provides easy access to the some of the world's best shore diving. For palm-reef huts, candlelight and cheap rooms, backpackers head a little further north to the unspoiled beaches that are just a stone's throw across the water from Saudi Arabia.

Best of Egypt Nile Valley & Red Sea

Top 20 things to see and do

❶ Pyramids of Giza

Three phenomenal ancient burial structures under the surveillance of the Sphinx rise up from a sandy plateau on the very edge of Cairo. Few sightseeing experiences top being dwarfed by the colossal Great Pyramid of Cheops, the only one of the Seven Wonders of the ancient world that still stands. Page 96.

❷ Egyptian Museum

Displaced by tomb robbers and archaeological excavation, some 136,000 ancient pharaonic materials, including the mummified remains of kings, queens and crocodiles, are now cocooned inside this must-visit museum. Be there when it opens and head straight to the Tutankhamen galleries in an attempt to beat the crowds. Page 77.

❸ Khan El-Khalili

'The Khan' is the vast maze of souks that are an essential ingredient of any visit to Cairo. Dating back to 1382 and traditionally divided by professions, it has streets that almost exclusively sell gold, silver, copper, perfume, spices, clothes or touristy souvenirs. It's traditional to start your bargaining at a third of the quoted price. Page 83.

1 Pyramids of Giza.

3 Khan El-Khalili.

6 Abydos.

8 Nile cruises.

❹ Saqqara Step Pyramid

If you can squeeze in one extra sight before leaving the Cairo region, make it this. Set within the vast necropolis of the first pharaohs, King Zoser's stepped pyramid illustrates exactly how the ancient architects made the leap from simple underground tombs to the audacious concept of the Pyramid of Cheops at Giza. Page 100.

❺ Pyramids of Dahshur

This is how pyramids appear in your imagination. The monoliths of the Red Pyramid and the Bent Pyramid loom mightily at Dahshur, all the more so when the sun sinks into the desert horizon turning the expanse of sky pink and the pyramids a steely grey, until eventually they melt completely into the darkness. Page 100.

❻ Abydos

As the holiest town of all for the ancient Egyptians, pilgrims were journeying here as far back as 2181 BC. The stunning temple of Seti I is its centrepiece, housing some of the most exquisitely carved reliefs of any monument in the country. Details in the faces, jewellery and hairstyles are utterly transfixing. Page 138.

❼ Luxor's West Bank

For many visitors, touring the sun-baked temples and snug subterranean burial chambers of the Theban Necropolis and the Valley of the Kings is Egypt's archaeological highlight. Concealed within the West Bank's arid landscape of limestone hills and valleys, these miraculous remains display the leviathan human effort that the ancients lavished on their dead. Page 126.

❽ Nile cruises

A meander along the ancient and enchanting Nile is a must and there are craft and cruises to suit every traveller's taste. Local feluccas sailing at sunset are one of Egypt's most splendid sights and they're the authentic way to take in the temples between Luxor and Aswan. For comfort choose a cruise boat, for colonial elegance a *dahabiya*. Page 156.

❾ Aswan High Dam

The contrast between the view of the narrow river channel looking towards Aswan on the downstream side of the dam and the vast area of Lake Nasser, almost like an open sea, as you look upstream, could not be more marked. Page 162.

❿ Lake Nasser

If funds allow, take a luxurious and unforgettable cruise. The juxtaposition of crystalline blue water teeming with life and the harsh, dry desert outlining it is striking and makes man-made Lake Nasser a treat to explore. Besides the wide variety of migrating birds, there are fox, gazelle and huge crocodiles that live off the shallows and shores. Page 172.

Introducing the region

① Abu Simbel

Just 40 km north of the Sudanese border, the magnificent Sun Temple of Ramses the Great looks out over Nasser's vast sapphire water. Stay overnight to appreciate the utterly sleepy atmosphere and have a chance of seeing the temples in total isolation before the tour groups pass through. Page 169.

② Island temple of Philae

Few would dispute that among the most beautiful and romantic monuments in the whole of Egypt are the Philae temples, which were built on Philae Island as an offering to Isis. If you see just one sound-and-light show on your travels, let it be this one. Page 159.

③ Red Sea monasteries

These isolated pilgrimage sites lay hidden in the folds of the Red Sea Mountains, attracting thousands of Coptic Christians and travellers who toured the monasteries' exquisite frescoes and the tiny caves where the saints supposedly once lived. Page 197.

④ Live-aboard diving safaris

Covering the same incredible sites as the daily boats, but hitting them at different times of the day to avoid the crowds, live-aboards offer a far more intimate diving experience. Page 63.

⑤ El Quseir

A sleepy coastal village dominated by a 16th-century fortress, where daytime swimming and snorkelling is followed by an evening *sheesha* on the beach. It has a unique atmosphere that combines a sense of history and a tangible presence of Islam that is heightened by the sound emanating from its 33 mosques. Page 193.

⑥ Ras Mohammed

Where the land is barren and the water an explosion of colour, Egypt's renowned national park is every scuba-diver's dream come true. This extraordinary ecosystem encompasses virtually every life form thriving in the Red Sea, including

15 El-Quseir.

16 Ras Mohammed.

the brightly coloured fish that live on the coral reef, turtles and deep-water species including sharks, tuna and barracuda. Page 65 and 201.

⑰ Wreck diving
Satellite images indicate over 1800 wrecks on the bed of the Red Sea, most of which lay at rest around the dangerous Straits of Gubal at the mouth of the Gulf of Suez. Experienced divers can access sites including Second World War casualty Thistlegorm, re-discovered by Jacques Cousteau in 1956, from Hurghada or Sharm El-Sheikh. Page 224.

⑱ St Catherine's Monastery & Mount Sinai
The site of Moses' burning bush was marked by an Orthodox monastery in the 10th century. Attracting pilgrims and visitors ever since, it is one of Egypt's most important sites. Behind it, 3700 steps lead up to the summit of Mount Sinai, where Moses received the wisdom of the Ten Commandments. Sunrise or sunset here is spectacular. Page 206.

⑲ Dahab
With a name meaning 'gold' in Arabic, Dahab shimmers as a watersports and chill-out zone. Boasting world-class windsurfing conditions, challenging trekking and bouldering, plus an addictive diving culture, travellers linger here to over-indulge in adrenaline rather than on an all-inclusive package deal. Page 202.

⑳ Sinai desert safaris
Set off inland from Dahab by jeep or camel with a Bedouin guide for treks around the Sinai, sleeping in the surrounding oases and dining under diamond-studded skies on handmade bread, coal-cooked meat and vegetables. While a few hours are sufficient to absorb the desert's tranquillity over a cup of sweet tea, take a few days and you will reset your soul. Page 226.

20 Sinai desert safaris.

Month by month

A year in Egypt Nile Valley & Red Sea

This is, of course, a desert country where the sun shines the whole year round. So while the timing of your visit does not illustrate your propensity to hot or cold weather, it probably does say something about your available budget. Egypt's year, best described in terms of 'winter' and 'summer', swings from high to low tourist season. The thought of exploring exposed tombs and temples with little shade, or stewing under poolside parasols, simply doesn't appeal to the majority of European holidaymakers. They'd much rather pay high season prices to avoid the long, hot summer months. Alternatively, visitors who can face higher temperatures find that flights and hotel prices are slashed or are at least negotiable during this time, and what's more the monuments and Red Sea dive sites will be far quieter.

Winter: October to April

Temperature-wise, October to April is generally the best time for travelling in Egypt. Cairo will be at its coolest between December and February, but daytime temperatures rarely sneak below 20°C. Admittedly, the sporadic cloudy haze over the city doesn't make this prime time for photographing the Giza Pyramids against clear blue skies. Precipitation is obviously fleeting (which contributes to the high of the Red Sea), but the few rainy days there are fall mainly in January and February. Also at this time of year in Cairo you could experience, on one of those rare days in March and April, a *khamsin* (hot winds that can whip up a sandstorm) blowing into town from the deserts.

The temperature increases as you travel south, with Luxor always 10°C warmer than the capital. It's these moderate temperatures and perfect bone-warming sunshine enjoyed by the Nile Valley during the winter that make it peak season for the Nile cruises. In fact, there's a running joke in Aswan, 'we have the best weather in the world… in the winter.' And it's true. In December, temperatures average a lovely 30°C.

Things are a little different in the Sinai interior where, during the winter months, the mountains and the sands of the desert are freezing at night, and, while sleeping under the stars is still possible, you have to be well prepared for the cold.

Meanwhile on the Red Sea coast the climate is more forgiving with temperatures consistently hovering around 26°C. While divers who have become well-acquainted with Egypt's dive sites during summer might notice that the soft coral

Dakhla oasis.

are slightly flaccid and the fish a little less animated at this time of year, there's an increased chance of seeing manta rays during their mating season – January and February, to the north of Hurghada.

Summer: May to September

As urban life heats up during summer in the capital, to uncomfortable temperatures in the high 30s, Cairnes engineer their escape to the coast (although normally not before the year's lively *moulid* celebrations have drawn to a close in May).

Be prepared for scorching heat if planning to explore the Nile Valley during these months – it can hit 50°C in Aswan between June and August. Hunt out a swimming pool for cooling dips; the Nile is not an option! Temperatures are lower on the Red Sea coast – in the mid to high 30s. Most hotels have pools and, if not, crystal-clear open

water abounds. Scuba-divers should note that, during summer, the colliding currents off Sharm El-Sheikh, at the Ras Umm Sidd site for example, bring about an abundance of pelagic (ocean going) marine life. While on dry land in late summer, thousands of white stork stop over at Ras Mohammed to rest during their annual migration to East Africa.

The holy month of Ramadan can make for special memories of summer in Egypt, see page 46. Residents will work different hours to normal during the day, and at night there's a festival atmosphere with fairy lights decorating the streets. Dependent on the lunar calendar, it is predicted the month-long festival of Ramadan will start 11 August 2010 and 1 August 2011.

Screen & page

Egypt in film & literature

Cleopatra
Joseph Leo Mankiewicz, 1963
No matter how historically inaccurate, it is Elizabeth Taylor's portrayal of the Queen of the Nile – dramatic with jet-black blunt fringe and thick winged eyeliner – that remains seared to the collective imagination. Otherwise this long-winded production is better known for the on-set extra-marital affairs between its leading lady and gent than for its cinematic genius.

Death on the Nile
John Guillermin, 1978
Agatha Christie's famous 'who done it' showcases dazzling Egyptian backdrops as the cast cruise between Luxor and Aswan, while the murderer picks them off one by one.

Raiders of the Lost Ark
Steven Spielberg, 1981
In this classic action-adventure movie everyone's favourite archaeologist, Indiana Jones, travels to Cairo and into the desert to thwart the dastardly plans of relic-obsessed Nazis.

The English Patient
Anthony Minghella, 1996
This Oscar winner, set in the Egyptian desert, plays out the dying memories of a troubled mapmaker who was injured in a plane crash during the Second World War. Ralph Fiennes, Juliette Binoche and Willem Dafoe star.

The Mummy and The Mummy Returns
Stephen Sommers, 1999, 2001
The core of the Mummy series, set in 1926 and then 1933 Egypt (yet filmed elsewhere, including in Morocco and Jordan), these all-action blockbusters unleash swarms of flesh-eating scarabs and the none-too-impressed resurrected mummy of High Priest Imhotep. Brendan Fraser and Rachel Weisz star.

Film locations in Egypt, or are they?

Huge taxes levied on foreign film companies since the 1990s mean that although films are set in Egypt they are never actually filmed in Egypt. The English Patient is a case in point, using Tunisia to stand in for the Egyptian desert. Despite this, the awesome scenery still inspired an influx of tourists to visit the Gilf Plateau in Egypt's Western Desert.

The Nile.

Yousef Chahine
Any film (there are 37) by the director Yousef Chahine will be a quality initiation into Egyptian cinema, and some of his masterpieces are available with subtitles. Look for *Al Nasser Salah-Ad-Din* and *Iskandriya Ley*? (Alexandria Why?).

Books

Letters from Egypt
Lady Lucie Duff-Gordon, 1863-1865
As inspiring as they are fascinating, these collected letters share the experiences of a lone female expat living in 19th-century Luxor.

Flaubert In Egypt: A Sensibility on Tour
Gustav Flaubert, 1872
A collection of personal writings characterized by a signature turn of phrase that's as humorous today as it was scandalous in the mid-1800s. It recounts the writer's 1849 journey through the bazaars and brothels of Cairo, and down the Nile.

Palace Walk
Naguib Mahfouz, 1956
From the Don of Arabic literature, who passed away in 2006 after aggravating the Islamists with his critiques of the establishment for so many years. The Nobel Prize winner's novels aren't always that accessible to the Western reader, but this slim volume is a good entry point into Mahfouz's world and the backstreets of Cairo where he grew up.

The Key to Rebecca
Ken Follet, 1981
A pulse-racing adventure story set in the Second World War that teams up a Jewish girl and a stalwart hero to stop the Nazis unlocking the secrets of Cairo. It's a good beach read.

In An Antique Land
Amitav Ghosh, 1998
Having lived in the tiny Egyptian village of Lataifa in the 1980s, this Man Booker Prize shortlister has woven the magic of everyday life into a biography of the country that stretches from the Crusades to Operation Desert Storm.

Apricots On the Nile – A Memoir with Recipes
Colette Rossant, 2002
Memories of the culinary kind from a food writer who cooked, shopped and feasted on Egyptian cuisine for ten years while living with her grandmother in Cairo. Includes mouth-watering recipes.

The Yacoubian Building
Alaa-Al-Aswany, 2002
Set in a real-life building on Sharia Talaat Harb in Cairo, this novel is racy as well as illuminating. A compelling and gritty debut novel, it caused a stir in the Arabic world when it was first published.

Contents

About the region

Bedouin man preparing dinner
in the Egyptian desert.

History

First Dynasty

The key to the development of a complex civilization lay in the water and soils of the Nile Valley. By 3000 BC, the Nile was supporting a dense sedentary agricultural society which produced a surplus and increasingly allowed socio-economic specialization. This evolved into a system of absolute divine monarchy when the original two kingdoms were amalgamated by the victory of King Menes of Upper Egypt who then became the first pharaoh. King Menes declared that Memphis, about 15 km to the south of modern-day Cairo and deliberately located on the border of Upper and Lower Egypt, would be his new capital. Despite this symbolic unification, the rivalry between the two parts of Egypt continued until the end of the Early Dynastic Period.

Wonders of the Old Kingdom

The three Fourth Dynasty giant pyramids of Cheops, Chephren and Mycerinus erected on the Giza plateau still hold the world in awe (see pages 98 and 99). Less touristy Dahshur boasts King Snefru's Red and Bent pyramids (see page 100), while Saqqara charts the evolution of the pyramid from stepped to smooth-sided (see page 100).

The Old Kingdom

What began with the Third Dynasty, ushered in a major period of achievement. A series of strong and able rulers established a highly centralized government and the 'Great House', per-aha from which the word pharaoh is derived, controlled all trade routes and markets. The sun god Re was the most revered deity and until now it was common practice for leaders to be buried in underground mausoleums (mastabas).

First Intermediate Period, the Middle Kingdom & the Second Intermediate Period

By the end of the Old Kingdom, the absolute power of the pharaohs had declined. Local leaders ruled their own provinces and a second capital emerged at Heracleopolis. Few great monuments were built in this very unstable First Intermediate Period.

During the 11th Dynasty, Menutuhotep II reunited the country once again, creating a new capital at Thebes (Luxor). Remains from this era, the Middle Kingdom, demonstrate its prosperity. Then during the five dynasties of the Second Intermediate Period, central authority disintegrated and Egypt was controlled briefly by Asiatic kings known as the Hyksos, who introduced horses and chariots to the country.

Zoser's Pyramid, Saqqara.

The New Kingdom

The New Kingdom, spanning the 18th-20th Dynasties and based at Thebes, ushered in a period of unparalleled wealth and power. During these 400 years the kingdom prospered and expeditions led to the creation of a huge empire. Military campaigns in Western Asia by Tuthmosis III, now known as the Napoleon of Ancient Egypt, brought Palestine, Syna and Nubia into the empire and their wealth and cheap labour poured into Thebes. During this period Akhenaten renounced the traditional gods in favour of a monotheistic religion based on the sun god Re but his boy-king successor Tutankhamen immediately reverted to the former religion and its principal god Amun. After the military dictatorship of Horemheb, a general who seized the throne, royal power was restored by Ramses I. Ramses II, a most prestigious builder,

Ancient Egyptian excavations

The temple complex of Karnak (see page 119) and the Valley of the Kings (see page 127) are just two of the astounding remains of the era. Also study the surviving patches of fresco that decorate the walls of Queen Hetshepsut's funeral temple. The fruitful expedition to Punt, now part of Somalia, made during her reign is depicted (see page 130).

reigned for 67 years. Following the death of Ramses III, the last great pharaoh, effective power moved increasingly into the hands of the Amun priests and the empire declined. The pharaohs' power was diminished through intra-dynastic strife, decline in political grip on the levers of power and loss of control of day-to-day administration.

Dynasties in Egypt up to 30 BC

Early Dynastic (3100-2686 BC
First Dynasty (3100-2890 BC; Memphis)
Menes
Second Dynasty (2890-2686 BC)

The Old Kingdom (2686-2181 BC)
Third Dynasty (2686-2613 BC)
King Zoser (2667-2648; Step Pyramid, Saqqara)
Huni
Fourth Dynasty (2613-2494 BC; Pyramids of Giza)
Snefru
Cheops (Khufu)
Chephren (Khafre)
Mycerinus (Menkaure)
Shepseskaf
Fifth Dynasty (2494-2345 BC)
Unas
Sixth Dynasty (2345-2181 BC)
South Saqqara Necropolis
Teti
Pepi I
Pepi II

First Intermediate (2181-2050 BC)
Seventh Dynasty (2181-2173 BC)

Middle Kingdom (2050-1786 BC)
Eleventh Dynasty (2050-1991 BC)
King Menutuhotep II (Creation of Thebes; Luxor)
Twelfth Dynasty (1991-1786 BC)
Amenemhat I(1991-1961)
Senusert I (1971-1928)
Senusert II (1897-1878)
Amenemhat III (1842-1797)
Queen Sobek-Nefru (1789-1786)

Second Intermediate (1786-1567 BC)
Fifteenth Dynasty (1674-1567 BC; capital Avaris)

New Kingdom (1567-1085 BC; Thebes)
Eighteenth Dynasty (1567-1320 BC;
Temples of Luxor and Karnak)
Amenhotep (1546-1526)
Tuthmosis I (1525-1512)
Tuthmosis I (1512-1504)
Tuthmosis IV (1425-1417)
Amenhotep III (1417-1379)
Amenhotep IV (Akhenaten; 1379-1362)

Tutankhamen (1361-1352)
Ay (1352-1348)
Horemheb (1348-1320)
Nineteenth Dynasty (1320-1200 BC)
Ramses I (1320-1318)
Seti I (1318-1304)
Ramses II (1304-1237)
Seti II (1216-1210)
Siptah (1210-1204)
Tawosert (1204-1200)
Twentieth Dynasty (1200-1085 BC)
Sethnakht (1200-1198)
Ramses III (1198-1166)
Ramses IV (1166-1160)
Ramses V (1160-1156)
Ramses VI (1156-1148)
Ramses VII (1148-1141)
Ramses IX (1140-1123)
Ramses XI (1114-1085)

Late Dynastic (1085-332 BC)
Twenty-second Dynasty (945-715 BC)
Twenty-fifth Dynasty (747-656 BC)
Shabaka (716-702)
Twenty-sixth Dynasty (664-525 BC)
Necho II (610-596)
Twenty-seventh Dynasty (525-404 BC;
Persian occupation)
Cambyses (525-522)
Darius I (521-486)
Thirtieth Dynasty (380-343 BC)
Nectanebo I (380-362)
Nectanebo II (360-343)

Late (332-30 BC; Macedonian Kings, capital Alexandria)
Alexander III (The Great; 332-323)
Philip Arrhidaeus (323-317)

Ptolemaic Era (323-30 BC)
Ptolemy I (Soter 323-282)
Ptolemy II (282-246)
Ptolemy III (246-222; Edfu Temple)
Ptolemy IV (222-205)
Ptolemy V (205-180; Kom-Ombo Temple)
Ptolemy VII (180-145)
Ptolemy VIII (170-145)
Ptolemy IX (170-116)

The difficult problem of border security for Roman administrators was solved by creating the limes, a border region along the desert edge which was settled with former legionaries as a militarized agriculturalist population.

Alexander the Great

During the Late Dynastic Period the succession of dynasties, some ruled by Nubians and Persians, became so weak that Alexander the Great had little difficulty in seizing the country. Although he did not spend long in Egypt his new capital city of Alexandria, where he is believed to be buried, still flourishes. His empire was divided among his generals and Ptolemy established the Ptolemaic Dynasty which ended with the reign of Cleopatra VII, the last of the Ptolemies before Egypt became a province of the Roman Empire.

The division of power between Rome and Constantinople resulted in the virtual abandonment of Egypt. Egypt's autonomy led to the development of the Coptic Church, which was independent from both the Byzantines and the Romans, and whose calendar dates from AD 284 when thousands were massacred by the Roman emperor Diocletian.

Occupied Egypt

Greeks & Phoenicians
In North Africa, Egypt's failure to expand westward permitted other developments to occur. The coastal area became the arena for competition between those Mediterranean civilizations which had acquired a naval capacity – the Greeks and the Phoenicians. Indeed, this became the future pattern and resulted in the history of the region being described in the terms of its conquerors.

The Greeks had begun to colonize the Egyptian and eastern Libyan coastline as part of their attempt to control Egyptian maritime trade. Greeks and Phoenicians competed for control of the old coastal areas in Libya and eventually created an uneasy division of the region between themselves. The Greeks took over Egypt's Ptolemaic Kingdom which was created on the death of Alexander the Great in 323 BC, incorporating Cyrenaica (in Libya) into their new kingdom. The Phoenicians created a new and powerful maritime commercial empire based at Carthage (in Tunisia), with outlying colonies to the west, right round to the Atlantic coast at Lixus (Larache).

The Roman Empire
Control of Egypt and North Africa passed on once again, this time to the rapidly expanding city-state of Rome. Control of the Ptolemaic Kingdom passed to Rome because of Roman interest in its agricultural produce and Egypt became a province of Rome in 30 BC.

The difficult problem of border security for Roman administrators was solved by creating the limes, a border region along the desert edge which was settled with former legionaries as a militarized agriculturalist population. Thus, although the border region was permeable to trade, resistance to tribal incursion could be rapidly mobilized from the resident population, while regular forces were brought to the scene. The limes spread west from Egypt as far as the Moroccan Atlantic coast.

Saints' caves & the Coptic Mona Lisa

Experience a more meditative existence in the caves of St Anthony and St Paul, both Coptic pilgrimage sites on the Red Sea (see page 197). The eyes in a portrait of the Virgin Mary hung just inside Cairo's Hanging Church follow you as you criss-cross the nave and along the aisles (see page 93).

About the region

Christianity

Egyptian Christianity became the major focus of the development of Christian doctrine. After the Council of Chalcedon in AD 451, the Coptic Church became the main proponent of Monophysitism (the belief that there is only one nature in the person of Jesus Christ; that he is not a three-in-one-being), while Donatism (direct giving, official largesse) dominated Numidia, an area approximately the size of present-day Algeria. At the same time, official Christianity in Egypt – the Melkite Church (adherents to the Council of Chalcedon) – combined with the Coptic Church to convert areas to the south of Egypt to Christianity.

The Islamic Period

In AD 642, 10 years after the death of the Prophet Mohammed, Arab armies, acting as the vanguard of Islam, conquered Egypt. To secure his conquest, the Arab commander, Amr Ibin Al-As, immediately decided to move west into Cyrenaica, part of Libya, where the local Berber population submitted to the new invaders. Despite a constant pattern of disturbance, the Arab conquerors of Egypt and their successors did not ignore the potential of the region to the south. Nubia was invaded in AD 641-642 and again 10 years later. Arab merchants and, later, Bedouin tribes from Arabia,

Islamic treasures

To see minarets and fortifications dating back to 1176, the Citadel of the Mountain in Cairo is a must-visit (see page 88). Sultan Hassan's mosque and mausoleum offers a doubly impressive combination of the city's highest minaret and arguably its most impressive Islamic art (see page 87). Perhaps standing out against the countless others is Cairo's oldest and vastest mosque, that of Ibn Tulun (see page 90).

Below: Mosque of An-Nasr Mohammed, Cairo. Opposite page: Amr Hassanein, Cairo.

were able to move freely throughout the south. However, until AD 665, no real attempt was actually made to complete the conquest, largely because of internal problems within the new world of Islam.

The Muslim seizure of Egypt was, despite the introduction of Islam, broadly welcomed by the Copts in preference to remaining under the Byzantine yoke. Islam slowly prevailed, as did the introduction of Arabic as the official language, although there remained a significant Coptic minority. Cairo became the seat of government and emerged as a new Islamic city. The new faith was only fleetingly threatened when the Christian Crusader armies attacked Cairo and were repelled by Salah Al-Din (AD 1171-1193).

The Great Dynasties

The Fatimids

The first of the great dynasties that was to determine the future of North Africa did not originate inside the region. Instead it used North Africa as a stepping stone towards its ambitions of taking over the Muslim world and imposing its own variant of Shi'a Islam. North Africa, because of its radical and egalitarian Islamic traditions, appears to have been the ideal starting point. The group concerned were the Isma'ilis who split off from the main body of Shi'a Muslims in AD 765.

The Fatimids took control over what had been Aghlabid Ifriquiya, founding a new capital at Mahdia in AD 912. Fatimid attention was concentrated on Egypt and, in AD 913-914, a Fatimid army temporarily occupied Alexandria. The Fatimids also developed a naval force and their conquest of Sicily in the mid-10th century provided them with a very useful base for attacks on Egypt.

After suppressing a Kharejite-Sunni rebellion in Ifriquiya between AD 943 and AD 947, the Fatimids were ready to plan the final conquest of Egypt. This took place in AD 969 when the Fatimid general, Jawhar, succeeded in subduing the country. The Fatimids moved their capital to Egypt, where they founded a new urban centre, Al-Qahira (from which the modern name, Cairo, is derived) next to the old Roman fortress of Babylon and the original Arab settlement of Fustat.

Hillalian invasions & after the Fatimids

Despite Fatimid concerns in the Middle East, the caliph in Cairo decided to return North Africa to Fatimid control. Lacking the means to do this himself, he used instead two tribes recently displaced from Syria as his troops. The invasions took place slowly over a period of around 50 years, starting in AD 1050 or AD 1051, and probably involved no more than 50,000 individuals.

The Hillalian invasions were a major and cataclysmic event in North Africa's history. They destroyed organized political power in the region and broke up the political link between Muslim North Africa and the Middle East. They also damaged the trading economy of the region. More than any other event, the Hillalian invasions also ensured that Arabic eventually became the majority language of the region.

Fatimid power in Egypt did not endure for long. They were forced to rely on a slave army recruited from the Turks of Central Asia and from the Sudanese. They found it increasingly difficult to control these forces and, eventually, became their victims. In AD 1073, the commander of the Fatimid army in Syria, which had been recalled to restore order in Egypt, took power and the Fatimid caliph was left only with the prestige of his office.

The Seljuk Turks took advantage of this weakness and Egypt soon fell under their sway. Control of Egypt passed to Salah Ad-Din Ibn Ayyubi in AD 1169 and for the next 80 years the Ayyubids ruled in Cairo until they, in their turn, were displaced by their Mamluk slaves.

Mamluks

The first Mamluk Dynasty, the Bahri Mamluks, were excellent administrators and soldiers. They expanded their control of the Levant and the Hijaz and extended their influence into Nubia. They cleared the Crusaders out of the Levant and checked the Mongol advance into the Middle East in the 1250s. They also improved Egypt's economy and developed its trading links with Europe and Asia. Indeed, the fact that the Mamluks were able to control and profit from the growing European trade with the Far East via Egypt was a major factor in their economic success.

The Ottomans in North Africa

Occupied Egypt

The Ottomans emerged with some strength from the northwest heartlands of Anatolia in the 15th century. By 1453 they controlled the lands of the former Byzantine Empire and 65 years later took over Syria and Egypt before expanding deep into Europe, Africa and the Arab Middle East. The Syrian and Egyptian districts became economically and strategically important parts of the empire with their large populations, fertile arable lands and trade links.

The great benefit of the Ottoman Empire was its operation as an open economic community with freedom of movement for citizens and goods. Traders exploited the Ottoman monopoly of land routes from the Mediterranean to Asia to handle the spice, gold and silk from the East, manufactures from Europe and the slave and gold traffic from Africa. Ottoman tolerance of Christian and Jewish populations led in Palestine/Syria to the growth of large settlements of non-Muslims. Arabic continued as the local language and Islamic culture was much reinforced. Elaborate mosques were added to the already diverse architectural heritage.

Until the late 18th century the Ottoman Empire was wealthy, its armies and fleets dominant throughout the region, but after that date a marked decline set in. European powers began to play a role in politics and trade at the expense of the sultan. The empire began to disintegrate. During the 19th century with Egypt under the Khedives, the famous Mohammed Ali and his successor Ismail, were only nominally under the sultan's control. Egypt adopted Western ideas and technology from Europe and achieved some improvements in agricultural productivity. The cost was ultimate financial and political dominance by the French and British in this part of the empire. In Palestine, too, colonial interventions by the French in Syria and Lebanon reduced Ottoman control so that by the start of the First World War the collapse of the Ottoman Empire was complete and the former provinces emerged as modern states, often under a European colonial umbrella.

Mohammed Ali & the Khedivate Dynasty

In Egypt, the Ottoman administration soon found itself struggling against the unreconstructed remnants of Mamluk society. By 1786, the Ottomans had destroyed the Mamluk factions and restored central control. Then in 1798, Napoleon's army conquered Egypt, delivering a profound cultural shock to the Muslim world by demonstrating, in the most graphic manner, the technological superiority of Europe. In 1805 Mohammed Ali was appointed governor and lost no time in breaking away from the Ottoman Empire to found a new dynasty, the Khedivate, which stayed in power for nearly 150 years.

Mohammed Ali sought to modernize Egypt and to expand its power. He brought in European military advisors, destroyed the remnants of the old political elite in Egypt and instituted wide-ranging economic reforms. In the Sudan, Mohammed Ali's Egypt was more successful; after the initial invasion in 1820, some 40 years were spent consolidating Egyptian rule, although, in 1881, the experiment failed.

Above: Colonial buildings in Ismailia, Canal Zone.
Opposite page: Mosque of Mohammed Ali, Cairo.

Legacy of a Khedivate leader

Khedive Ismail (1863-1879), son of Ibrahim Pasha, is considered one of the great builders of modern Egypt. Enthusiasts of triumphant engineering feats can't resist a visit to his Suez Canal. It is listed among Egypt's greatest riches and is still the greatest navigation route on the planet.

About the region

By that time, Egypt itself had succumbed to the financial pressures of its modernization programme. Borrowings from Europe began, with the inevitable consequence of unrepayable debt. In addition, Britain realized the potential importance of Egypt for access to its Indian Empire, particularly after the Suez Canal was opened in 1869. A debt administration was instituted in 1875, under joint British and French control. In 1881, a nationalist officers' rebellion against what they saw as excessive European influence in the Khedivate, provoked a British takeover which lasted until 1922. Following British military commander General Gordon's death in Khartoum and the consequent British campaign against the Mahdist state in the Sudan, which culminated in the Battle of Omdurman in 1898, Britain instituted an Anglo-Egyptian condominium over Sudan.

Colonialism

The British occupation of Egypt introduced a regime which, as the well-known historian Ira Lapidus said, "managed the Egyptian economy efficiently but in the imperial interest". Railways were built and widespread irrigation was introduced; the population virtually doubled in 35 years; private property was increasingly concentrated in the hands of a new elite; and the foreign debt was repaid. Industrialization was, however, neglected and Egypt became increasingly dependent on cotton exports for revenue.

Social and political relations were not so smooth. The British occupation of Egypt coincided with a wave of Islamic revivalism. At the same time, a secular nationalist tradition was developing in Egypt which crystallised into a political movement at the end of the 19th century and was stimulated by Egyptian resentment at British demands on Egypt during the First World War.

At the beginning of the First World War, the potential vulnerability of the Suez Canal and the strategic implications of the Turkish-German alliance led Britain to increase its control over Egypt by declaring it a protectorate. This led to the emergence, over the following 20 years, of both Arab and Egyptian nationalist movements which eventually procured nominal independence for Egypt in 1936, although Britain reserved the right to protect the Suez Canal and defend Egypt. By the end of the Second World War, this complex political system had outlived its usefulness and in 1950 Egypt unilaterally abolished the Canal Zone Treaty.

The Desert War 1940-1943

Italy, the colonial power in Libya, at the outbreak of the Second World War, invaded Egypt in the closing weeks of 1940 thus beginning a long period of fighting between the Axis powers and Great Britain in North Africa. Italian, and later German, strategic plans were the displacement of Great Britain from Egypt, the destruction of Great Britain from Egypt, the destruction of Britain's imperial communications links through Suez, and the opening up of the Middle East oilfields to Axis penetration.

The Italians were soon expelled from Egypt and much of eastern Libya but were powerfully reinforced in 1941 by the arrival of German troops that rapidly drove the British back to the Egyptian frontier by April. The German formations were led by General Rommel with skill and audacity. Rommel's eastward advance was slowed by the protracted resistance of the garrisons, first Australian then British and Polish, at Tobruk. Meanwhile, the main armies fought pitched battles around the Libyan-Egyptian border until Rommel withdrew temporarily in December 1941. He used his improved lines of communication in the west to prepare a counter attack and pushed east again as far as Gazala, near to Derna, in January and February 1942 and, after a pause, into Tobruk and deep into Egypt in June. His advance was finally held at El-Alamein after a fierce battle. Rommel made a final attempt at Alam Halfa east of El-Alamein to push aside British and Commonwealth forces and break through to the Nile Valley in August 1942 but failed in the face of strong defensive effort and his own growing losses of men and equipment.

The balance in the desert war changed mid-1942 as the allies gradually won superiority in the air and had more freedom of movement at sea. The Germans and Italians began increasingly to suffer from shortages of equipment, while the health of Field Marshal Rommel caused concern. On the allied side, General Montgomery took over leadership of allied forces and began a build-up of the Eighth Army sufficient to overwhelm the well-trained and experienced Afrika Korps.

Montgomery opened his attack at El-Alamein on 23 October 1942 and after 11 days of hard fighting the Axis army was beaten back and retreated by rapid stages to the west to make a last, unsuccessful, stand in Tunisian territory.

Postcolonial Egypt

In 1952 the constraints of the British mandates, and the frustration following the defeat in the 1948 Arab-Israeli war, led to the emergence of a new class of young army officers who staged a bloodless coup overthrowing King Farouk and ousting the remaining British troops. The new leader, Colonel Gamal Abdel Nasser, inherited a politically fragmented and economically weak state burdened with an ever-increasing demographic problem.

When the World Bank, at the behest of the USA, refused to help finance the construction of the new Aswan High Dam in 1956, Nasser nationalized the Suez Canal in order to raise the necessary revenues. This sent shock waves throughout the world and led to the Suez Crisis in which an Anglo-French force invaded and temporarily occupied the Canal Zone. Nasser's dreams of development were hampered by Egyptian/Israeli tensions including the shattering Egyptian defeat in the 1967 war. He died in 1970 and was succeeded by Anwar Sadat. Sadat was aware that Egypt could not sustain the economic burdens of continual conflict with Israel so, despite the partially successful October 1973 war which restored Egyptian military pride, he sought peace with his neighbour. In 1977 he made a historic trip to Jerusalem and laid the foundations for the 1979

Camp David Peace Accords which enabled Egypt to concentrate on her own economic development and firmly allied Egypt with the USA. While he was applauded abroad he was considered a traitor in the eyes of the Arab world and Egypt was diplomatically isolated. His assassination by Islamic fundamentalists in October 1981 brought vice-president Hosni Mubarak to power.

The derelict Tiring Building, Midan Ataba, Cairo.

Art & architecture

In Egypt, even more so than in other states of the Middle East, the extant pre-Islamic heritage in architecture is considerable – readily visible in the pyramids, temples and tombs scattered across the country. With the arrival of Islam, Egypt enjoyed a continual diversity of architectural styles as each successive dynasty introduced new fusions of imported and local building techniques.

Early Islamic period

The transition from felt to stone

It must be remembered that the early Islamic conquerors were soldiers and often migrant pastoralists in lifestyle. The nomadic tradition, for all its emphasis on a minimum of light, transportable materials has, over time, produced exciting artefacts in the form of tents, particularly the black tent which survives still in the desert outposts of Egypt. Immediately after the conquest of Egypt by Amr Ibn Al-As in the seventh century, the Islamic armies used the existing Egypto-Roman stock of citadels, forts and housing at Fustat (now part of Old Cairo), which enabled some of the historical legacy of the area to survive.

The mosque

At the heart of Islamic architecture is the mosque, and the elaboration of Islamic architecture centring on the mosque took place despite the men of the Arab conquest being essentially unlettered nomads and warriors. To redress the shortcomings of the Arab armies, their rulers imported skilled architects, masons and tile workers from established centres of excellence in the empire – Persians, Armenians and others. Together, these itinerant teams of artisans and their Islamic patrons developed a wonderful and distinct style of building form and decoration which is among the great legacies of Islam.

To make sense of a visit to a mosque, the following principles and guidelines might be useful. The word 'mosque' implies a place of prostration, thus the architecture of mosques, like that of traditional Christian churches, was designed to induce quiet and contemplation, above the noise and bustle of everyday life. Muslims pay particular attention to this solemn sanctity of the mosque. Behaviour is muted and decorous at all times, particularly during services.

Egyptian contributions to the mosque

Egyptian mosques in particular show great variety of decoration and some differences in ground plan. Even to the untutored eye, five principal styles of mosque can be seen in most Egyptian cities; Fatimid (AD 967-1171), Ayyubid (AD 1171-1250), Mamluk (1250-1516), Ottoman (1516-1905) and modern (1905-present).

The Fatimids left as their monument the great Mosque of Al-Azhar in Cairo, square in plan with a roofed sanctuary on twin-pillared colonnades. After their overthrow a new mosque style grew up in Egypt, reflecting the mosque as a major public building by scale and ornamentation. Unlike all previous mosques, it provided a separate teaching room for the four great schools of Orthodox Islam in a pair of mosques, each with a double *liwan* (vaulted arcade). Look out for the discordance between the alignment of the adjacent street and the *liwans*, resulting from the need to set the *qibla* (mosque wall) facing Mecca.

The legacy of the Mamluks includes the Madresa of Sultan Hassan built in 1356-1360. It is an Islamic building on a giant scale with the tallest minaret in Cairo. Architecturally, it is also distinct for its simplicity and for the separate *liwans*, entrances to which are all offset from the magnificent *sahn* (courtyard).

Enduring elements of the mosque

While all mosques vary in detail of layout and decoration, the basic floor plan remains more or less uniform. In addition to the great mosques used for public prayer on holy days, there are local mosques of plain construction, many with architectural modifications to suit regional conditions of climate, culture and the availability of building materials in Egypt. The basic layout even here is uniform, though the ornamentation and wealth in carpets in the sahn may well vary.

Mosque of Amr Ibn Al-Aas, Cairo.

Above: Ahmed Ebn Tolon ancient minaret.
Opposite page: Fayoum portrait.

The Ottomans ruled for many years (16th century-19th century) during which Egypt experienced a flood of new architectural ideas – the use of light as a motif, and the deployment of slender pillars, arches and minarets of Turkish origin. The Mosque of Suleyman Pasha, dated to 1528, was the first Ottoman mosque to be built in Cairo exhibiting these features. That of Mohammed Ali Pasha was one of the last, with its tall octagonal minaret and fine Ottoman dome.

The modern period is represented by the Al-Rifai Mosque in Cairo, completed in 1911, which blends Mamluk with contemporary architecture.

The *ma'dhana* (minaret)

Providing a high point from which the prayer *muezzin* (leader) calls the faithful to their devotions five times each day, the minaret is also the principal topographic marker in the Egyptian landscape. The minarets of the Egyptian mosque are quite distinct despite reflecting influences from elsewhere in the Islamic world. They generally have three separate levels including a base of square section, overlain by a multi-faced column usually octagonal in shape surmounted by a circular tower, itself terminating in an elaborate miniature pavilion. The finial is provided by a small gilded spire carrying a crescent.

The private house

Although there was some inertia in the architectural style and building techniques in Islamic Egypt, aided by the Ottoman imperial practice of adopting local building types without change, the private houses belonging to great families and powerful personages showed much individuality alongside strong elements of continuity. All houses had a central courtyard which was reached indirectly through a corridor from the street. The house entrance was usually via a studded door to a lobby or pair of small rooms designed to ensure that no one from the street could either view or easily enter the inner courtyard or rooms. Around the central courtyard were clustered all the principal rooms. Libraries were important in the houses of public figures, while some great houses had internal *hammam* (bath areas). In lower-class dwellings this same formula was repeated but on a smaller scale and without the baths and libraries.

Cairo has many fine historic houses in various states of repair, rarely seen by visitors simply because they are overshadowed by so many wonderfully attractive public buildings. Sadly many of the older grand houses in diverse styles borrowed from France, Greece and Italy of the 18th and 19th century are now demolished and few examples remain for which there is public access.

Today, many larger houses are laid out using an offset entry system just like the older Islamic houses.

Finding mud-brick for construction purposes is getting difficult as a result of prohibitions on brick-making, so low-rise houses are roughly constructed in cement blocks. Increasingly, better off Egyptians are abandoning the traditional house for apartments in tower blocks.

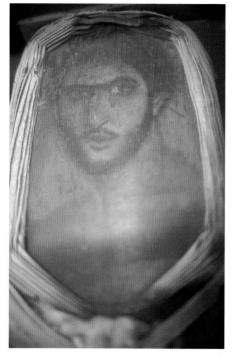

Graeco-Roman artworks – the Fayoum portraits

These touchingly realistic portraits or funeral masks were executed in tempera or encaustic – a mixture of paint and wax – on wooden bases. Painted by Greek artists between 30 BC and AD 395, they are among the earliest portraits known. You will find examples of them in Room 14-UF of Cairo's Egyptian Museum (see page 77).

(see page 77)

Western artists in Egypt

A great entourage of scientists, writers and artists accompanied the French occupation of Egypt in 1798, which continued until 1802, opening this hitherto largely protected Islamic country up to a new audience. These Orientalist artists and writers of the 19th century were confronted in Egypt, and elsewhere in North Africa, with sights and scenes of what appeared to be a startlingly different culture. They recorded what they saw for an audience at home that was eager to catch glimpses of these unknown lands.

In addition to the French, the British imperial mission in 19th-century Egypt brought its own harvest of 'Orientalist' works of art. John Frederick Lewis (1805-1875) spent 10 years in Egypt and was a prolific British painter of watercolours of ancient monuments such as Edfu, Upper Egypt and scenes of contemporary Cairo life such as *A Turkish School in the Vicinity of Cairo*.

David Roberts (see page 162) was another British master of the sketch and oil painting who voyaged along the Nile in 1839. *Temple at Dendereh* and *The Island of Philae* are fine examples of his work. There are many inexpensive cards and books with reproductions of his illustrations. They show very clearly parts that have disappeared and parts that are now too high to view, and give an excellent idea of the coloured decoration.

Latecomers to Egypt were William Holman Hunt (1827-1910), who was a founder member of the Pre-Raphaelite Brotherhood and who visited Egypt in 1854-1856. His paintings were enlightened by his view of the archaeological sites of Egypt and the Levant, with notable pieces such as *The Great Pyramid* and *Entrance to the Temple of Amun*.

In the 20th century the German artist, Paul Klee (1879-1940), was influenced by his travels in Egypt in 1928-1929, from which he took not merely symbols into his paintings but ideas of a holistic universe. His *Legend of the Nile* encapsulated his Egyptian experiences in a single modern picture in pastel.

Egypt Nile Valley & Red Sea today

Windsurfing at Dahab, Sinai.

Prime Minister Mubarak & economic policy

Hosni Mubarak's victory in the first multi-candidate election held in September 2005 won him a fifth six-year term. Previously, he was re-elected by majority votes in a referendum – a foregone conclusion as voters were asked to either vote 'yes' or 'no', though there was no opposing candidate. International and domestic pressure led to a democratization of the electoral process, allowing other candidates to stand against the incumbent president. In most circumstances Egypt's electoral system is designed to ensure that the National Democratic Party (NDP), which Hosni Mubarak leads, commands a majority in the Assembly and prevents any opposition from making a serious challenge. It was a landslide victory for Mubarak. Criticisms of the elections include reports of NDP vehicles ferrying public employees in to vote for Mubarak, and voters being bought in poor and rural areas.

Despite Mubarak's liberal stance on economic policy and the promise of reform, Egypt's economic potential remains hindered and the standard of living low. For some years Egypt has depended on predominantly US and European foreign aid, which still accounts for up to 50% of food supplies needed annually from abroad that enable Egypt to feed itself. Ultimately it seems that Egypt will have to continue to rely on its current principal sources of foreign exchange – oil, tourism, Suez Canal fees, and expatriate remittances – for its economic salvation.

Tourism

A primary source of foreign currency, tourism directly employs one million people in Egypt, in addition to all the income tourists bring in outside of their hotels and restaurants. With almost 13% of Egypt's workforce kept employed by spending visitors, the perpetual wavering of the industry has weighed heavy on the state of the economy. The 1997 Luxor massacre was the first serious blow,

What the locals say

Spending our time dwelling on and rehashing old disasters is a waste of time and spreads fear and depression. Dreaming and talking of plans and desires for the future is time well spent, if you don't spend all day on it! Now is the only reality we have and living in the now is time well spent while fear is a waste of time. Those who want to come to Egypt will always find a way and come here no matter what the obstacles.

Mara, *Mara House, Luxor*

resulting in a drop from 4.5 million visitors in 1996 to less than 3.5 million the following year. It recovered only to slump again after 9/11 and the Palestinian uprising in Israel. The War on Iraq resulted in another serious setback, as did the Sinai bombings in 2004-2005. The latest area to suffer is the Western Desert in the fallout from the September 2008 kidnapping of 19 tourists and Egyptians in the Gilf Kebir.

New restrictions on travel may well be imposed, preventing freedom of movement for the 45,000 annual visitors who want to explore the oases or take a desert safari. In the face of enhanced security, the situation is likely to remain quite calm. Nonetheless, since Egypt is in the centre of one of the world's hotbeds of unrest, tourism will continue to rise and fall. But history indicates that no matter how far it falls, tourists do eventually come back and, if the number of hotel rooms is any indicator of people's predictions, with more than 70,000 rooms in mid-construction, optimism is high.

Nature & environment

The River Nile is a narrow green ribbon, threading its way through the middle of Egypt's incredibly diverse landscape from the Delta region right up to and beyond the border with Sudan. It is flanked by seemingly endless desert sands that sweep away to the western horizon on one side and on the other, beyond the majestic mountains of the Eastern Desert, to a coastline fringed with extensive coral reef.

The River Nile

The Nile in Egypt is entrenched in a narrow valley below the surrounding land and has only one cataract at Aswan. In its last 325 km before entering its Delta the Nile tends to keep to the east bank with the main cultivated zone of the valley on the west bank. Most irrigation requires water to be lifted from the river by traditional means such as the *saqiya*, *shadoof* or by mechanical pumps. The Nile Delta is the heartland of Egypt. It covers a great silt plain built up by the river over centuries. The Delta stretches 160 km from the vicinity of Cairo north to the Mediterranean coast and 250 km across the Mediterranean end of the wedge. The main distributaries in the Delta are the Western Rosetta and Eastern Damietta 'mouths', which are the axes of intensive irrigation networks.

The flow of the Nile has been influenced by fluctuations in rainfall in the countries where the river has its sources, in the Ethiopian highlands and Lake Victoria in Uganda. It is possible that long-term climatic change is involved, indicating that the flow in the river might never recover to the average of 84 cubic km in the period 1900-1959 (the 1984-1987

The River Nile.

The Nile at Aswan.

level of less than 52 cubic km). The water flow during floods has always varied, as we know from inscriptions in pharaonic times, but recent trends are worrying for the states that rely on the river.

There are over 190 varieties of fish in the River Nile, the most common being the Nile bolti with coarse scales and spiny fins and the Nile perch, frequently well over 150 cm in length. Bolti are also found in Lake Nasser. Other fish include the inedible puffer fish, lungfish (which can survive in the mud when the waters recede), grey mullet and catfish (a popular catch for domestic consumption but some species can give off strong electric shocks). Decline in fish numbers is blamed on pollution, over-fishing and change of environment due to the construction of the Aswan Dam.

Essentially a linear oasis stretching for hundreds of kilometres, the Nile Valley provides outstanding birdwatching, particularly from the slow-moving cruise boats, which are literally 'floating hides'. Apart from the wide range of herons and egrets, specialities include the African skimmer, Egyptian geese, pied kingfisher and white pelican. Even the tombs and monuments are rewarding for the ornithologist, yielding Sakar falcons, Levant sparrowhawks and the black-shouldered kite.

Cobras & crocodylus niloticus

Fortunately the only place you are likely to see an Egyptian cobra (*Naja haje*) is decoratively, on the head dress of Egyptian divinities and sovereigns. There are also other cobras in Egypt. The smaller black-necked spitting cobra sprays venom up to the eyes of its attacker – causing temporary blindness and a great deal of agony. Sightings are confined to the region south of Aswan. The Innes cobra is exceedingly rare, recorded in particular around St Catherine's Monastery.

Crocodiles, the largest reptile in Africa, were worshipped as the god Sobek who was depicted as a man with a crocodile's head. The Ancient Egyptians kept them in lakes by the temples and fed them the best meat and fish and even wine. Special creatures were decked with jewels, earrings, gold bracelets and necklaces. The problem was these cold-blooded creatures needed to come out of the river to bask in the sunshine and feed – and they could move at a surprising speed on land. Children became easy prey.

Today these 900-kg creatures can no longer reach the major part of Egypt. They cannot pass the Aswan dam but they exist to the south of this barrier in large numbers.

About the region

Deserts

Cairo, some 150 km from the sea, has an annual average rainfall of 25 mm and a maximum temperature of 35°C. Progression southwards brings even greater extremes. At Aswan rainfall drops away to 1 mm per year and average maximum temperatures rise to 37°C. The profound aridity of Egypt outside the Nile Valley makes it absolute desert for the most part, relieved only where water occurs such as the oases of the Western Desert.

In the desert environment, annual plants have a very short lifespan, growing, blooming and seeding in a few short days, covering the ground, when moisture content permits, with a patchy carpet of low-lying blooms. Desert perennials are sparse, tough and spiny with deep root systems. Where rain is a rare occurrence, plants and animals

What the locals say

The Sinai Desert is one of those places where there is a powerful relationship between the environment and the human spirit. The Bedouins have been a part of this unique, delicate ecosystem for thousands of years and their view of the environment is informed by nomadic tradition and ancient wisdom that embodies a profound understanding of sustainability. For example, there is a tribal law that prohibits cutting green trees. You can only cut a dry tree, taking only the amount of wood you need and no more.

Harby, *harbysplace.com*, *Wadi Mahash in Nuweiba*

Desert dunes.

Landscape between Dahab and St Catherine, Sinai.

Salt lake in Siwa oasis.

have developed a short life cycle combined with years of dormancy. Many animals in the desert areas are also nocturnal, taking advantage of the cooler night temperatures.

When rain does arrive, the desert can burst into life, with plants seeding, flowering and dispersing within a few weeks or even days. Rain will also stimulate the hatching of eggs that have lain dormant for years. Perhaps the most remarkable example of adaptation is shown by the camel. Apart from its spreading feet which enable it to walk on sand, the camel is able to adjust its body temperature to prevent sweating, reduce urination fluid loss and store body fat to provide food for up to six months.

The Red Sea

The Red Sea supports 800 species of tropical fish not to mention reef and hammerhead sharks, moray eels, slender barracudas and manta rays. Here, while sport and commercial fishermen chase after tuna, bonita and dolphin, scuba-divers pay to explore the fringing coral reefs and view the paintbox selection of angel, butterfly and parrot fish and carefully avoid the ugly scorpion fish and the even more repulsive stone fish.

Inland, the slowly widening major fault line running along the length of the Red Sea created the dramatic jagged charcoal peaks

and mountains of the Eastern Desert, a belt stretching for about 1250 km from the southern tip of the Suez Canal. These mountainous desert expanses are the final frontier before Saharan Africa and deep in their folds thrive ibex and gazelle, while nomadic tribes live a traditional lifestyle little changed in 6000 years.

The Sinai Peninsula

Described by some as '24,000 square miles of nothing', travellers to this triangular peninsula soon come to find that in 'nothing' there is so much. Not only does its southern coast feature some of the best diving in the world, Sinai's landscape also anchors Egypt's highest mountain, Jebel Katrina, next to St Catherine's Monastery, which reaches 2228 m at its summit.

Hyenas and jackals still thrive in the Sinai. Wild cats are also found, as are mountain gazelle, which inhabit locations above 2000 m. Seize the opportunity to hike through the mountains before everyone realizes that this is one of the earth's last unspoilt places, proffering isolation and an intimacy with nature.

Festivals & events

Whether stemming from religious, commemorative or cultural roots, each of these enthusiastically observed events will undoubtedly add an extra dimension to your experience of Egypt.

January

New Year's Day (1st)
A public holiday.

Christmas (7th)
Christmas for Coptic Christians is preceded by 43 days of fasting, ending on 6 January (Christmas Eve) with a midnight service and a celebratory meal. Christmas Day, after church, is a time for visiting family and friends. Coptic Christmas Day is a public holiday.

Epiphany (19th)
A feast day for Coptic Christians marking the arrival of the Magi. A public holiday.

Cairo International Book Fair
Held at the Exhibition Grounds in the district of Nasr City. This major meeting of the publishing world has been held annually since 1969.

The Islamic year

The Islamic year (Hejra/Hijra/Hegira) is based on 12 lunar months that are 29 or 30 days long depending on the sighting of the new moon. The lengths of the months vary therefore from year to year and from country to country depending on its position and the time at sunset. Each year is also 10 or 11 days shorter than the Gregorian calendar. The approximate dates of the major Islamic festivals are listed here.

February

Ramses II birthday, Abu Simbel (22nd)
The first of only two days per year when the morning sun penetrates the inner sanctum of Ramses II's temple, illuminating the seated statues of Ramses II himself, Amon Ra (the sun god), and Ra-Harakhty (god of the rising sun). The fourth statue, that of Ptah (god of the underworld and darkness) aptly remains in shade. Thousands of people convoy south for the event.

Mouloud (26 February 2010 / 15 February 2011)
The birthday of the Prophet Mohammed is enthusiastically celebrated. A public holiday.

March

El Fayoum National day (15th)
A public holiday.

April

Easter Sunday (4 April 2010 / 24 April 2011)
Easter follows 55 days of fasting during which
no animal products may be eaten, wine or coffee
drunk, nor food or drink consumed between sunrise
and sunset. On Good Friday altars are draped with
black and candlelight processions take place
at dawn – commemorating Jesus' entry into
Jerusalem. Easter Sunday celebrations including
church services and a breaking of the fast.

Sham El-Nessim (20 April 2010 / 5 April 2011)
The first day of spring, or as it's also known, Sniffing
of the Breeze, is celebrated with family picnics.

Liberation of Sinai (25th)
Marks the withdrawal of Israeli soldiers from the
peninsula on this day in 1982 following the signing of
the Israel-Egypt Peace Treaty. A public holiday in Sinai.

Moulid of El-Hussein
The mosque of Hussein in Cairo's Khan El-Khalili is
the focus of his annual moulid. One of the city's most
important, chaotic and intense festivals, it is held over
a fortnight during the month of Rabi El-Tani and
attracts thousands who camp in the streets.

May

Labour Day (1st)
A public holiday.

June

Evacuation Day (18th)
When the British left Egypt in 1954. A public holiday.

Moulid of Abu El-Haggag.

July

Moulid of Abu El-Haggag
Luxor's biggest *moulid* (religious birthday/
festival) has parades, processions, stick-fighting,
zikrs (repetitive prayers) and all the other traditional
entertainments that you don't get to see very often
as a tourist. It is held on the East Bank during the
first fortnight of the month before Ramadan.

Anniversary of 1952 Revolution (23rd)
Remembering the military coup d'état that
resulted in the Egyptian Republic. A public holiday.

Alexandria National Day (26th)
A public holiday.

About the region

Eid El-Fitr (8 September 2010 / 30 August 2011)
The end of Ramadan, also called Aïd Es Seghir. As the sun sets during the holy month and everyone ventures inward to break fast, it offers a rare and delightful occasion to wander through barren Cairo streets. For the rushed or impatient traveller, note that travel facilities immediately before and after Ramadan are often very congested since families like to be together especially for the Eïd Al-Fitr.

Wafa El-Nil

Cairo's annual celebratory festival translates as 'Fidelity of the Nile' and is rooted in the Ancient Egyptians' veneration of their life-sustaining River Nile.

October

International Festival of Documentary Films
(annual dates vary)
This annual event and competition takes place in the Suez Canal city of Ismailia. Film-makers from around the world enter their most recent work for Best Long and Short Documentary, Short Feature, Animation and Experimental Film.

Armed Forces' Day (6th)
Parades and military displays are held in commemoration of the Egyptian Army, most notably Egyptian successes during the 1973 Yom Kippur War. Parades and military displays feature. A public holiday.

Suez Day (13th)
A public holiday.

Ramses II's Coronation (22nd)
All eyes again turn to watch the morning sun's rising rays illuminate statues deep within Ramses' mighty Sun Temple at Abu Simbel (see Ramses II's birthday, page 44).

August/September

Beginning of Ramadan
(11 August 2010 / 1 August 2011)
Ramadan, the ninth month of the Muslim calendar, is a month of fasting for Muslims. The faithful abstain from eating between dawn and sunset for about one month until an official end is declared to the fast and when Eïd Al-Fitr, a three-day celebration, begins. During the fast, especially if the weather is bad or there are political problems affecting the Arab world, people can be depressed or irritable. The pace of activity in official offices slows down markedly, most closing by 1400. You may want to stay out of the area during Ramadan and particularly the Eïd Al-Fitr, but for the patient and curious traveller, it can be a fascinating time. As the sun sets during the holy month and everyone ventures inward to break fast, it offers a rare and delightful occasion to wander through barren Cairo streets. For the rushed or impatient traveller, note that travel facilities immediately before and after Ramadan are often very congested since families like to be together especially for the Eïd Al-Fitr.

Eid El-Adha (27th 2009 /16th 2010 / 6th 2011)
Also called Aïd El-Kebir, the celebration of Abraham's willingness to sacrifice his son coincides with the culmination of the Hajj in Mecca. A public holiday.

Moulids

There is nothing more uplifting than witnessing a *zikr* at a *moulid*. As the *munshi* sings and chants, he transports the swaying devotees into another realm and all inhibitions are lost as young and old, rich and poor, men and women, move together in praise of Allah. It's a real eye-opener to a side of Egyptian society that is hidden far beneath the layers of everyday life, a chance for people to cut loose and express intense spiritual joy. Other *moulid* activities are more prosaic and create a carnival atmosphere around the mosque, with rickety fairground rides, stick fighters and food stalls.

Cairo International Film Festival
(annual dates vary)
Stars and sovereignty of the silver screen have been converging on the capital for this annual festival since 1976. Top prize is the Golden Pyramid award (cairofilmfest.org).

December

Islamic New Year
(18th 2009 / 7th 2010 / 26th 2011)
The new year, or Al-Hijra, begins on the day that Mohammed began his journey from Mecca to Medina. A public holiday.

Victory Day (23rd)
Egyptian's mark the end of the 1957 Suez Crisis. A public holiday.

Above: Devotees at the moulid of Sayiddnah Nafisah, City of the Dead, Cairo. Opposite page: Tent of Ramadan, El Hussein mosque, Cairo.

Sleeping

Tourism is one of Egypt's major industries so it's no surprise that accommodation is widely available at the main sites, cities and all of the major beach resorts. With prices to suit all pockets, the options vary from de luxe international hotels to just floor or roof space for your sleeping bag. Eco-establishments have also begun popping up in Sinai and the Western Desert, a few of which are mega-luxurious, while others offer a more rustic experience.

Accommodation at Nature Camp, Bir Al Matar in Bahariyya oasis.

Hotels

Most quality hotel chains are represented and offer top-class facilities. There are also many cheap hotels with basic rooms ranging from the clean to the decidedly grimy. Mid-range accommodation is a bit more limited, though the occasional gem exists. There is a pronounced seasonality in demand for accommodation and in the winter holiday months the main tourist areas can be very busy and the choicest hotels fully booked. Advanced reservations are recommended, especially for luxury hotels. Finding cheap accommodation is easy throughout the country, even in high season, but ask to see the room first before checking in.

Prices for the top-class hotels are on a par with prices in Europe while mid-range hotels are generally cheaper in comparison. Note that while price is a reasonable reflection of the type of hotel and service you can expect, some hotels are expensive but very ordinary while others are wonderful and quite cheap. International hotels have an uncomfortable habit of changing owner and name. Be prepared for this and if confused ask for what it was called before.

In almost every case, the advertised room price (that charged to the individual traveller) is higher than that paid by the package tourist. Bargaining is common, especially when tourists are thin on the ground. At hotels three-stars and higher, credit cards are almost always accepted. Tax and a service charge will be added to your accommodation bill, apart from in budget hotels or unless it is clearly stated as inclusive.

Floating accommodation

If you consider the Nile, Lake Nasser and the coral-rich Red Sea to be Egypt's major draws why not spend your whole trip on the water? For cabins on a *dahabiya* or a cruise ship, see pages 176 and 181; for space on a *felucca* see page 181; and for live-aboards, page 63.

Youth Hostels

There are 17 hostels in Egypt's main historic and tourist towns that are open year round. Overnight fees range from US$1.5-9 and often include breakfast. Rules generally include no alcohol or gambling, single sex dormitories and lights out between 2300-0600. Booking is recommended during peak travel times. They are a great place to meet Egyptians, but are generally a couple of kilometres out town and horribly busy during student holidays. Information from Egyptian Youth Hostels Association, 1 El-Ibrahimy St, Garden City, Cairo, T02-2796 1448, iyhf.org.

Camping

Sites of varying quality do exist around Cairo and Sharm El-Sheikh while camping Bedouin-style under virgin sky forms part of most organized desert safaris and treks. A few popular destinations, Dahab and Marsa Alam among them, have what are misleadingly called 'camps'. These are generally very cheap and sometimes have charming grounds that offer small concrete rooms or simple bamboo huts for just a few euro per night.

Adrere Amellal Ecolodge, Siwa oasis.

Eating & drinking

From *fuul* stalls to the more elaborate Western style menus of high-end restaurants and all-inclusive hotels, every palete and pocket is catered for. The majority of travellers find satisfaction somewhere in the middle ground, frequenting low-key eateries that serve up simple and the filling food. This is food typified by mounds of freshly baked flat bread dunked into dishes of tasty dips or wrapped around chargrilled chicken or lamb.

Breakfast, lunch & dinner

Order an Egyptian breakfast and you'll usually receive *fuul* – fava beans simmered slowly overnight – often topped off with a hard-boiled egg. Depending upon your hotel or food outlet, this tasty take on the first meal of the day might also include falafel with *tahina* (sesame seed dip). Continental breakfasts are also widely available, especially in beach resorts and international hotels.

Lunch is dominated by rice and bread, accompanied by vegetables and either meat or fish. Mezzas, a selection of small salads, are served at the beginning of the meal and include *tahina*, *babaghanoug* (*tahina* with mashed aubergines),

Top: Alf Leila, Dahb.
Above: Bedouin-style seating, Funny Mummy, Dahab.

olives, local white fetta-style cheese, *warra einab* or stuffed vine leaves, and *kobeiba*, fried bulgar wheat stuffed with meat and nuts.

Lamb pieces grilled over charcoal on a skewer, and *kofta*, minced lamb, are common main dishes. As are chicken and pigeon, the latter considered a local delicacy when stuffed with rice and nuts. Fish is commonly eaten in coastal regions and is often superb.

Main dishes include *molokhia*, finely chopped mallow leaves, prepared with garlic, spices and either rabbit or chicken, and a good deal more tasty than its glutinous texture suggests; *fatta*, layers of bread, rice, chunks of lamb or beef, yogurt, raisins and nuts, drenched in a vinegar garlic broth; *koshari*, a poor man's feast that will fill a belly for hours, comprises macaroni, rice and lentils covered with fried onions and a spicy tomato sauce; and *mahshi*, vegetables, typically aubergines, tomatoes, green peppers, and courgettes, stuffed with rice and mincemeat. For the less adventurous, Western-style food (other than pork) can be found in many restaurants, and high-end hotels have fantastic international cuisine (but for the price you would pay at home).

Snacks

Good options exist if you need to munch on the move or find some light sustenance between scuba-dives. *Fuul* and *ta'amaya* constitute cheap Egyptian fast food with the addition of *shawarma*, sliced lamb kebab sandwiches. Also good are local dips and *torshi* (brightly coloured pickled vegetables such as turnips, carrots and limes) mezze-style, with a basket of bread. Bread is the staple of the Egyptian diet, its Arabic name *ai'iish*, means life.

Fitir, sold in most cafès and also in special fatatri cafès, are thin dough pancakes made to order with either sweet or savoury fillings.

Fruits, like vegetables, are seasonal although there is a wide variety available all year round. Winter offers dates of various colours ranging from

Fuul up

This snack of fava beans could really be the national dish of Egypt. Some of the best *fuul* comes from the colourful carts on wheels, which station themselves in the same places every day so hungry customers can gather round. The *fuul* is ladled out of a vast pot, hidden in the depths of the cart and heated from below, before being mashed with spices, oil, lemon, salt and pepper – and a boiled egg if you fancy it. Tourists rarely sample a plate, but the vendors will be pleased and surprised if you do. It's probably best to avoid the chopped side salad.

yellow to black, citrus fruits, small sweet bananas, pears, apples, and even strawberries. Summer brings plums, peaches, figs, pomegranates, guava, mangoes, grapes, melons and a brief season, for a few weeks in May, of apricots.

Desserts

One of the best of all is *Om Ali*, or Mother of Ali, a warm pudding of bread or pastry covered with milk, coconut, raisins, and nuts. But try the oriental pastries including *atayef*, deep-fried nut-stuffed pancakes; baklava, honey-drenched filo pastry layered with nuts; *basbousa*, a syrupy semolina cake often filled with cream and garnished with pistachio nuts and *konafa*, shredded batter cooked with butter and stuffed with nuts.

About the region

Hot drinks

The streets of Cairo and all Egyptian towns are awash with local *ahwas* (coffee shops) where men gather to smoke *sheesha* and drink *shai*, play *towla* (backgammon) or dominoes, and while away the hours. The most famed is Fishawis in Cairo, which gathers people from all walks of life into a crowded den of mottled mirrors where numerous hawkers add to the cacophony of noise (see page 107). More down-to-earth places might not have as wide a variety of drinks, but you should always find hot/cold *karkade* (hibiscus), mint tea and potent *ahwa*. Coffee shop chairs are the same classic wooden design across the country, usually with Cleopatra's head on the seat and the name of the shop scoured into the back.

Shai (tea) is taken strong without milk and spoonfuls of sugar, or with mint (*shai bil na'ana*). Instant coffee, just called 'Nescafé', is available. The thick Turkish coffee (*ahwa*), often laced with cardamom or cinnamon, should be ordered either *saada*, with no sugar; *arriha*, with a little sugar; *mazbut*, medium; or *ziyada*, with extra sugar. *Mazbut* is the most popular.

Cold drinks

There are the usual soft options, Coca-Cola, Pepsi, 7-Up and Fanta. Of more interest are the traditional *ersoos* (liquorice juice); *asir limon*, tangy and delicious but highly sweetened lemon juice; *karkade*, made from the dried petals of the red

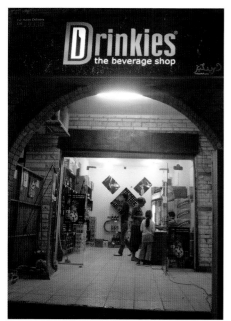

Above: Drinkies in Assalah, Dahab. **Opposite page: Don't be** *shai.*

for both brands remains variable depending on the batch. There are a few local wines, the reds are very drinkable and the whites less so. Local spirits are bottled to resemble international brands, and include an ouzo called Zibib, a rum 'Zattos', and a 'Big Ben' gin. Beware of local liqueurs that don labels and names resembling Western brands such as 'Jhony Wakker' and the like they have been known to contain alcohol so strong that they can cause blindness if drunk to excess.

Practical information

Islam has strictly observed rules governing what things may be consumed by the faithful. The Koran forbids the eating of pork and drinking of wine (interpreted as an outlawing of all alcohol). Non-Muslim visitors are not included in these controls and international food is provided in the majority of tourist hotels.

Vegetarianism is not a concept with which all Egyptians are familiar, and while vegetable dishes are plentiful it is difficult to avoid tiny pieces of meat or meat stock. Even the wonderful lentil soup, like most Egyptian soups a meal on its own, often has the addition of a chicken stock cube. Fortunately, basic staples such as *koshari*, *fuul* and *taamaya* are omnipotent in any town. In the smaller oases, a diet of rice, salad and potatoes or courgettes stewed in tomato sauce is tasty but can get repetitive.

hibiscus; and *tamarhindi*, from the tamarind. Freshly squeezed juice stands are located throughout all cities, and mean you can drink seasonal pomegranate, mango, or orange juice for just E£2-3 a glass.

Tap water in the urban centres is generally safe to drink, but so chlorinated it's intolerable for a lot of travellers. Be prepared for shortage or restriction of water in more rural areas. Cheap bottled water is widely available. Check that the seal is intact and that the bottle has not been refilled.

Alcohol

Although Egypt is a Muslim country, alcohol is available. While five-star hotels are beginning to import beer in barrels, the local 'Stella' beer is the most popular sold, with the better-quality 'Stella Export', in half-litre bottles. Nonetheless, quality

Entertainment

Bars & clubs

You won't have to look too hard to find somewhere suitable for your evenings out in Egypt. Cairo's scene encompasses the plush bars and discos of the Downtown and Zamalek districts (often run by or affiliated with major four- and five-star hotels), locals' drinking holes and alcohol-free *ahwas*. Cairo's most popular venues include the lounge bar on the 40th floor of the Grand Hyatt, Jazz Up at the Nile Hilton, the Fontana Hotel bar and the Odean Palace Hotel's Rooftop Bar.

Similarly, several of Luxor's hotels have rooftop bars offering exquisite views of the town and the Nile, particularly at sunset. However, none of these really rival the terrace at the historic Winter Palace for a sunset drink. The Royal Bar inside the hotel has plenty of period atmosphere too. Discos also exist in the major hotels, but with the exception of Sinouhe, they are often fairly empty. Quite a few 'authentic' pubs have sprung up over the last few years on Luxor's East Bank, generally British-themed and close enough to one another to warrant an evening tour. There are also plenty of *ahwas* scattered about the souk.

On the Red Sea coast, El-Gouna has the standard hotel bars and several funky places to go for a drink. Hurghada, besides the main hotel restaurants which feature discos and serve alcohol, has a handful of discos and around 100 bars. Hed Kandi Beach Bar and Little Buddha are particularly good places to tag onto the clubbing crowd. Beer and booty-shaking are the norm in Sharm El-Sheikh, or more precisely in the adjoining resort of Na'ama Bay where the majority of the nightlife is located. For a more traditional evening, there are plentiful cafés and *ahwas* offering *sheesha*, Arabic music, tea, coffee and often beer.

Catering for less mainstream clientele, Dahab's bars and cafés ply a young and varied crowd of travellers and expat watersports instructors with cold beers, *sheesha* and backgammon boards, usually in Bedouin-style settings. Chill-out tunes and the occasional fire poi display try to revive the hippie ambiance of old. Most stay open until people leave to move onto to the handful of small lively clubs.

Beer and booty-shaking are the norm in Sharm El-Sheikh, or more precisely in the adjoining resort of Na'ama Bay where the majority of the nightlife is located.

A Tannoura whirling dervish dancer.

Children

'Are our kids too young? Will they get much out of it?' These are questions that many parents worry about when considering a holiday here. Obviously, school-age children who have covered ancient Egypt in the classroom will be blown away by seeing the real thing, but that doesn't mean younger travellers will find it boring. The secret is to combine fact with fun.

Divide your time in Cairo between the Pyramids of Giza and the Egyptian Museum. Make a beeline for the dazzling treasures of teenage pharaoh Tutankhamen and the grizzly, engrossing Royal Mummy Room. In Giza innocent eyes won't register the 'over-zealous touts' or the encroaching Cairo suburbs. Instead they'll see the Great Pyramid of Cheops simply for what it is, a towering Ancient Wonder of the World. Dampen their urge to climb the thing by buying tickets to explore the pyramid's long, cramped 'secret' passages.

Tip…

Current information on cinemas and performances can be found on icroc.com, in the *Egyptian Gazette*, and the monthly glossy *Egypt Today* magazine.

Also, build your itineraries around mini-adventures, like sailing on a *felucca* or riding a camel. At Luxor's West Bank try to select a few of the most enigmatic sites, such as the Temple of Hatshepsut and the tombs of Ramses I and Ramses VI – both of which have burial chambers with elaborately painted scenes of animal-headed gods.

Cinema

Cairo has around a dozen cinemas that show films in English. Unfortunately Arabic films rarely have subtitles. Commercial cinemas change their performances every Wednesday and screenings

Popular music

While Western music is popular with the cosmopolitan upper class, the vast majority of Egyptians prefer their own indigenous sounds.

Classical Arabic music Sung in classical Arabic, it is highly operatic, poetic and characterized by a soloist backed by mass ranks of violinists and cellists and a large male choir.

Shaabi, or 'popular' music is that of the working classes, particularly the urban poor. It has retained a traditional form but through stars such as Shaaban Abd Al-Reim – who was catapulted into fame with his song *I Hate Israel* – it broke convention by speaking in plain and often raunchy language about politics and the problems of society.

Al-Musika Al-Shababeya or 'youth music' is popular with the middle and upper classes and is sometimes imitated in the Shaabi. It is a mixture of Arabic and Western influences, underpinning typical Arabic singing and Arabic instruments such as the dof drum and oud lute with a Western beat.

Egyptian ethnic music You might come across the music of Upper Egyptian, the rhythms of which are based on the wooden horn, *mismar saiyidi*, and two-sided drum nahrasan, and Nubian music, which has an African feel.

are generally around 1030, 1330, 1530, 1830 and 2130 and sometimes at 2400, especially on weekends. Cultural centres have one or two screenings per week.

Gay & lesbian

Being openly gay as an Egyptian male is almost unheard of and, while not actually illegal, foreign men should exercise caution when in the country. The authorities veer away from persecuting foreigners, but Egyptian partners will not be immune – as the infamous busting of Queen Boat, a floating nightclub in Cairo, in 2001 proved. Since then, the scene has gone more underground and we are not going to recommend venues to meet people. Lesbian culture is so subdued that women on the look out will have to look far. For more information visit gayegypt.com. But do not access it from Egypt, as the authorities are known to monitor some gay sites.

Below: The moulid of Sayiddnah Nafisah, City of the Dead, Cairo. Opposite page: Live music in Aswan.

Music & dance

For a slick belly-dancing performance by one of the famous stars, head to one of Cairo's five-star hotels. A cover charge usually applies (E£300-600, depending on the venue) that includes the show and a multi-course meal. During high season (winter), all of Luxor's five-star and most four-star hotels have some kind of 'live' music or belly dance floor show. This also applies to the package-holiday resort hotels in El-Gouna, Hurghada and Sharm El-Sheikh.

Cairo's cheaper venues reside in floating restaurants on the Nile, in the strip of dodgy nightclubs along Pyramid Road and tucked away in seedy alleyways Downtown. Women are fine to visit these places but only when accompanied by men, and everyone should be wary about being ripped-off for drinks or snacks.

The Whirling dervishes of the El-Tannoura Dance Troupe are a Cairo must-see (if you can

Live music venues

Hoteliers and restaurant owners across Egypt will procure performers to entertain guests around the pool or in the restaurant, particularly in high season. However, here are a few suggestions if you are in these areas and are actively seeking live music.

Cairo   Arab Music Institute; Darb Al-Asfa; El-Sawy Culture Wheel, the Opera House (see page 108).

Aswan   Nubian House restaurant; Eskaleh guesthouse (see page 179).

You can also often listen to Nubian musicians while watching the *feluccas* from the Corniche.

suspend any desire for authenticity). Sponsored by the Ministry of Culture, it's a spectacular show (see page 109). Staring at the colourful spinning can put you into a trance.

Shopping

Shopping at an Egyptian *souk* (market) is a must and Cairo has the ultimate *souk* experience: the Khan El-Khalili, a labyrinthine criss-crossing of hundreds of covered alleys and tiny stalls manned by sharp-witted merchants adept at spotting what catches your eye. At 'the Khan', as in most of Egypt's traveller hubs, you'll find everything that your heart desires for sale, piled high next to tourist kitsch that no visitor really needs. There are also plenty of opportunities to spend your money on locally produced goods being sold by the producers themselves or from 'fair trade' shops.

Cotton & textiles

Higher-end stores in luxury hotels and shopping malls around Cairo have stores that sell linens and clothes. For colourful tapestries, scarves and bags, the city's Khan El-Khalili is a good place to start. If you want a *gallabiyya*, formal or otherwise, wander around the shops surrounding Al-Azhar mosque in Cairo. For handmade rugs, check out the many stores lining Sharia Saqqara, near the Giza Pyramids.

Making papyrus.

Herbs & spices

A visit to the spice market (Souk Al-Attarin) is highly recommended both for the visual impact and the tremendous aromas. Anything that could possibly be wanted in the way of herbs, spices, henna, dried

Tip...

There is almost always a distinction between the goldsmiths and the silversmiths and there are also shops, designated in Egypt by a brass camel over the door, which produce jewellery in brass or gold plate on brass for the cheap end of the market.

Bottles of sweet-smelling perfume to sample.

and crushed flowers and incense are on display, piled high on the ancient pavements in massive burlap bags or secreted away in tin boxes in various drawers inside. Ask if what you want does not appear to be in stock but do not be fobbed off with old merchandise – fresh spices are always available. Prices are extremely low by Western standards and shopkeepers are prepared to sell small amounts, weighing out the purchase into a little paper cornet. Saffron is the best buy, far cheaper than at home, but sometimes only the local rather than higher-quality Iranian saffron is available.

The main street of Cairo's spice market at Khan El-Khalili runs parallel to Sharia Al-Muizzli Din Allah beginning at the Ghuriyya. Here, many of the shops have been in the same family for over 200 years. Some of the owners are also *etara* (herbalists), practising offering cures for everything from bad breath to rheumatism. Cairo's most famous herbalist, however, is Abdul Latif Mahmoud Harraz, 39 Sharia Ahmed Maher, near Bab El-Khalq. Founded in 1885, the shop attracts a devoted following throughout the Middle East.

Jewellery

Today the main jewellery bazaar is a dedicated section at the centre of Cairo's Khan El-Khalili, but every Egyptian town has its own jewellers and jewellery *souk*. Gold and silver jewellery is usually sold by weight and, although there might be an additional charge for more intricate craftsmanship. Jewellers also sell a great number of silver items, at the cheaper end of the tourist market, as 'ethnic' jewellery.

In Sinai, necklaces, tie-dyes and fabric bags are the hallmark souvenirs of Dahab and are sold in small bazaars on the main bay. The local Bedouin girls sell pretty cotton bracelets along the shore and in the beach cafés. Just don't shop in Dahab when tour groups from Sharm El-Sheikh are in town – everything doubles in price.

Herbs and spices

The Arabic names for some common herbs and spices are:

Basil	rihan
Cardamon	habbahan
Cayenne	shatta
Chilli	filfil ahmar
Cinnamon	erfa
Coriander	kosbara
Cumin	kamoon
Ginger	ginzabeel
Marjoram	bardakosh
Mint	naanaa
Oregano	zaatar
Paprika	filfil ahmar roumi
Rosemary	hassa liban
Saffron	zaa'faran
Turmeric	korkom

Music

Recordings of Egyptian music are available in all cities from small roadside kiosks (often bootleg), market stalls, or record shops. For Saidi and Nubian albums, you'll find the largest selection in Upper Egypt around Luxor and Aswan. The latter's endless Sharia Souk is considered a good place for musical instruments, ancient stereos and local music to play in them. Most music merchants blare out tunes at all hours. If you want to listen to a particular album, just ask. CDs should cost somewhere around E£20.

Perfume

You'll probably smell the perfume stalls before you see them. They're all over Khan El-Khalili and most carry an extraordinary variety of smells – ranging from rose to Egyptian musk to replicas of famous scents. Ask around at different stalls for the going price before purchasing. Elsewhere, in the more relaxing confines of a perfume shop, assistants will attentively unstopper row after row of glass jars so that you can sample their heady 'essence of flowers', blends and aromatherapy oils.

The art of bargaining

Haggling is a normal business practice in Egypt and is run as an art form, with great skills involved. Bargaining can be fun to watch between a clever buyer and an experienced seller but it is less entertaining when a less-than-artful buyer such as a foreign traveller considers what he/she has paid later! There is great potential for the tourist to be heavily ripped off. Wise to the wealth and gullibility of tourists, most dealers start their offers at an exorbitant price. The price then drops by a fair margin but remains at a final level well above the real local price of the goods.

To protect yourself in this situation be relaxed in your approach. Talk at length to the dealer and take as much time as you can afford to inspect the goods and feeling out the last price the seller will accept. Do not belittle or mock the dealer – take the matter very seriously but do not show commitment to any particular item you are bargaining for by being prepared to walk away empty-handed. Never feel that you are getting the better of the dealer or feel sorry for him. He will not sell without making a profit. Also it is better to try several shops if you are buying an expensive item such as a carpet or jewellery. This will give a sense of the price range. Walking away – regretfully of course – from the dealer normally brings the price down rapidly but not always. Remember to use common sense when bargaining – the few pounds you save may be a week's salary to others.

Who sells seashells?

The answer is nobody should sell shells because nobody wants to buy. The sale of shells and coral is illegal, and large fines and long prison sentences can result if you are successfully prosecuted. Removing anything living or dead from the water in Protected Areas is forbidden. The Environmental Protection Association, along with operators of dive centres and hotels are desperately trying to educate visitors – they know they have a better chance of educating the tourists not to buy than the locals not to sell.

Last of the tarboush workshops, Sharia Al-Muizz, Cairo.

Activities & tours

Are you as equally fascinated by the wonders of natural history as those of ancient history? If so, splitting your time between appreciating the temples and the Red Sea's coral gardens and/or the desert interior lets you experience the absolute best of both worlds. That said, it's unlikely that those who travel with their sights firmly set on adrenalin–fuelled sports will even set foot near a pyramid. Why not? Because the calibre of Egypt's scuba-diving, wind- and kitesurfing along the Red Sea coast, plus hiking, bouldering and rock climbing the desert interior and in Sinai, is equally wondrous in its own right.

Diving

Climatic and geographic features make the Red Sea *the* place to scuba-dive and snorkel and many tourists come to Egypt with no intention whatsoever of seeing the monuments on land. Sites include sheer drop-offs, eel-gardens, coral-encrusted wrecks, gullies and pinnacles: a new world (see Diving in the Red Sea, page 64).

Tip...

A 3 mm or 5 mm wetsuit is recommended for most of the year but something thicker is required for winter (18°C) or for a prolonged series of dives.

Manta Rays spotted by divers at a Na'ama Bay scuba school.

Red Sea Diving College, Na'ama Bay.

What the locals say

If you are too afraid, or stressed from your journey here, you simply won't be able to dive. But if you relax you will be fine.

Ossama Mahmud,
Scuba diving instructor, Hurghada

Keeping kids happy

As little as half a day's snorkelling in the Red Sea could turn your water baby into an aspiring marine biologist. With healthy coral reefs often just a few feet from the beach or hotel jetty, parents can introduce little ones to countless species of weird and wonderful sea life in its natural environment. They'll happily count the 'Nemos' (clown fish) that snuggle into softly swaying anemones, and befriend (but never touch or intimidate), the shy puffer fish that swim in and out of crevices.

The minimum age for learning is 10, although children as young as eight can take the plunge with a PADI Bubblemaker try-dive (in a swimming pool and to a maximum depth of 2 m). Children aged 10+ can enrol in the Discover Scuba Diving program – but again only in a pool. To dive in the sea, kids aged 10-14 must take a Junior Open Water Diver course (four days in a pool).

Diving prices & courses
Scores of dive shops in Sharm El-Sheikh, Hurghada and Dahab offer relatively affordable scuba-dive courses that can have you certified in five days.

Daily dives
Diving costs €40-65 per day (€30-55 per day if booking five days or more), depending on the season and whether you are booking from Hurghada, Sharm El-Sheikh or Dahab (which are cheaper) or Marsa Alam, further south.

PADI diving courses
The prices quoted for PADI courses should include all diving equipment and materials. The Open

Water course takes five days – three days of theory and work in confined water or a deep swimming pool to put the theory into practice and two days in the ocean completing four open-water dives. Courses requiring certification are an extra €35 per certificate. You will also need a log book (€8 or included in your course) to record your dives.

Other courses
Open Water Certification: €280-340. Advanced Open Water Certification (three days): €190-225. Medic First Aid (one day): €60. Rescue Diver Certification (three-four days): €240-270. Dive Master Certification: €600-650. Under Water Naturalist: €100. Night Diver: €100-150. Multi-level Diver: €100. Reef Diver: €100. Wreck Diver: €200.

Live-aboards
This method of accessing the dive sites permits divers to reach more remote locations in smaller groups so, in theory, less disturbance is caused.

Most live-aboard agents extend all year round over the northern waters from Sharm El-Sheikh and Hurghada to Ras Mohammed, Gulf of Suez, Tiran Straits and Port Sudan. In summer they chart south from Marsa Alam to the more isolated reefs and islands. Summer is the best time to dive in the south when the winds and currents are not so strong and the water temperature (here at the Tropic of Cancer) reaches about 30°C. Boats from Hurghada tend to head northwards to Abu Nawas and Thistlegorm, eastwards to Ras Mohammed or southwards to Safaga.

Diving in the Red Sea

Imagine swooping like an aquatic Peter Pan through surreal citadels of corals and giant anemones, gazing with goggle-eyed wonder at shoals of tropical fish and maybe glimpsing a hammerhead shark or a turtle. That's the vision that lures the million or more experienced and novice divers to Egypt's Red Sea coastline year after year, and these are the five most famous dive sites to which advanced divers gravitate to live out the dream. They are not suitable for inexperienced or newly qualified divers.

Butterfly fish in the Red Sea.

Top 5 dive sites

❶ The Brothers

Deep divers pilgrimage to sleepy El-Quseir or join charter live-aboard from Hurghada to a site where reef walls plunge to 900 m and sharks are of various sorts are often reported. The famous Brothers reefs, islands about 1 km apart, 67 km off the shore northeast of El-Quseir, are overwhelmed by soft coral rainbows and water so clear it doesn't seem to exist. They were off limits for a few years until authorities developed a protection plan, a newly decreed Protected Marine Area – special permission to dive is required.

Two exposed parts of the same reef, the Brothers offer what some say is the absolute best diving in the Red Sea. On Big Brother, the larger of the two, there's a stone lighthouse constructed by the British in 1883 (and still working).

The dramatic underwater pinnacle that is Little Brother can have ripping currents, but arrive on a calm day and you won't believe your eyes. There are vast fan corals and caves, and the visibility goes on forever. Keep your eyes on the big blue yonder for sharks – a flash of silver out in the channel could turn out to be a majestic scalloped hammerhead. Note: renowned for serious pelagics and hefty currents.

❷ Elephinstone Reef, or Sharks' House

Accessed from Marsa Shagra and Marsa Alam, or by live-aboard, Elephinstone's well-deserved reputation is partly built on how rarely you actually get to dive it and partly because it's rare not to see one of seven species of sharks, including tigers and hammerheads. This mysterious reef, one of various striking offshore reefs with great sloping walls, is seen by only the luckiest or most persistent divers: if the wind is up your boat won't be able to make it there; if the currents are too strong or in the wrong direction, you won't be able to descend.

On the day that you manage to make this dive, you have the chance of seeing some of the most impressive pelagic around – such as Oceanic whitetip sharks – that make it famous.

Tip...

Less qualified and/or experienced divers can take shallow dives off the shore, with Movenpick's Subex Dive Centre (see Sleeping, page 209) at El-Qadima Bay, which has a varied topography and fauna; also shallow, about 10 km further south, is the more sheltered El-Kaf.

Rocky Valley Beach Camp, El Hamarwan Village, 14 km north of El-Quseir, have a good little set-up and run PADI open-water courses. There is a reef off the beach for shore diving and they also rent snorkelling masks and fins for E£15 per day.

Shore diving, Dahab.

Dives start at depth, to see if there are any large animals beneath the plateau, and are usually rewarded with schools of chevron barracuda and glimpses of various reef shark. Ascent takes you to the most magnificent wall of soft and black corals with masses of fish, including coral trout and pipefish.

❸ The 'Ras'

Of the 20 acclaimed sites in Sinai's Ras Mohammed National Park, those loosely known as 'Ras' excite divers the most. The Ras is actually the twin peaks of Shark Reef and Jolanda, their joint status springing from the fact that most dives start on one and finish on the other: starting as a drift dive where a wall drops dramatically into the blue and passing over a saddle into technicolour coral gardens.

A large Napoleon Wrasse in the Ras Mohammed.

Ras Mohammed National Park

A small peninsula that juts out from Sinai's most southerly tip, Ras Mohammed is the point where the waters of the shallow (95 m) Gulf of Suez meet the deep waters (1800 m maximum) of the Gulf of Aqaba. The strong currents have resulted in a truly extraordinary ecosystem that encompasses virtually every life form thriving in the Red Sea. Besides the huge variety of brightly coloured fish that live on the coral reef, deep water species like sharks, tuna and barracuda also come to feed. The beaches around the marine gardens are also beautiful. There are some clean shallow sheltered coves perfect for snorkelling as well as more exposed stretches where wind and strong currents necessitate caution. For general visitor details also see page 201.

Tip…

Some visitors are upset by the number of boats containing inexperienced snorkellers, which scare away marine life. Come on a safari boat if you are a diver, so you can arrive as the sun comes up and beat the crowds – then your first dive can be enjoyed in relative solitude.

At **Shark Reef**, hanging on the southernmost tip of the Sinai Peninsula, currents split along the site resulting in a hugely varied spectacle of life. Depending on the season, you'll see whatever you could see in the Red Sea: sharks, turtles, thousands of schools of fish, a wonderland. Onto the coral gardens at **Jolanda** where a freighter of the same name (the wreck of which has dropped far deeper than recreational divers can go) sprawled toilets around the ocean floor. It is nothing short of surreal to wander amid the wonders of the sea and a bunch of porcelain toilets.

❹ The Straits of Tiran
Slap bang in the middle of the Gulf of Aqaba and an hour or so sailing from Na'ama Bay, the straits of Tiran include Jackson which has a 70-m drop-off, Woodhouse, Thomas and Gordon reefs. There are fantastical coral walls, both of hard and soft coral, extremely lively with fish, while in the deeper waters the chance of seeing a dolphin pod is high. The residue of a few wrecks including Sangria and Laura are scattered about the strait. Many large pelagic fish including sharks are common, and two of the reefs here also the permanent residences of Hawksbill turtles.

Hushasba, southwest off the island of Tiran is shallow with a sandy floor and sea grass. Note: The currents can be strong in this area.

❺ The Blue Hole
Scuba and mono-finned free-divers, travel by 4WD the 7 km north of Dahab to descend into the Red Sea's very own Blue Hole – the most famous, and unfortunately infamous, dive in the area. The Blue Hole (literally a void in the coral) is just a few metres from the shore and over 80 m deep, although the majesty and life of the place is far closer to the surface. Deeper than any recreational diver should ever go, at about 60 m down, there's an arched passageway to the other side of the hole. Every year there are stories of advanced divers who die from nitrogen narcosis or carelessness while attempting this dive – attempting to go through it obviously strongly discouraged.

Sadly an abundance of careless snorkellers (and not all of them are) has taken its toll on the Blue Hole's coral, so much so that many divers recommend descending at the nearby Bells site. **The Bells**, still wonderfully rich with coral and large fish, is just north of the Blue Hole, along a coral cliff that leads to the hole. Combine these two sites with the self-explanatory Bells to Blue Hole dive.

Tip...
If you want to dive the Blue Hole or the Canyon, go early. Ideally do them as early morning dives on separate days, rather than two on the same day.

Responsible diving

Damage has been caused to the coral reefs around the coast by divers taking trophies, anchors being dropped onto the living corals and rubbish being thrown into the water. The regulatory bodies set up to prevent this damage to the environment have had little effect – it is up to those who delight in this eco-system to preserve it for the future by diving responsibly.

Check you are weighted correctly As the Red Sea is a semi-enclosed basin it has a greater salt content than the open ocean. The extra salinity requires heavy weights, thus buoyancy checks are essential.

Avoid all contact with coral These living creatures can be damaged by the slightest touch.

Remove nothing from the reef In Egypt this is taken so seriously that boat captains can lose their license if either shells or pieces or coral are brought on board.

Always move with care Careless finning stirs the sand and can smother and kill the softer corals.

Do not feed the fish Introducing an unnatural imbalance to the food chain can be fatal.

Do not purchase souvenirs of marine origin Do not encourage trade in dead marine objects, which is illegal in Egypt.

Be mindful in caves Air bubbles trapped in caves can kill the marine creatures who extract their oxygen from the water.

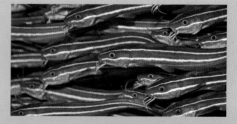

Above: Sunrise balloon trip over Luxor. Opposite page: Wind-surfing on the lagoon in Dahab, Sinai.

Desert safaris

Nearly 20,000 people each year make an expedition into the desert. One of the most commonly explored is Sinai with its vibrant-coloured canyons and ancient sacred peaks. The Eastern Desert is also becoming increasingly popular, where the stern grey mountains hide unexpected and magical *wadis*, and nomadic tribes still roam. Jeep tours are usually cheaper than camel safaris, some tour companies and local desert guides provide absolutely everything for as little as US$30 per person per day (and, depending on what you want, up to US$150 per person per day). Trips generally include food, sleeping bags/blankets and transport (whether it's camel or jeep) and give you the freedom to create your own adventure.

Hot-air balloon rides

Floating above the Valley of the Kings in a hot-air balloon while dawn breaks over the patchwork of fields, desert sands and villages of Luxor's West Bank has to be a highlight of any visit to Egypt. After crossing the Nile in the dark and ascending to dizzying heights (300 m), you can spy down on the farmers starting work in the fields, women cooking on fires, rooftops where washing and dates lie drying and the ruins of temples. The morning light is magnificent – the mountains are positively glowing by the time the trip comes to an end. Lower prices mean that more tourists can afford a ride than in the past, and the skies are now strung with balloons – an impressive and magical sight in itself.

Normally collection is from your hotel and the flight lasts between 45 and 60 minutes. Trips are subject to weather conditions over which there is no control – make sure your tour agent offers a refund in case of cancellation. Agility is required to climb into the basket and children under 138 cm (4ft 6in) are not accepted. Luxor has several balloon companies, see page 146, and hotels can usually make the arrangements for you.

Snorkelling

If you lack the funds or inclination for scuba, snorkelling can be just as fulfilling. Equipment can be rented at diving centres and purchased in many beachfront stores. Look for easy entry into the water so you won't have to splice your feet and kill the coral on your way in. Access is significantly easier during high tide. In the shallows, you will find a vast array of wondrous creatures, corals that open and close, fish that kiss your goggles, exquisite rainbow colours and patterns. Check weather conditions carefully before tagging onto a dive boat, as choppy seas and strong currents can make the experience risky, and there is unlikely to be any supervision.

Trekking, bouldering & rock climbing

The best place for trekking in Egypt is the interior of Sinai. Options range from an afternoon or late-night meander up Mount Sinai to treks of several weeks through the mountainous interior. Scaling majestic summits and camping in lush wadis and gardens, treks are led by local Bedouin tribesmen who also do the cooking and share their knowledge of the local flora and fauna.

A good linear route goes from St Catherine's to El-Tur on the western coast, scaling Jebel Umm Shomar (the second-highest peak in Egypt) on the way, but there are countless other options and circular routes, which can be tailored to suit trekkers' preferences. Desert Divers in Dahab (desert-divers.com) offer guided climbs and bouldering excursions, try-climbs and courses to get beginners started.

Windsurfing & kitesurfing

In addition to underwater pursuits, Egypt offers excellent spots for windsurfing and kitesurfing. Ras Sudr on the western coast of the Sinai and Safaga on the Red Sea coast are both known for their reliable year-round gusts. The lagoon south of Dahab is also a popular spot for learning to windsurf or kitesurf.

Contents

Cairo

The setting sun behind the Pyramids of Giza .

Introduction

T he largest city in the Middle East and Africa and one of the most populous in the world, Cairo has an estimated 16 million souls living in a place designed for two million. The Nile runs like a vein through it, sustaining hearts and bellies as it has for millennia. On either bank extraordinary remains of civilizations past – thousands of years of pharaonic, Coptic and Islamic history – comingle with the dwellings and lives of modern Egyptians.

It's little wonder that it has multiple personalities. Parts of the capital want to hold hands with the most cosmopolitan world cities, boasting the splendours of the past; others just want to get by. A walk around the city is a walk through thousands of years: from the colossal Pyramids of Giza at the edge of the Western Desert to the Old Coptic Quarter on the east bank; through the alleys of Islamic Cairo, gushing with life and hundreds of ancient monuments to the downtown quarter where the stunning façades of 19th-century buildings remind onlookers of the profound influence of European occupiers. And in between the ancient monuments and modern buildings, *souks* and *ahwas*, bazaars and *falafel* stalls fill crevices where the contagious energy of Cairo, perhaps the city's greatest attraction of all, looms on as it always has.

What to see in...

...one day
Start early for the Tutankhamen galleries at the **Egyptian Museum**, followed by the **Pyramids of Giza**. Head next into Islamic Cairo for the **Khan-El Khalili** experience and some mint tea and *sheesha* at Fishawis, before climbing the spiralled minaret at **Ibn Tulun mosque**. Close the day with dinner, drinks and views from the 40th floor of the Grand Hyatt.

...a weekend or more
More time allows for losing yourself in the streets of Islamic Cairo, dense with mosques and mausoleums, before relaxing in a local *ahwa* for the afternoon or taking a **Nile cruise** as the capital lights up for the evening. Tour the mighty **Citadel** and pop into the **Hanging Church**, and spend time viewing even more ancient Egyptian architecture at the outlaying pyramids at **Saqqara** and **Dahshur**.

Ibn Tulun mosque.

Essentials

❶ Getting around

By foot Downtown Cairo is a condensed area, so walking is a good way to see the heart of this city, while wandering the narrow streets of Islamic Cairo is what Cairo is all about. But try to minimise your exposure to the heat and heavy traffic by taking public transport and/or a taxi rather than walking from district to district.

Buses Operate daily from 0530 to 0030, extended hours during Ramadan. Packed to bursting point are the hop-on, hop-off inner-city buses and minibuses. There are also microbuses that are private van-like vehicles with a navigator who shouts out the destination as it drives along. A few air-conditioned buses connect the main *midans* (squares) to Heliopolis and the airport. They are a bit more expensive (a flat E£2), but more pleasant.

Metro E£1 to go anywhere. Stations are marked with a big red 'M', with signs clearly marked in both English and Arabic. There are two lines: El-Marg–Helwan and Shobra–Giza, with a third planned. Trains have a women-only carriage. Noteworthy stops are Sadat (for Downtown); Attaba (Islamic Cairo); Mar Girgis (Old Cairo).

Taxis Easy to use and by Western standards, extraordinarily cheap are the ramshackle black and white chequered cars. Functioning meters are rare so always agree a fare before entering. Point-to-point trips in the centre shouldn't cost more than E£5; one district to another E£10-15; Downtown to Giza Pyramids E£20 or the airport E£35-50. Book yellow cabs and blue cabs with air conditioning and working meters by calling T16516 or T19155. Good for longer distances (say to the airport), more expensive for short hops. Service taxis follow specific routes and carry up to 7 passengers. Fares range from 50 pt-E£1.

Calèche Not for getting around in but nice for an evening's exploration (E£30 per hr).

⊖ Bus station The main terminal is **Turgoman**, Sharia Shanan in Bulaq. Signed the 'Cairo Gateway' although no one calls it that, it is within walking distance of Midan Ramses (E£3-5 taxi from Midan Tahrir). Also Aboud Station, Sharia Ahmed Helmi, 3 km north of Ramses (E£5 taxi from Ramses, E£10 from Downtown).

❷ Train station The main station is **Ramses Station**, Midan Ramses, T02-2575 3555. An English-speaking office (T02-2579 0767) helps with schedules and tickets.

❺ ATMs Most banks are in Downtown, or in more affluent districts such as Mohandiseen, Zamalek, Dokki or Heliopolis. Barclays, Citibank, and HSBC are all present, with branches in Garden City and Zamalek. Also, at Ramses train station.

⊕ Hospital There are several including **Cairo Medical Centre**, 4 Sharia Abou Obeida El-Bahr, Midan Roxy, Heliopolis, T02-2258 1003/0566;

⑤ CAIRO METRO

River Nile

New El-Marg
El-Marg
Ezbet el-Nakhl
Ain Shams
El-Mataria
Helmiyet el-Zeiton
Hadayek el-Zeiton
Saraya el-Kobba
Hammamat el-Kobba
Kobri el-Kobba
Manshiyet el-Sadr
El-Demerdash
Ghamra

Shubra El-Khelma
Kolleyet El-Zera'ah
El-Mazalat
El-Khalafawi
St Teresa
Rodel Farag
Massara
Orabi

Imbaba
El Sudan
Mohandissen

Cairo Airport
Salah Salem
Al Azhar
Port Said
El Ahram
Kolleyet el-Banat
Cairo Stadium
Cairo Fairgrounds
Abbasiya

Dokki
El-Behous
Cairo University
Faisal
Giza
Giza Suburban
Sekiat Mekkey
El Monieb

Mohamed Naguib
Saad Zaghloul
Sayyida Zeinab
El-Malik el-Saleh
Mar Girgis
El-Zahraa
Dar el-Salam
Hadayek el-Maadi
Maadi
Thakanat el-Maadi
Tura el-Balad
Kozzika
Tura el-Asmant
El-Massara
Hadayek Helwan
Wadi Hof
Helwan University
Ain Helwan
Helwan

LEGEND

Line 1
Line 2
Line 3 Under Construction
Line 3 Proposed
Train Station

Downtown traffic on Sharia 26 July, Cairo.

Anglo-American Hospital, by Cairo Tower, Gezira, T02-2735 6162.

✚ **Pharmacies** Ali and Ali, (9 outlets and delivery service), T02-27604277, and **Isa'f Pharmacy**, Sharia Ramses, T02-574 3369, (no delivery). Both open 24 hrs.

✉ **Post office** The main office is in Midan Ataba (open Sat-Thu 0800-1500). Send packages from the office in Midan Ramses (open Sat-Thu 0800-2100).

ℹ **Tourist information** The main office is 5 Sharia Adly, near Midan Opera, T02-2391 3454. Also at the airport (24 hrs); Ramses Train Station (T02-2579 0767); Giza Train Station (T02-3570 2233); Pyramids of Giza (T02-3383 8823).

Stick to your plan

Outside the airport independent travellers often encounter a barrage of unsolicited offers from self-declared tour guides, drivers, hotel vendors, and the like. The greatest thing to fear is getting severely overcharged for a taxi ride or being lured to a dingy hotel room. Avoid eye contact, firmly say *la'a shukran* (no, thank you), and stick to the plan you made in advance.

Downtown, Zamalek & Gezira

The non-stop pulsing heart of the modern city radiates out from the central Midan Talaat Harb, its boulevards and gracious five- and six-storey buildings inspired by fin de siècle Paris. Streams of traffic and consumers pack the streets way into the small hours, and independent travellers are drawn here for the budget hotels and the shops and restaurants that stay open late into the night. The predictable lines of the *kherti* (male touts) fall on the deaf ears of visitors, more taken by the ethereal architecture that surrounds them, who traverse between museums or towards Sharia 26th July in Bulaq, where a cacophony of car horns, lines of fruit carts, and endless rails of clothes spill off the pavement.

Below: The Nile, Zamalek Island and Cairo Tower. Opposite page: Entrance to the Egyptian Museum.

Egyptian Museum

Takes up the north side of Midan Tahrir, enter from the sculpture garden, egyptianmuseum.gov.eg. Ticket office open daily 0900-1645 (museum until 1830, last entry 1645), 0900-1600 during Ramadan. Tickets E£50, E£25 for students. Extra E£100/E£50 for the Royal Mummy Room. Guided tours last 2 hrs, E£50-70 per hr. Cameras and video not permitted. Metro: Sadat.
Map: Downtown Cairo, B4, p80.

Called El-Mathaf El-Masri in Arabic and sometimes, mistakenly, referred to as the Cairo Museum, this is one of Egypt's greatest wonders for tourists and scholars alike and a must if only for a few hours. Café and restaurant facilities are available on the 1st floor, via a souvenir shop. Note GF = ground floor; UF = upper floor. Rooms and galleries are both described as 'Rooms'.

A two-hour tour will give you enough time to take in the ground floor followed by a visit to the Tutankhamen Gallery. Allow at least four hours for a full initial viewing of both floors. Although it is taken over by coach parties most of the time, try to visit the museum early in the day or last thing in the afternoon.

The pride of the museum – the **Tutankhamen Collection** – is contained in rooms 3, 4, 6, 7, 8, 9, 10, 15, 20, 25, 30, 35, 40 and 45 on the Upper Floor. These remarkable treasures, found intact by the Englishman Howard Carter in 1922, were saved from grave-robbers by the tomb's position low in the valley hidden under that of Ramses VI and by the construction of workmen's huts across its entrance. Unlike most other archaeological finds before 1922, the treasure was retained in Egypt and considering that he only reigned for nine years, between the ages of nine and 18, the mind boggles to imagine what Seti I's tomb, for example, must have contained. The Tutankhamen exhibit is particularly in demand and it might be necessary to queue for entry.

If you can afford the extra ticket, the elegant Royal Mummy Room contains what is left of some

Five of the best

Treasures of a Boy King

❶ **King Tut's death mask** wears a ceremonial beard and a headdress knotted at the back of the neck. The blue stripes are in intensely blue lapis lazuli, and there is a gold upright cobra and vulture head above the brow. Room 3-UF.

❷ **The golden throne** Extraordinary. Coated with sheets of gold and ornamented with semi-precious stones. Room 35-UF.

❸ The **Innermost coffin** rendered in gold and semi-precious stones with coloured glass. In the Osiride form of a mummy with crossed arms carrying divine emblems, the body is covered by carved feathers and the representations of Upper and Lower Egypt – the vulture and cobra. Room 3-UF.

❹ Life-size **Ka statues** of Tutankhamen, wearing *khat* headdress and gilded kilt can be found in the antechamber guarding his tomb. Entrance of Room 45.

❺ A **Golden Canopic chest** made of wood gilded with gold and silver is ornately decorated with family and hunting scenes. Room 9/10-UF, display 177.

Outside the Egyptian Museum.

Tip...

Even if you are planning to go to Luxor or Aswan where *feluccas* are an essential ingredient of any visit, it's still mesmerizing to have a night-time sail while in Cairo when the city is at its most beautiful. Bargaining is the norm, but a standard price is around E£70 per hour. Tips are expected. *Feluccas* for hire dock in front of the Nile Hilton, Downtown, and near the Four Seasons in Garden City.

of the most famous pharaohs of them all. Eleven mummies are on display, some still shrouded in their wrappings, but most have had at least their faces unwrapped and seem to rest peacefully in the climate-controlled cases. Best preserved are Seti I and Ramses II, whose hair appears to have been tinted, while the mummies of queens Hodjmet and Henttawy are still wearing their wigs.

Including Tutankhamen's treasures and the royal mummies, the museum hosts a staggering 136,000 items, split across two floors. Those in the set of galleries 11, 12, 6 and 7 are mainly from the 18th Dynasty. Objects from the 19th and 20th Dynasties are displayed in Rooms 9, 10, 15, 14 and 20-GF. The best of the Late Period (1085-332 BC) is concentrated in Rooms 25, 24 and 30-GF. And the central atrium of the museum (Rooms 13, 18, 23, 28, 33 and 38-GF) is used to exhibit mega-statues from a mixture of periods, most eye-catching of which is a 7-m-high representaton of Amenhotep III and his wife Queen Tiy.

Adjacent to the Tutankhamen galleries, and well worth looking out for, are some of 146 touchingly realistic portraits excavated by Sir Flinders Petrie. They were of children, men and women of all ages. They date from Graeco-Roman times, 30 BC to AD 395; when the deceased was embalmed the portrait would be attached to the coffin or mummy case. Room 14-UF.

Zamalek & Gezira

This island in the Nile was unoccupied until the middle of the 19th century when Khedive Ismail built a magnificent palace and landscaped its surrounds into sprawling royal gardens populated by exotic animals. These days, the palace is part of the Marriott hotel and Zamalek, the northern part of the island, is a leafy, upmarket residential area popular with expats and the Egyptian elite. There are many decent restaurants (some of them floating), welcoming places for a drink and excellent shopping (books, art and souvenirs). Gezira occupies the southern half, mostly taken up by the grounds of the Gezira Club and the Opera House complex, plus there are some attractive gardens along the river and the landmark Cairo Tower.

Cairo Tower

Sharia Hadayek Al-Zuhrey, Gezira.
Daily 0900-0100, E£60. Metro: Opera.
Map: Central Cairo popout map, B4.

The 187-m tower with a lotus-shaped top is a prominent icon of the Cairo skyline, especially at night when it is lit with waves of neon lights that constantly change colour. It was built with Soviet help in 1957-1962 and has just undergone a revamp. Although the revolving restaurant at the top and café are decent, it is the viewing platform that is most impressive. Providing the pollution is not too bad, you can look east across the modern city centre to the minarets and mosques of Islamic Cairo and to the Muqattam Hills beyond; to the west the Pyramids and desert sprawl out on the horizon. It's a great view of the city at night.

Bulaq

A separate suburb in the 19th century, Bulaq used to be the commercial port of Cairo when Sharia 26th July was an avenue lined with flowering trees leading tourists to Shepheard's Hotel. It was also visited by soldiers from the canal zone who frequented the prostitutes in the 'seven houses' of Bulaq, as they were the cheapest in the city and easily linked to the barracks by train. The women had to have regular medical check-ups and would first visit the *hammams*, singing songs on the way from the brothels as they rode along in carts.

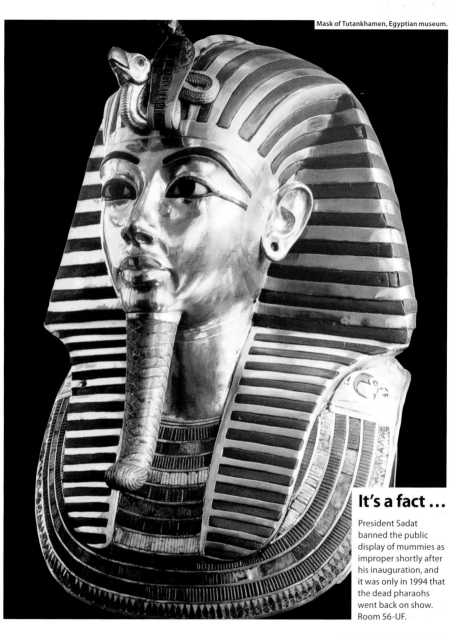

Mask of Tutankhamen, Egyptian museum.

It's a fact …

President Sadat banned the public display of mummies as improper shortly after his inauguration, and it was only in 1994 that the dead pharaohs went back on show. Room 56-UF.

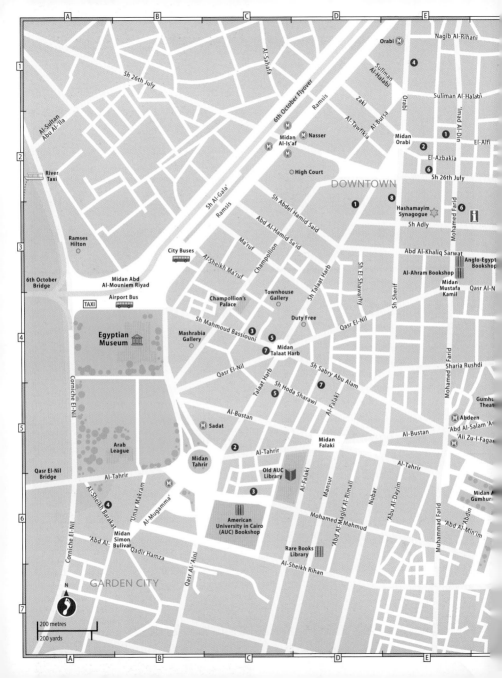

Downtown Cairo listings

❶ Sleeping
1 Bluebird *42 Sharia Talaat Harb, 6th floor* D3
2 Canadian Hostel *5 Sharia Talaat Harb* C5
3 Dahab Hotel *26 Sharia Mahmoud Bassiouny, 7th floor* C4
4 Garden City House *23 Sharia Kamal El Dinn Salah* A6
5 Lialy Hostel *8 Midan Talaat Hard, 2nd floor* C4
6 Pension Roma *169 Sharia Mohammed Farid* E3
7 Sara Inn Hostel *21 Sharia Yousef El-Guindi* D5
8 Talisman *39 Sharia Talaat Harb* E2
9 Victoria *66 Sharia El-Gumhoriyya* F1
10 Windsor *19 Sharia Alfi Bey* F2

❶ Eating & drinking
1 Akher Sa'a *8 Sharia El-Alfi* E2
2 Alfi Bey *3 Sharia El-Alfi* E2
3 Cilantro's *31 Sharia Mohammed* C6
4 El-Tabei *31 Sharia Orabi* E1
5 Felfela *15 Sharia Hoda Sharawi* C5
6 Gad *13 Sharia 26 July* E2
7 Greek Club *3 Sharia Mahmoud Bassiouni* C4

Islamic Cairo

Built with defence purposes in mind, the streets of the Islamic city are narrow and, in addition to looming Mamluke mausoleums and age-old mosques on every corner, the feeling of having stepped back in time is deepened by the ceaseless trading, shouting and everyday life all around. The ancient Al-Azhar Mosque and the nearby *souk*s in the Khan El-Khalili district are at the centre of modern-day Islamic Cairo. The area's defining chaos may be somewhat dimmed as palm trees are planted and faux-Arabesque street lighting takes the place of swinging single light bulbs, but fortunately, these changes haven't encroached too far into the mayhem. South of Al-Azhar the streets are still an absorbingly dirty labyrinth filled with the rickety tables of vendors and hordes of people browsing in the shadows.

Sayyidnah Hussein Mosque.

Islamic Cairo.

In the city of a thousand minarets, where do you begin? Broadly speaking, the most important sights to visit in Islamic Cairo lie in a broad belt to the east of the main Sharia Port Said. Use Al-Azhar as a dividing line, exploring to the north and south of it in turn.

Khan El-Khalili

Most shops are shut on Sun, some shut on Fri. Metro: Ataba. Microbus or a 15-min walk from Midan Ataba along Sharia Al-Azhar (under the flyover) or down Sharia Muski.
Map: Central Cairo popout, H3.

Although it also refers to a specific street, Khan El-Khalili is the general name given to the vast maze of individual *souks* that are an essential ingredient of any visit to Cairo. The Arab/Islamic system of urban planning traditionally divided the *souks* by professions or guilds and while the system is less rigid now there is still a concentration of one particular trade in a particular area. Khan El-Khalili includes streets that almost exclusively sell gold, silver, copper, perfume, spices, cloth or any one of a number of particular products.

Known to locals simply as 'the Khan', this has been the main *souk* in Cairo since 1382 when it was first created around a *caravanserai* by Amir Jarkas Al-Khalil, the Master of Horse to the first of the Burji Mamluk Sultans, Al-Zahir Barquq (1382-1389). The *caravanserai* attracted many foreign and local traders and expanded rapidly, to become a base for the city's subversive groups and was consequently frequently raided.

Today the main area of the *souk* has tourist shops but a few of the streets to the west are more authentic. Here you will find gold, silver, copperware, leather goods, perfume oils, alabaster, boxes, herbs and spices. It is essential to bargain with the majority of traders, although not those selling precious metals which are sold by weight. On a bracelet, for example, a small percentage is added for workmanship, and this is the only thing that is negotiable.

Tip...

As this is a particularly conservative area it's wise to dress especially modestly. Women should wear clothes that cover their legs and arms and should bring along a headscarf for use in mosques. Men should avoid shorts and sleeveless T-shirts. Shoes must be removed for entry into mosques.

Mosque of Al-Azhar

Sharia Al-Azhar.
Sat-Thu 0900-1500, Fri 0900-1100/1300-1500. Tip any guides. No bare legs, shawls are provided for women. Metro: Ataba. Microbus or walk along the underpass from Midan El-Hussein below Al-Azhar.
Map: Central Cairo popout, H4.

A famous and very influential mosque and university whose leader, known as the Sheikh Al-Azhar, is appointed for life and is Egypt's supreme theological authority. The mosque was built in AD 970 and established as a university in AD 988 which, despite a counter-claim by Fes' Qarawiyin Mosque in

Around the city

Morocco, may make it the world's oldest university. With the exception of the main east *liwan*, however, little remains of the original building.

The entrance is through the Barber's Gate (where students traditionally had their hair shaved), which opens out on to the 10th-century Fatimid *sahn* (courtyard) overlooked by three minarets which can be climbed for excellent views over the surrounding area.

During the Shi'a Fatimid era (AD 969-1171), the university was used as a means to propagate the Shi'a faith in a predominantly Sunni city, but it fell into disrepair under Salah Al-Din and his successor Ayyubids (Sunni Muslim rulers), before being reopened by the Bahri Mamluks (1250-1382) and eventually becoming a bastion of Sunni orthodoxy.

Later, during the rise in Arab nationalism in the late 19th and early 20th centuries, Al-Azhar became a stronghold for independent thinkers and it was from here that in 1956 President Nasser made his speech against the Suez invasion.

North of Sharia Al-Azhar

Sayyidnah Hussein Mosque

North side of Midan El-Hussein.
Closed to non-Muslims. Tip the shoe attendants.
Metro: Ataba. Map: Central Cairo popout, H3.

This is Cairo's official mosque where some 10,000 people pray daily, and President Mubarak worships on important occasions. It is named after, and contains the head of, the Prophet Mohammed's grandson Hussein. The rest of his body is perhaps in Iraq. His mosque is the focus of his annual *moulid*, one of Cairo's most important, chaotic and intense festivals that is held over a fortnight during the month of Rabi El-Tani, attracting thousands who camp in the streets.

Tip...

Gather as much small change as you can, as although entry to almost all mosques is free, *baksheesh* is expected if you climb minarets. Up to E£20 may be demanded, but E£5 is acceptable.

Al Azhar Mosque.

Qalaoun Complex

Sharia Al-Muizz Li Din Allah.
0900-1700, closed at the time of writing but due to be open soon. Metro: Ataba.
Map: Central Cairo popout, H3.

The earliest and most impressive *maristan-madresa-mausoleum* was built by Sultan Al-Mansur Qalaoun Al-Alfi. Built on the site of the Fatimid's Western Palace, the complex took just 13 months to complete in 1284-1285. Visit the mosque/*madresa* first, which has Syrian-style glass mosaics on the hood of the *mihrab* and is a beautifully proportioned and impressive space. But save yourself for the beauty of the mausoleum as it's like stepping inside a jewellery box. The restored ceilings are brilliantly coloured and gilded, tinted glass casts subtle light, ancient granite pillars and marble inlays all ornament the interior, while the dome soars 30 m above.

Al-Nasir Complex

Sharia Al-Muizz Li Din Allah.
Restoration work was ongoing at time of writing.
Metro: Ataba. Map: Central Cairo popout, H3.

Started by Sultan Kitbugha in 1295 and finished by Al-Nasir during his second reign in 1304, an era commemorated by over 30 mosques and other public buildings throughout the city. The complex consists of a mosque, *madresa* and tomb and a *qibla* wall, which still has its original decoration and Kufic inscriptions. The fabulous Gothic doorway was filched from one of the Crusader churches at Acre by Al-Nasir's elder brother, Khalil.

Barquq Complex

Sharia Al-Muizz Li Din Allah.
Metro: Ataba. Map: Central Cairo popout, H3.

Built in 1384-1386. An impressive marble entrance and the silver-encrusted bronze-plated door lead through an offset corridor to the *sahn*, which has four *liwans* arranged in a cruciform shape. The *qibla liwan*, to the east, is divided into three aisles by four ancient pharaonic columns that support beautifully

Mausoleum of the Qaloun complex, Islamic Cairo.

carved and painted ceilings. Upstairs are cells for the Sufi monks who once inhabited the building. To the north of the *madresa* a door leads to the mausoleum where Sultan Barquq was originally buried before being transferred to a specially built mausoleum in the Northern Cemetery (see page 91).

Beit Al-Suhaymi

Darb Al-Asfar, T02-2574 3373.
Daily 0900-1700, 0900-1500 during Ramadan.
E£25, E£15 for students, includes Beit Kharazati next door and Beit El-Gaafar nearby.
Metro: Ataba. Map: Central Cairo popout, H3.

One of the finest examples of a luxurious Mamluk mansion in Cairo, it was lived in until 1961. Beautifully restored, it has a lovely courtyard and a *haramlik* (harem) for the women with superb tiling and a domed bathroom. It is also the wonderfully atmospheric venue for folk music and songs every Sunday at 2000, plus occasional special events and performances particularly during Ramadan.

Around the city

The Northern Walls

Between Bab Al-Nasr and Bab Al-Futuh.
For keys and a 'guide' enquire by Bab Al-Nasr, at the wooden shack; E£5 *baksheesh* should cover things. Map: Central Cairo popout, H3.

The northern walls and gates of the Fatimid city are a masterpiece of military architecture (although they were never actually put to the test by a siege) and are monumentally impressive when viewed from the main street beyond. At present, access is through the square-towered Bab Al-Nasr (Gate of Victory). From the towers there are views out to the Bab Al-Nasr cemetery opposite, an organic mixture of tombs and ramshackle houses. Walking the dark 200-m-long stretch of wall between Bab Al-Nasr to Bab Al-Futuh you appreciate how soldiers could move between the two towers under cover, stealthily firing arrows through slits in the walls.

South of Sharia Al-Azhar

The Ghuriyya: Mosque-Madresa & Mausoleum of Al-Ghuri

Sharia Al-Azhar, next to the footbridge.
Mosque-*madresa* daily 0900-2000; free, *baksheesh* expected; Mausoleum and Sabil-Kuttab daily 0900-1700; E£20, E£10 for students. Metro: Ataba. Map: Central Cairo popout, H4.

The magnificent complex of Sultan Al-Ashraf Qansuh Al-Ghuri, comprises the mausoleum to the east of the street and the mosque-*madresa* to the west. Built in 1504-1505, this was the last great Mamluk public building before the Ottoman conquest.

The mausoleum's interior of black and white marble appears almost art deco, the floor is a patchwork of patterns and the walls are carved in an arabesque design. The dome up above was the crux of the restoration process. Having already collapsed three times since it was first built, the current project opted for a flat drum-topped solution that can be seen from the roof but not from below. From the sabil-kuttab you can climb to the roof to look at the clothes market and admire the mosque opposite.

The stripy exterior of the mosque-*madresa* is stunning. Watch prayer-time from the balcony above the women's section at the rear, and from the minaret (*baksheesh* will be expected to unlock the door) are fantastic views over Al-Azhar, all the way to the Citadel.

Bab Zuweila

Sharia Al-Muizz Li Din Allah.
Daily 0830-1700, E£20, E£10 for students. Map: Central Cairo popout, G4.

Built by Badr Al-Gamali in 1092 when Fatimid fortifications were being reinforced, this was one of the three main gates in the city walls. At 20 m high, with a 4.8-m wide multi-storey arch between two solid stone towers topped by twin minarets, it is a beautiful and impressive sight. From the top of the minarets there is an excellent view over the surrounding area and the adjacent mosque.

The Tentmakers' bazaar

Continue walking south of Bab Zuweila along what is officially known as Sharia Al-Muizzli Din Allah but which, like so many other long roads, changes its name in different sections. At this point is Sharia Al-Khiyamiyya, or the Tentmakers' bazaar. Probably the city's best preserved example of a roofed market, a multitude of coloured printed fabrics are sold here.

Mosque of Sultan Al-Muayyad Sheikh

Ahmed Mahir, immediately to the west of Bab Zuweilai.
Map: Central Cairo popout, G4.

Built on the site of the old Kazanat Al-Shamaii prison where Al-Muayyad had been incarcerated several times because of his love of alcohol when he was a Mamluk slave-soldier. On being released after one particularly unpleasant stretch, he vowed to replace the prison with a mosque, which he began in 1415 after becoming Sultan. Sometimes known as the Red Mosque because of the colour of its external walls, it was one of the last to be built in the ancient large enclosure style before the Turkish style was adopted as the norm. Superb bronze-plated wooden entrance doors open into a vestibule with an ornate stalactite ceiling.

Behind the mosque is a lane, known as Bab El-Khalq after a medieval gate that has long since vanished, where in the weeks before Ramadan the shops display row upon row of lanterns in every possible size, shape and colour.

The Museum of Islamic Art

Midan Bab Al-Khalq.
Closed for renovation at time of writing.
Metro: Mohamed Naguib, or 20-min walk or 5-min taxi west of Bab Zuweila along Sharia Ahmed Maher.
Map: Downtown Cairo. H5, p80.

This museum has been undergoing lengthy renovations, and when (or if) it will open again is still unclear. It is worth checking the current situation when in the vicinity, as it contains the rarest and most extensive collection of Islamic works of art in the world. Among over 75,000 exhibits, of particular interest are: the Fatimid panels that depict animals and birds because, unlike the Sunni Muslims, the Fatimid Shi'a had no objection to portraying living things; doors originally from the Al-Azhar Mosque; a Mamluk astrolabe used by Muslim navigators and the oil lamps from the mosque of Sultan Hathor.

Mosques of Sultan Hassan & Rafail

Midan Salah Al-Din, directly below the Citadel.
Sat-Thu 0800-1630, Fri 0800-1100 and 1500-1630.
During Ramadan until 1430. Entrance to each E£25, E£15 for students.
Map: Central Cairo popout, G6.

These two adjacent mosques present themselves best at dusk when the atmosphere becomes charged with the *adhan* (call to prayer) and the very air seems to shimmer around their colossal forms. The Sultan Hassan Mosque, completed in

Tip...

Turn right (east) at Bab Zuweila into Sharia Darb Al-Ahmar (Red Road) for a fascinating and unspoilt 1¼-km walk straight to the Citadel (see page 88).

Above: Mosques of Sultan Hassan and Rafail from the Cairo Citadel.
Opposite page: Bab Zuweila.

1363, is one of the largest mosques in the world and was at times used as a fortress, being conveniently placed for hurling rooftop missiles at enemies in the Citadel. The marble *minbar* here is one of the finest in Cairo, its height accentuated by hanging lamp-chains. The original glass lamps from these chains can be found in the Museum of Islamic Art in Cairo and in the Victoria and Albert Museum in London. A bronze door with gold and silver motifs leads to the mausoleum of Sultan Hassan, a room of grand proportions dominated by a 21-m-diameter dome. As Sultan Hassan was murdered and his body never recovered, two of his sons are buried here in his place. The three-section 86-m minaret by the mausoleum is the highest in Cairo, with each new section decorated at its base with stalactites.

Despite its appearance, the Al-Rifai Mosque, directly to the east of Sultan Hassan Mosque, was only started in the late 19th century and finished in 1912.

The Citadel

Enter via Bab Al-Gabal.
Sat-Thu 0800-1600 winter, 0800-1700 summer, last entrance to museums 1530. E£40, E£20 for students, plus tips for guides and shoe attendants. Bus No 72 or minibus No 154 from Midan Abdel Mounim Riyad (near Midan Tahrir); ask taxi drivers for 'Al-Qala'a', with a guttural 'q'. Map: Central Cairo popout, H7.

The Citadel (also known as *Al-Qala'a Al-Gabal* – Citadel of the Mountain – or *Al-Burg*) perches on the steep slopes of the Muqattam Hills, its multiple minarets piercing the skyline and the silver (tin) dome of the Mosque of Mohamed Ali glinting in the sun. It was begun by Salah Al-Din in 1176 as part of an ambitious general fortification plan that included enclosing the whole city with a new wall that could be controlled from the main fort.

Later the Citadel was abandoned until the Mamluks' arrival, when it became the Sultan's residence and the base of the Burgi Mamluks (1382-1517). In the 14th century Sultan Al-Nasir Mohammed (1310-1340) added a number of

Five of the best

Citadel gates, towers & museums

❶ **Bab Al-Azab**, enclosed by a pair of round-headed towers, stands on the west side of the Citadel. It was the original entrance to the Southern enclosure and has brass-bound wooden doors dating from 1754.

❷ The **Ayyubid walls and towers** around part of the northern enclosure are from the time of Salah Al-Din (1176-1183). The dressed stone walls are 10 m high, 3 m thick and 2100 m in circumference interspersed with half-round towers.

❸ **Burg As-Siba**, or **Lions' Tower** Built in 1207 by the Mamluk Sultan Baybars, this tower is so called because it is decorated with a frieze of stone lions, the sultans' heraldic symbol.

❹ The **National Police Museum** has some strange and interesting exhibits of policing problems ranging from assassination attempts to the protection of Egyptian antiquities. The view from the terrace takes in the Pyramids on the left through to the minaret of the Mosque Al-Fath in Midan Ramses to the right – hope for a clear day.

❺ **Seized Museum** Items confiscated from dealers in the antiquities black market, span the history of Egypt, from pharaonic painted wooden sarcophagus and funerary beads through to Byzantine, Islamic and European gold coins and a set of official seals from the reign of the Mohammed Ali.

The Citadel.

Ceiling of the Mohammed Ali Pasha Mosque.

buildings including a mosque and later, because of the development of warfare and the use of canons, the Turks undertook major reinforcements. The most recent modification to the Citadel was by Mohammed Ali Pasha (1805-1840) who built an impressive mosque on the site of the original palaces. The whole complex is still under military control and there are large areas that are closed to the public.

The architecture of **Mohammed Ali Pasha Mosque** was strongly influenced by the Ottoman mosques of Istanbul with the characteristic high, slender, octagonal minarets and covered by an imposing dome with four half-domes on each side. Once inside, after readjusting to the dim lighting, note the unusual inclusion of two *minbars*. The large wooden construction, carved, painted and gilded, was installed by Mohammed Ali. It was too large to erect in the conventional space by the *mihrab* and was placed under the central

Tip…

If you're squeezing in a short visit to the Citadel start off by exploring its most interesting features – the Mosque of Mohammed Ali Pasha, which provides an amazing view west over Cairo, and the restored Sultan Al-Nasir Mohammed Mosque.

dome making the weekly sermon inaudible to most of the congregation. In 1939 King Farouk installed a smaller alabaster *minbar* carved with a geometric pattern – to the right of the *mihrab*.

The **Sultan Al-Nasir Mohammed Mosque**, built between 1318 and 1335, is certainly the best preserved Mamluk building in the Citadel and is claimed to be one of the finest arcade-style mosques in Cairo, the arches being supported by pharaonic and classical columns plundered from elsewhere. The two distinctive minarets, one above each entrance, are covered in the

Around the city

upper part with green, blue and white ceramic tiles attributed to craftsmen from Persia as are the onion-shaped bulbs on the tops of the minarets.

Look out for a small square tower to the northwest of the marble-floored courtyard. Here is a clock that was a gift from King Louis-Philippe of France in 1846 in exchange for the obelisk now in the Place de la Concorde in Paris. The clock has never worked.

Mevlevi Dervish Theatre

Al Hilmiyya.
Walk over the crossroad from the Palace of Amir Taz. Map: Central Cairo popout, G6.

Also known as the Cairo Tikiyya, and lovingly and painstakingly restored over many years by a joint Italian-Egyptian team. Part of the Rumi sect, the whirling dervishes who lived and practised here came to Egypt just after the Ottoman conquest, and were the last of the sect to be dissolved in 1945. The interior is decorated with botanic designs, while the flying birds on the dome represent the liberation of the soul from a materialist life. It's the perfect place to re-energize, as is the peaceful Turkish garden outside.

Mosque of Ibn Tulun

Ibn Tulun.
Daily 0800-1700. E£1 for shoe-covers to wear inside the mosque. Bus No 72 or minibus No 154 from Midan Abdel Mounim Riad to the Citadel via the Saiyyida Zeinab area and then past the mosque; taxi from Downtown (E£5-10). Map: Central Cairo popout, F7.

The largest place of worship in Cairo – external measurements are 140 m by 122 m – and the oldest to retain its original features is this mosque, built between AD 876-879. The cosmic proportions and austere interior make it stand out among a million other mosques in the city. Its central courtyard is 92 m square yet despite its huge size, the overall impression is of harmony, simplicity and

sobriety. Kufic inscriptions, almost 2 km long, circle the mosque walls several times below the roof and relay about 20% of the Koran. The marble-plated *mihrab*, added in the 13th century, is surrounded by a glass mosaic frieze. Directly above is a small wooden dome. Legend says that the mosque's sycamore beams were previously part of Noah's ark. The *minbar*, presented by Sultan Lagin in 1296, is a fine work of art. The minaret has an unusual outside spiral staircase, which appears to be a copy of the one at Samarra in Iraq; the view from the top over the surrounding area is excellent and worth the climb. It's fine to keep footwear on (no covers required) for climbing the minaret.

Al-Azhar Park

Entrance gate is on Salah Salem.
Daily 0900-2300, except Wed 0900-2200.
E£5. Taxi from Downtown (E£10).
Map: Central Cairo popout, H5.

Called in Arabic *Hadiyka Al-alzar* (which will help taxi drivers), the park is amazingly lush, with shrubs, trees and flowers in abundance, and full of Cairene families enjoying the palm-lined walkways and children's play area. It is an emerald-green success story built on top of an immense, centuries-old mound of the Islamic city's rubbish dump.

Come to the park for sunset and you will get sweeping views across the city as monuments are lit up and the green neon lights of minarets glow.

Mosque of Ibn Tulun, Islamic Cairo.

Cities of the Dead.

It's a fact…

Muslim graveyards have no flowers unless they grow wild by chance. Instead of buying flowers to decorate family graves on their routine weekly visit, relatives will, instead, often give a simple dish to the poor to provide a meal for their children.

The fabulous Hilltop Restaurant on the northern hill is worth splashing out on, or the Trianon café outside is a delightful place to sit with a cool drink (though there's a minimum charge of E£35 and painfully slow service). An urban plaza with car parking, a café, retail area and a new museum is planned for the park. This new **Museum of Islamic Cairo** (due to open in 2011) will prepare visitors for the experiences awaiting them in the lanes of the old city.

Cities of the Dead

The Cities of the Dead is the name given by Europeans to Cairo's two main cemeteries that spread north and south from the Citadel. Half a million people are thought to live among the mausoleums and tombs of the sprawling necropoli, and the communities here have shops, electricity and schools. Residents tend to be comparatively poor and, although certainly not dangerous, it is obviously advisable not to flaunt your wealth, to dress modestly and remember that these are people's homes. It's one of few intimidating places in Cairo (lone women will feel conspicuous, either sex will feel more comfortable with company) and somewhere you can get very lost after dark.

Al-Qarafa Al-Kubra

From Sultan Hassan Mosque head south towards Sharia Imam Al-Shafi for about 1.5 km, more pleasant by taxi (E£3-4) than on foot.

The Al-Qarafa Al-Kubra (Southern Cemetary) is older, but there are relatively few monuments to see. The Mausoleum of Imam Al-Shafi is the focus of a visit, with splendid marbling and a quite

astounding dome, gilded and painted red and blue, and topped by a metal boat. The Imam Shafa'i was born in Palestine in AD 767 and was the originator of the Shafi'ite School of Islamic jurisprudence, one of the four great Sunni Schools of Law. His tomb lies to the north of the building. Its religious focus is a delicate 20th-century sandalwood screen or *maqsurah* and a marble stela. These are kissed by visiting Muslims as a sign of faith.

Al-Qarafa Al-Sharqiyyah

Taxi direct; or walk east along Sharia Al-Azhar from the Al-Azhar mosque for 15 mins until you reach the roundabout junction with Sharia Salah Salem and then north for 250 m. Head for the dome and minaret.

The Northern Cemetary, known locally as *Al-Qarafa Al-Sharqiyyah* (the Eastern Cemetery) because it was east of the old city, has been the burial place of the sultans since the 14th century. It contains a number of the most beautiful mausoleums in the city, including **Mausoleum of Sultan Al-Zahir Barquq** (daily 0900-2000). It was the first royal tomb to be built in the necropolis. To the south is the *madresa* and **Mausoleum of Sultan Al-Qaitbay** (daily 0900-1700), which is a magnificent example of 15th-century Arab art and one of Egypt's most beautiful monuments from the Arab era.

Old Cairo & Roda Island

What began as a defensive Persian settlement around 500 BC grew into a large town bearing the name Babylon-in-Egypt. Under the Arabs it became the Fortress of the Beacon. Today, this historical district goes by two far less exciting if perfectly apt names, Old Cairo or Coptic Cairo. Come here on a Sunday for an appreciation of Coptic culture as Coptic Cairenes wander from holy sight to holy sight.

Leaving Mar Girgis station, you are confronted by two circular Roman towers some 33 m in diameter which comprised the west gate of the fortress. Built on what was at that time the east bank of the Nile, now 400 m further west, the towers sit on foundations now smothered beneath 10 m of Nile silt and rubble. Between them is the Coptic Museum, while the Hanging Church is entered to their right and the modern Church of St George to their left. The other main churches and synagogue of Ben Ezra are accessed via a little flight of sunken steps.

Tip...

Certainly the easiest and cheapest way to get to Old Cairo is via the metro which drops you right in front of the Coptic quarter. For more of an adventure, river-taxis leave Maspero Dock between 0700-0800, E£1, and call at Mar Gigis five stops later.

The Coptic Museum

Sharia Mari Girgis, copticmuseum.gov.eg.
Daily 0900-1700, 1500 during Ramadan. E£40, E£20 for students. Metro: Mar Girgis (St George); taxi from Downtown E£10.
Map: Greater Cairo popout, D5.

This museum was founded in 1908 as a means of preserving Coptic artefacts and Egypt's Christian heritage against the acquisitive activities of local and foreign collectors. It gives an interesting insight into the evolution of Christian (and to some extent secular) art and architecture in Egypt in the period AD 300-1800, as well as demonstrating the interchange of ideas with the larger Islamic community.

In the Old Wing, the building itself is as rewarding as the artefacts. The ceiling carvings throughout this section are from Coptic houses in Old Cairo and have been incorporated into the building along with panels and tiles. Rooms 20-22 are a highpoint of the museum. They contain the icons, spanning a huge range of iconographic styles – Byzantine, Greek, Cretan, Syrian and more. Room 23 has some unimaginably heavy and ornate keys from the monastery doors of Middle Egypt, plus jewellery, intriguing lamps fashioned into animal shapes, and a wealth of incense censers – so important in the Coptic liturgy – swinging on chains.

Displays, arranged thematically across two floors in the New and Old Wings, are best tackled in an anticlockwise direction, starting on the ground floor. Reckon on about three hours for a thorough viewing or an hour to just whip around. It's a good idea to go over lunchtime, when the museum is virtually empty.

The Hanging Church

Sharia Mari Girgis.
Daily 0900-1700. Coptic masses Fri 0800-1100 and Sun 0700-1000. Free guided tours – ask staff if anyone is available. Metro: Mar Girgis (St George); taxi from Downtown E£10.
Map: Greater Cairo popout, D5.

Beside the Coptic Museum, the other main attraction in Old Cairo is the Hanging Church (*Al-Mu'allaqah* or 'The Suspended One'). It is so called because it perches on top of the three stone piers of the semi-flooded Roman Water Gate from where the Melkite bishop Cyrus, the last Byzantine viceroy, fled by boat as the Muslim army arrived. A painting of the Virgin on the right-hand wall greets you. A Coptic 'Mona Lisa,' her eyes will follow you when you move from side to side. Against the left-hand wall are relics of saints contained in cylindrical vessels wrapped in red cloth: it is to these you can appeal for blessings. To the right of the altar is a room that is built over the eastern tower of the southern gateway of the old fortress – there is a cordoned-off hole in the floor, through which you can see 13 m down to appreciate the fact there are no foundations – just date palm trunks holding the church up.

A mosaic in the Hanging Church.

The Church of St Sergius

From the convent of St George,
turn right at the end of the lane.
Daily 0800-1600. Metro: Mar Girgis.

This fifth-century church is dedicated to two soldiers, St Sergius and St Bacchus, who were martyred in Syria in 303. It lies some 3 m below street level and its architecture follows the style of a traditional basilica with the nave divided from the side aisles by two rows of six monolithic pillars. The partially flooded crypt, the only remaining vestige of the original church, is intriguing because it is claimed that the Holy Family sought refuge here during their flight to Egypt. It has always been a popular place of pilgrimage and a special Mass is held annually on the 24th day of the Coptic month of Bechens (1 June) to commemorate the flight.

Ben Ezra Synagogue

South of the Church of St Barbara.
Daily 0900-1600. Metro: Mar Girgis.
Map: Greater Cairo popout, D5.

Ben Ezra Synagogue in the former sixth-century Church of St Michael the Archangel, which itself had been built on the site of a synagogue destroyed by the Romans. Hence, this is the oldest surviving synagogue in Egypt. In the 12th century it was sold back to the Jews by the Copts in order to pay taxes being raised to finance the Ibn Tulun mosque. The synagogue is built in the basilica style with three naves and an altar hidden by doors, which are wonderfully worked and encrusted with ivory.

Church of St George

Enter via the first door on the left of the main
entrance to the Coptic museum.
Daily 0800-1600. Metro: Mar Girgis.

The Church of St George is a modern construction from 1904 and the only circular church in Egypt, so shaped because it is actually built on top of the north tower of the old fortress. Part of the Monastery of St George, which is the seat of the

Souk El-Fustat

If you are going to walk from the main Coptic sights to the mosque and monasteries to the north, you will pass by this *souk*. It's about 400 m north of the metro station, on the right-hand side of Sharia Saydi Hassan Al-Anwar, before the Mosque of Amr. You can't miss the freshly constructed building, which provides workspaces for local artisans (metal workers, leather workers, glass blowers, etc) in an attempt to keep traditional crafts alive.

Tip...

With alfresco wicker seating, whispering trees and good lemon juice (*asir limon*), Café Saint George is a bit expensive but the best place to re-group after seeing so many churches.

Greek Orthodox Patriarchate of Alexandria, the church is the scene of one of the largest Coptic *moulids* in Egypt on 23 April (St George's Day). It is worth a quick look for the brightly stained glass, piped music and heady scent of incense.

Mosque of Amr Ibn Al-As

500 m north of Mari Girgis metro station.
Map: Greater Cairo popout, D5.

The original Mosque of Amr Ibn Al-As was built in AD 642 by the commander of the Arab army that captured Egypt in that year. Built near to both Babylon-in-Egypt and the Arabs' encampment (Fustat), it is the oldest mosque in Egypt and one of the oldest in the entire Islamic world. As is often the case in the older mosques the interior includes many pillars taken from ancient Egyptian monuments. As a result the whole mosque is a hybrid with parts of the fabric dating from before the conquest of Egypt until the 19th-century alterations.

Coptic Orthodox Cathedral

Off Sharia Ramses.
Metro: Mar Girgis.
Map: Downtown Cairo, G1, p80.

There are more than 100 Coptic Orthodox churches in Cairo but the special pride is the Coptic Orthodox Cathedral (1965) dedicated to St Mark. It can seat 5000 worshippers, houses the patriarchal library and accommodates the patriarch Pope Shenouda III.

Roda Island

Accessible by bridge from Garden City at the northern end and from Old Cairo at the bottom.

Roda has a couple of interesting sights, the eccentric Manyal Palace being chief amongst them. Strolling the 2 km between the palace in the north and the Nilometer to the south along mainly post-1950s streets is something few tourists find time to do, but it offers plenty of scope for a relaxing *sheesha* and *ahwa* in shady streets that are more peaceful than most.

Manyal Palace

Daily 0900-1630. E£20, E£10 for students. Currently closed for restoration and scheduled to reopen 2010. Map: Central Cairo popout, C7.

An oasis of tranquillity and well worth visiting, the palace was built in 1903 and is now a museum. It was the home of King Farouk's uncle Prince Mohammed Ali and comprises a number of buildings in various styles including Moorish, Ottoman, Persian, Rococo and Syrian. Upstairs are a number of luxurious rooms, of which the Syrian Room is the finest. The Royal Residence in the middle of the garden (stocked with rare trees brought to Egypt by Mohammed Ali) is a mixture of

Above: Manial Palace Museum. Opposite page: Chruch of St George.

Turkish, Moroccan, Egyptian and Syrian architectures and contains a number of rooms, nearly all of which are decorated with blue earthenware tiles.

The Nilometer

A small kiosk on the island's southern tip.
Daily 0900-1700. E£10, E£5 for students.
Map: Greater Cairo popout, C5.

On the southern tip of Roda Island stands a small kiosk containing the Nilometer, originally built in the ninth century BC. There has probably been a nilometer here since ancient times but this one was constructed in AD 861 and is considered the second-oldest Islamic structure in Cairo, after the Amr Ibn Al-Aas Mosque. The original measuring gauge remains today and there is exquisite Kufic calligraphy on the interior walls and an elaborately painted dome.

Giza

The newer suburbs on Cairo's west bank are chiefly comprised of post-1960 housing, interspersed with the occasional grand villa, crumbling mansion and pleasant green square. There are a few smaller, less frequented museums as well as some good restaurants, but of course the main draw of this side of the river is the three mighty pharaonic pyramids.

No matter how you approach them the first sight of these ancient memorials, incongruous triangles above the concrete block houses, transfixes even the most seasoned traveller. One of the first things that visitors to the Pyramids will notice is their unexpected proximity to urban Cairo. The second is the onslaught of hustlers that bombard the awe-struck onlooker. Despite the increased police presence that tries in earnest to subdue hawkers, and camel and horse hustlers, they still get through.

The Sphinx, Giza plateau.

Pyramids of Giza

Daily 0800-1600 winter, 0800-1800 summer.
Entry E£50, E£25 for students; to enter the
Pyramid of Cheops E£100, E£50 for students;
E£25/15 for the 2nd and 3rd pyramids.
For Sound and Light performances, see page 108.
Metro: Giza. Map: Greater Cairo popout, A6.

Of the Seven Wonders of the ancient world only
the Great Pyramid is left standing. Giza's are by
no means the only pyramids in Egypt but they are
the largest, most imposing and best preserved.
Herodotus, chronicler of the Ancient Greeks,
claimed that it would have taken 100,000 slaves
30 years to have constructed the great Pyramid
of Cheops, but it is more likely that the pyramid
was built by peasants, paid in food. Happily, the
high waters also made it possible to transport the
casing stone from Aswan and Tura virtually to the
base of the pyramids.

The enormous Pyramid of Cheops, built
between 2589-2566 BC out of over 2,300,000
blocks of stone with an average weight of two
and a half tonnes and a total weight of 6,000,000
tonnes to a height of almost 140 m, is the oldest
and largest of the pyramids at Giza. Maybe not
surprisingly, it can be seen from the moon.

The Pyramid of Chephren and Pyramid of
Menkaure date from 2570-30 BC. There is a theory
that the odd plan of the three Pyramids of Giza,
progressively smaller and with the third slightly
offset to the left, correlates to the layout of the
three stars of Orion's Belt. Highly controversial,
it suggests that the Ancient Egyptians chose to
reproduce, on land and over a great distance, a
kind of map of the stars.

The first thefts from tombs occurred relatively
soon after the Pyramids' construction, which was
undoubtedly an important factor in the preference
for hidden tombs, such as in The Valley of the
Kings, by the time of the New Kingdom.

Of the Seven Wonders of the ancient world only the Great Pyramid is left standing.

Tip...

Be first through the gates or the last person in before
the gates close, and head off to view the pyramids'
majesty from afar. The number of tourists who can
enter Cheops is limited so arrive early (morning
session 0800, then another batch at 1300; 250 at one
time in winter, 150 people in summer).

Above: Camel trekking to the Pyramids of Giza.
Right: Pyramids of Giza at night.

The Great Pyramid of Cheops (Khufu)

Originally the 230 x 230 m pyramid would have stood at 140 m high, but 3m has been lost in all dimensions since the encasing limestone was eroded or removed by later rulers who used the cemeteries like a quarry to construct the Islamic city.

Inside, after ascending the 36-m long corridor, which is 1.6 m high and has a steep 1:2 gradient, you arrive at the start of the larger 47-m long Great Gallery, which continues upward at the same incline – the sensation of being under six million tonnes of stone becomes overpowering at this point, it's definitely not for claustrophobics or those who dislike being hustled into moving too quickly by lines of other visitors. The gallery, whose magnificent stonework is so well cut that it is impossible to insert a blade into the joints, narrows at the top end to a corbelled roof and finishes at the King's Chamber, 95 m beneath the pyramid's apex.

It's a fact

Chephren's pyramid it is a few metres smaller than Cheops' Pyramid but its construction, on a raised limestone plateau, was a deliberate attempt to make it appear larger than his father's pyramid.

The room measures 5.2 x 10.8 x 5.8 m high and contains the huge lidless red granite sarcophagus, which was all that remained of the treasures when archaeologists first explored the site. It was saved because it was too large to move along the entrance passage and, therefore, must have been placed in the chamber during the pyramid's construction.

Wait around a while in the King's Chamber, if you can stand the heat, to let the crowds thin out and you'll start to get a sense of the mystique of the place that prompts some visitors to start chanting.

Pyramids of Cheops, Chephren and Menkaure, Giza.

Pyramid of Chephren (Khafre)   Built for the son of Cheops and Hensuten. The top of the pyramid still retains some of the casing of polished limestone from Tura that once covered the entire surface, providing an idea of the original finish and how the pyramid would have appeared to the earliest travellers – gleaming and white as they approached from the desert. The entrance to the tomb was lost for centuries until 1818 when Belzoni located it and blasted open the sealed portal on the north side. Although he believed that it would still be intact, he found that it had been looted many centuries earlier.

Pyramid of Menkaure (Mycerinus)   This is the smallest of the three Giza Pyramids and marks the beginning of a steep decline in the standards of workmanship and attention to detail in the art of pyramid-building. At the time of Menkaure's death (Chephren's successor) the pyramid was unfinished and the granite encasement intended to cover the poor quality local limestone was never put in place by his son Shepseskaf.

The Sphinx   We are extremely lucky that 'the Awesome', or 'Terrible One' (*Abu'l-Hawl*) still exists. It was built of soft sandstone and would have disappeared centuries ago had the sand not covered it for so much of its history. Nobody can be certain who it represents but it is possibly Khafre himself and, if this is the case, would be the oldest known large-scale royal portrait. Some say that it was hewn from the remaining stone after the completion of the pyramid and that, almost as an afterthought, Khafre set it, as a sort of monumental scarecrow, to guard his tomb. Others claim that the face is that of his guardian deity rather than Khafre's own.

Five of the best

Giza excavations & subsidiary pyramids

❶ South of the Pyramid of Menkaure are three smaller incomplete pyramids, the largest of which, to the east, was most likely intended for Menkaure's principal wife.

❷ In accordance with the pharaonic custom, Cheops married his sister Merites whose smaller ruined pyramid stands to the east of his, together with the pyramids of two other queens, both of which are attached to a similarly ruined smaller sanctuary.

❸ West of the Cheops Pyramid is an extensive **Royal Cemetery** in which 15 *mastabas* have been opened to the public after having been closed for over 100 years. A 4600-year-old female mummy, with a unique internal plaster encasement unlike that seen anywhere else, was discovered at the site.

❹ The **Sun Boat Museum** (open daily 0900-1600, E£40, E£20 for students) is at the base of the south face of the Cheops Pyramid where five boat pits were discovered in 1982. The boat on display, painstakingly reassembled over 14 years and an amazing 43 m long, is held together with sycamore pegs and rope. The scale and antiquity of the vessel is impressive and makes real the engravings of boats you will see on temple walls around Egypt.

❺ The **Mortuary Temple of Khafre** lies to the east and is more elaborate and better preserved than that of his father. Although the statues and riches have been stolen, the limestone walls were cased with granite, which is still present in places. There are still the remains a large pillared hall, a small sanctuary, outhouses and a courtyard.

Tip...

Horse and camel rides are available around the pyramids – fine if you are short on time or only want to take in their splendour from afar. For short rides offer no more than E£20 to be paid after your meander. AA and MG stables (past the entrance to the Sphinx) are among the more notable in Giza.

Easy side trips from central Cairo

Why stop at Giza when the region surrounding Cairo is dotted with ancient sites and excavation, including the Step Pyramid of Saqqara, and Dahshur's two sublimely-shaped monoliths. The approach to Saqqara, the vast necropolis of the first pharaohs, through a forest of date palms is as breathtaking as the multitude of hidden mastabas, ruinous courts and causeways, and the sand-strewn rungs of the step pyramid itself. Dahshur, unlike the Giza plateau, is surrounded by nothing but the grey and gold desert, and there's usually no one in sight but a few bored policemen. The easiest way to tour Cairo's triumvirate of pyramid sites in one day – Giza, Saqqara and Dahshur – is by taxi, costing around E£180-200.

Saqqara Step Pyramid

Daily 0800-1600. E£50, E£25 for students, includes Imhotep Museum, parking E£2. Organized tour (E£100, exclusive of ticket price, or less if booked through a budget hotel); Bus No 987 from Midan Tahrir or a microbus from Pyramids Road in Giza to Badrasheen, then a 1.5 km walk from the main road by the sign for Saqqara antiquities. Public transport can be difficult to come by late at night.

The Step Pyramid stands at the heart of an ancient funerary complex designed and built for King Zoser (Old Kingdom) under the control of Imhotep who many regard as the world's first architect. The pyramid, the first of its kind, can be seen as a prototype for the Giza Pyramids. It marked the evolution of burial tombs from *mastabas* with deep shafts for storing the sarcophagus to imposing elevated mausoleums. Although the fine white limestone casing has disappeared over time, the step structure is still clearly visible. The pyramid eventually reached a height of 62.5 m on a base of 109 m by 121 m, which although small compared with those at Giza, is still an amazing feat. The advances represented by Zoser's Pyramid were not in the building techniques or materials, which were already established, but the concept, design and calculations involved that made such a monument possible.

Shafts inside the pyramid are no longer open to the public and the area is currently under restoration.

Dahshur Pyramids

Daily 0800-1600 winter, 1700 in summer. E£25, E£15 for students.

Snefru (2575-2551 BC), first ruler of the Fourth Dynasty at the time of great pyramid construction, built these two pyramids. His constructive tendencies were continued by his son Cheops. You arrive first at the Red Pyramid to the north, named after the reddish local limestone used in

Tip...

Bring water and food for the day, as the restaurants surrounding the area tend to be very touristy and poor value for money.

The Red Pyramid at Dahshur.

the core. It is thought to be the first true pyramid to be constructed with sloping sides rather than steps, and is second in size only to the Great Pyramid of Cheops at Giza. A 28-m climb leads to the entrance, from where you plunge down a shaft to two antechambers, their sides as smooth as if they were built yesterday. A wooden staircase takes you up to the burial chamber, which was unused by Snefru or anyone else. Claustrophobics who passed up the chance to enter the Great Pyramid should give it a go, as there is no pushing and shoving to induce anxiety.

The Bent Pyramid (or Southern Shining Pyramid) gets its unusual shape from an obvious change in its angles. A number of theories have put forward to explain this: some think that the builders got tired and changed the angle to reduce the volume and so complete it sooner, others suggest that the change indicated a double pyramid – two pyramids superimposed. It is further hypothesised that the architect lost his nerve, as this pyramid was being built when the pyramid at Maidoum collapsed.

That too had an angle of 52° so a quick rethink was necessary. At the base it measures 188.6 m and the height is 97 m (originally 105 m). If construction had continued at the original angle it would have been 128.5 m high. The pyramid is also unique in having two entrances.

What the locals say

Dahshur's pyramids are about an hour south of Giza, but nobody ever really goes there, so you get the whole complex to yourself. Climbing down a pyramid's dark shaft is exhilarating, especially when you realize how much stone is piled on top of you. While there's not much to actually see inside, since they were gutted long ago, it's amazing to stand in the belly of such a massive, and famous, monument.

Andrew, *student,*
American University of Cairo.

Listings
Sleeping

Cairo has loads of interesting and decent cheap hotels, which means fierce competition, and brutal hotel touts. Lies are part of the game. You will be told hotels are full, or closed, or have doubled in price. Take control of the situation by choosing a place in advance.

Downtown, Zamalek & Gezira

Longchamps €€€
21 Sharia Ismail Mohammed, Zamalek, T02-2735 2311, hotellongchamps.com.
Map: Downtown Cairo, E2, p80.
Long-standing family-run hotel that is about the quirkiest in Cairo. Always popular, it's imperative to book in advance. Two shaded terraces offer peace, greenery and a cold beer, the restaurant is pleasant, the breakfast buffet highly recommended and there is a library. Rooms are very comfortable with new furniture, air conditioning, TV, fridge and a hint of the colonial flavour that permeates the public areas.

Talisman €€€
39 Sharia Talaat Harb, T02-2393 9431, talisman-hotel.com.
Map: Downtown Cairo, E2, p80.
This gem of a hotel is hidden down an alley parallel to Sharia 26th July. Look for the New Minerva hotel sign and once inside take the left-hand elevator up to rich, warm colours and tasteful Arabesque decor throughout. Each room is different and the lounge area is festooned with artefacts. The only almost-boutique hotel in Cairo, so book in advance. Free Wi-Fi.

Victoria Hotel €€€,
66 Sharia El-Gumhoriyya, T02-2589 2290, victoria.com.eg.
Map: Downtown Cairo, F1, p80.
A large pink hotel that's been around since the 1930s, but long red carpets, wooden floors and loads of chandeliers make it feel almost Victorian. High-ceilinged air-conditioned rooms have all necessary amenities. En suite

rooms are spacious and have tubs as well as showers. There's an internet café, cosy bar and an open-air coffee shop. The best deal for a three-star in the city, and although the location is a bit far from the heart of downtown it's an easy walk to Islamic Cairo.

Windsor €€€
19 Sharia Alfi Bey, T02-2591 5277, windsorcairo.com.
Map: Downtown Cairo, F2, p80.
Historic and atmospheric, well-run, family-owned hotel with clean air-conditioned rooms. Look at a few as they vary greatly, the de luxe rooms are stacked with antique furniture while others have drawers hanging off. Bathrooms are definitely on the small side, some cheaper rooms have their toilet outside the room. Breakfast included. One of the classiest and cosiest bars in the city, with barrel chairs, plenty of memorabilia and an interesting history. Michael Palin stayed here while going around the world in 80 days.

Garden City House Hotel €€,
23 Sharia Kamal El Dinn Salah, Garden City, gardencityhouse.com.
Map: Downtown Cairo, A6, p80.
On the edge of Midan Tahrir, yet this place feels well out of any backpacker scene. Large rooms have plenty of furniture and share huge balconies with a bit of a view. There's a sociable breezy restaurant area and general air of nostalgia

Hotel Longchamps

Great Value – Home away from Home.

www.hotellongchamps.com
hotel.longchamps@web.de
T: +20 2-2735-23-11 or 12
F: +20 2-2735-9644
21 Ismail Mohamed Street
Zamalek, Cairo / Egypt

throughout. Clean if old-fashioned doubles with bathroom, with or without air conditioning, breakfast included.

Pension Roma €€
169 Sharia Mohamed Farid, T02-23911088, pensionroma.com.eg.
Map: Downtown Cairo, E3, p80. Among the classiest of budget options, this old-world hotel is clean with hardwood floors and high ceilings that make up for no air conditioning. Staff are friendly and informative, lounge has TV, and it attracts an international and age-diverse group of travellers. Doubles with shared bath or private bath, and they can accommodate three or four people in larger rooms. Some balconies look down on the mayhem, breakfast included.

Pension Zamalek €€
6 Sharia Salah Al-Din, T02-2735 9318.
Spacious, old-fashioned rooms, some with air conditioning and heater, most with balconies, in very tranquil nook off Zamalek's

main drag. A family-run super-friendly hotel, every two rooms share a spotless bath. Laundry service and TV in the eerie salon. Breakfast included. Phone ahead as they're often booked up with long-stayers.

Sara Inn Hostel €€
21 Sharia Yousef El-Guindi, Bab El-Louq, T02-2392 2940, sarainnhostel.com.
Map: Downtown Cairo, D5, p80. A quiet, intimate, recently renovated hotel, centrally located with young staff. Warmly decorated, communal lounge with TV and internet access. Basic budget hotel breakfast. Can arrange cheap tours.

Bluebird Hotel €
42 Sharia Talaat Harb, 6th floor, T02-2575 6377.
Map: Downtown Cairo, D3, p80. Small family set-up in a top-floor hideaway with extremely clean rooms, all with fans. Choice of bathroom inside the room or spotless shared showers, and a communal kitchen, breakfast included. A cute little place.

Canadian Hostel €
5 Sharia Talaat Harb, T02-2392 5794.
Map: Downtown Cairo, C5, p80. Recommended for the super-friendly staff who offer good travel advice. Clean airy rooms are a little stark and gloomy, but breakfast is included, there's reliably hot water, cheap laundry (E£10) and internet (E£6 per hr).

Dahab Hotel €
7th floor, 26 Sharia Mahmoud Bassiouny, T02-2579 9104.
Map: Downtown Cairo, C4, p80. One of the cheapest beds in town, this rooftop hotel is amazingly successful in offering a little taste of Dahab in the middle of downtown Cairo madness. Small, very simple rooms on the rooftop, some with fans, have clean sheets and decent pillows. Bathrooms are clean and newly tiled. It's the garden that's special, a little oasis overflowing with flowers and plants, you can even hear birds chirping. Pure backpacker vibes, it's a good place to meet people. Breakfast E£8 extra.

Lialy Hostel €
8 Midan Talaat Harb, 2nd floor, T02-2575 2802.
Map: Downtown Cairo, C4, p80. A relatively new establishment right in the heart of everything, spotless, private, and homely – though rooms are very simple. The staff is young, well informed

Eating & drinking

and friendly. Hearty breakfast included, there's a great view over Midan Talaat Harb from the lounge. Internet, laundry (E£1 per piece). All bathrooms are shared.

Islamic Cairo

El-Malky Hotel €
4 Midan El-Hussein,
T02-2589 0804, elmalky.com.
Unquestionably the most pleasant of the three hotels around Midan Hussein, as well as being the best value at E£100 per room. You'll definitely need to book in advance. Except for the El-Hussein mosque, which sounds periodically, street noise isn't a problem. Rooms and baths are reasonably clean and include TV, telephone and fan, some with air conditioning. Breakfast included. Make sure you request a room with a balcony, as some have no windows, and check out the view from the roof.

Roda Island

Grand Hyatt Hotel €€€€
Corniche El-Nil, Garden City,
T02-2362 1717.
Excellently located on the north tip of Roda Island, looking down on *feluccas* circling on the river. There's a range of notable restaurants, including the Hard Rock Café, and one of the best views of Cairo from the revolving restaurant bar. They are serving alcohol again after the furore caused in May 2008 when the

Saudi owner turned the hotel dry and up to US$1 million of liquor was poured into the Nile.

Giza

Mena House Oberoi €€€€
6 Sharia Pyramids, El-Ahram,
Giza, T02-3377 3222,
oberoihotels.com.
An exquisite old-style hotel built in 1869, with sublime views of the Pyramids and set in luxuriant gardens. Excellent Indian (and other) restaurants, disco, casino, largest outdoor pool in Cairo, tennis, a nearby 18-hole golf course, horse and camel riding with experienced instructors. Take a room in the renovated older part for preference. If beyond your budget, it's still a delightful place to enjoy breakfast opposite the Pyramids.

Camping
Salma Camping
Because Cairo has very little undeveloped earth on which to pitch a tent and since there are so many budget hotels, there is little demand for camping. The only decent campground is **Salma Camping** (T02-2381 5062). It can be reached by turning off from Harraniya village on the road between the Pyramids and Saqqara. It has cabins, a camping ground, hot showers, a buffet and a bar. E£25 to pitch a tent; E£90 for a simple double cabin.

Downtown, Zamalek & Gezira

Abu Es-Sid €€€
157 Sharia 26th July, Zamalek,
T02-2735 9640.
Open 1300-0200.
Intimately lit sumptuous decor makes you feel like you've entered a harem, the cuisine is authentically Egyptian and it's a rare chance to smoke *sheesha* and drink alcohol at the same time. Egyptian men admit that Abu Sid is as close as it gets to their mum's cooking, try the *molokhayia*, a unique slimy green soup. However, it's not great for vegetarians and can get annoyingly busy.

L'Asiatique €€€
On Le Pacha 1901, Sharia Saraya
El-Gezira, T02-2735 6730,
lepacha.com.
Open 1900-0200.
Superb sushi and Thai cuisine on the floating, not cruising, Pacha paddle boat. A delightful, albeit pricey dining experience.

Paprika €€€
1129 Corniche El-Nil,
T02-2578 9447.
Open 1200-0100.
Paprika-based dishes of mixed Egyptian and Hungarian food. Near the TV and Radio Building, it's not uncommon to spot local Egyptian celebrities on the premises.

Taboula €€€
1 Sharia Latin America, Garden City, T02-2792 5261.
Subterranean lounge space, with warm lighting and faithfully Lebanese decorations, cushions, and pictures all around. The hot and cold *mezza* and meaty mains are as authentic as the interior and the menu vast. Serves alcohol.

Alfi Bey €€
3 Sharia El-Alfi, Downtown, in pedestrian precinct, T02-577 1888.
Open 0830-0200.
Map: Downtown Cairo, E2, p80.
Authentic Egyptian food, especially kebabs, koftas, lamb chops and shank, grilled and stuffed pigeon with pastas and rice. Smart waiters provide an efficient and friendly service, no alcohol served.

El-Bahrain €€
123 Sharia El-Roda, by the Fatima Hamada Cinema, Manial, T02-2532 2175.
Daily 1300 until late.
Their grandfathers were fishermen, and for the last four years this restaurant has been serving up the freshest of the day's catch. Pick your fish from the ice (ask for it to be cooked *mistakawi* style), accompanying salads are excellent and the shrimps some of the best you'll ever taste. The first floor restaurant is nothing flash, the usual marble and plastic surrounds, but it's great value.

Felfela €€
15 Sharia Hoda Sharawi, Downtown, T02-239 2833.
Open 0830-0130.
Map: Downtown Cairo, C5, p80.
One of downtown's most popular tourist restaurants, serves good, clean, local food and beer in a dimly lit, strangely funky environment. A good place for a first taste of Egyptian food on arrival. There is also a branch in Giza near the pyramids, as well as a takeaway stand next to the downtown restaurant (the lentil soup is delicious).

Greek Club €€
3 Sharia Mahmoud Bassiouni, Downtown, T02-2575 0822.
Open 0700-0200.
Map: Downtown Cairo, C4, p80.
Above Groppis on Midan Talast Harb, this is a deserved classic of the Cairo scene. Grand neo-classical interior, complete with moose head, there's no menu but dishes are standard kebab, salad, soups – nothing truly special, but the terrace (only open in summer) is a splendid vantage point over the *midan*. Beer is reasonable at E£12.

Sabai Sabai €€
1st floor at the Rive Gauche, 21 Sharia El-Maahad El-Swiesri, Zamalek, T02-2735 1846.
Open 1200-2400.
Genuinely Thai-tasting food, there's a huge and reasonably priced menu – you really will be stuck for choice – plus they will

turn any dish into a vegetarian option. It's not overly formal, tables are well-spaced, and decor is low-key ethnic. Good, for groups or couples.

Akher Sa'a €
8 Sharia El-Alfi.
Open 24 hrs.
Map: Downtown Cairo, E2, p80.
An all-Egyptian vegetarians' heaven. You can have a taste of every item they serve and still pay next to nothing.

El-Tabei €
31 Sharia Orabi, T02-2575 4391.
Open 0700-0100.
Map: Downtown Cairo, E1, p80.
Another cheap and good local favourite serving up *mezze* galore and, of course, *fuul* and *tameyya*. Especially recommended for its trustworthy salad bar.

Gad €
13 Sharia 26th July, T02-2576 3583.
Open 24 hrs.
Map: Downtown Cairo, E2, p80.
Always heaving, the tasty, cheap local grub includes excellent *fatir*, *fuul*, *tameyya*, and acclaimed liver sandwiches. Seating upstairs and will deliver almost anywhere.

Ahwas & cafés
Cilantro's
31 Sharia Mohammed Mahmoud.
Map: Downtown Cairo, C6, p80.
For a Western-style coffee downtown, the most pleasant environment is still upstairs at

Cilantro's despite the competition from Costa and Beano's nearby. There are a couple of tables out on the balconies and velvet 'snugs' for couples; it's unpretentious and has a clean toilet.

Mandarin Khadeer
17 Sharia Shargarat Al-Dor, Zamalek.
This place has the best ice cream and sorbets in Cairo. Mango and mandarin flavours come out on top.

Simonds
Sharia 26 July, Zamalek.
Open 0730-2130.
One of the oldest stand-up coffee shops in Cairo, it unfortunately underwent a disastrous refit in 2008 and little of the 1898 charm remains. Even

so, it is still a good place to read the paper, observe classic Cairo characters, and have decent cappuccino. The mini-pizzas and OJ are a great pick-me-up.

Islamic Cairo

Naguib Mafouz Coffee Shop & Khan El-Khalili Restaurant €€€
5 Sikkit El-Badestan, Khan El- Khalili.
Open 1000-0200.
The classiest place to relax after a day's wander through Islamic Cairo. Oberoi-managed (with air conditioning), serves Western and Egyptian *mezze* and meals. Prices for tea and coffee are inflated, but the surroundings justify going. Live Oriental music is featured on occasion. Minimum charges apply.

Egyptian Pancake House €€
7 Midan Al-Azhar.
Fiteer galore, savoury and sweet. Tuna, cheese, eggs, meat, chicken, cream, and even turkey cock are available fillings. Prices range from E£15-25.

Mohammed Ali's *fuul* cart €
Behind the Palace of Amir Bashtak, Sharia Al-Muizz, Midan Hussein.
Undoubtedly some of the best *fuul* going, as the queues further testify. Handy for basic refuelling north of the Khan, and an interesting place to take a break among dilapidated mansions.

Zizo €
Midan Bab El-Futuh.
Open 1200-0700.
Facing the north wall of Islamic Cairo. Said to have the best liver

Entertainment

sausage and fried brain in town, if that's your thing. This takeaway is a local landmark, very cheap and open through the night.

Ahwas & cafés

Fishawis
Smack bang in the middle of Khan El-Khalili.

Fishawi's is Cairo's longest-standing *ahwa*, claiming never to have closed since it first opened in 1773. If you only go to one coffee shop in Egypt, let it be this one. The place is filled with atmosphere, dangling chandeliers, cracked mirrors and characters that have been here for decades. Plus heaps of tourists. *Sheesha*, fresh juice, tea and Turkish coffee are all good, but at a steep price.

Giza

Barry's Oriental Restaurant €€€
2 Sharia Abu Aziza, Giza, T02-3388 9540.

Follow the road (Sharia Abu El-Houl) past the entrance to the Sphinx (on your right) to the very end, Barry's is above AA Stables, just ring the bell. Go for drinks, meat grills or *mezza* (if you're vegetarian, great *besara*) and the best view of sunset behind the pyramids in the world. You can even just about hear the Sound and Light show from the roof terrace. It's best to check the price of Saqqara and juices before you order them.

Bars & clubs

After Eight
6 Sharia Qasr El-Nil (past a kiosk down an unlikely looking alley), T010-339 8000.
Open 1200-0300. Sometimes later.

A real hotspot on the Downtown scene, this smoky little dive is one of few places in Cairo to hear good live music. On Thursdays a packed house enjoy *rai* favourites and originals you can dance to; DJ Dina (a woman) is on the decks on Tuesdays; there's Bashir and his band on a Nubian vibe on Sundays. There is a cover charge of E£100 on Thursday and E£50 on Sunday. Fully stocked bar, standard menu serving variety of meats and pastas through the night.

Buddha Bar
Sofitel El Gezirah, T02-2737 3737.

The place to be seen, but pricey (E£200 minimum charge). Dominated by a gargantuan gold Siddhartha, their sushi gets rave reviews and the bar serves until 0200.

Cairo Jazz Club
197 Sharia 26 July, T02-345 9939.
Many rate it as the best place in town for live local music. Each night has a theme or regular act. Loungey and hip, with plush decor and a small dance floor that doubles as a stage. On occasion there's live jazz.

El-Horriya
Midan Falaki, Bab El-Louk, Downtown.

About the only local *ahwa* that serves beer, Horriya is a true Cairo institution. Everyone comes here – old and young, foreign and local – to spew thoughts on the state of the country, play chess, and get rowdy as the night wears on.

Fontana Hotel
Midan Ramses, T02-2592 2321.
There is an open-air bar on the top floor looking down on the mayhem of the *midan* far below with *sheesha* and Stella at reasonable prices. There's also a 24-hour disco – one of the kitschiest you will ever see.

Grand Hyatt Hotel
(See page 104). Spectacular views over the city from the lounge bar on the 40th floor. No minimum charge before 1900, E£95 per person after that. You can stop for a drink or just have a wander round, and there's also a revolving restaurant upstairs open from 1900.

Hard Rock Café
By the Grand Hyatt Hotel, Corniche El-Nil, T02-2532 1277/81/85.
Open 1200-0400.
Provides all you expect from the place: standard Tex-Mex specials, celebrity guitars, funky costumes, live shows, karaoke, and theme nights. The dance

floor gets kicking after midnight. No minimum for foreigners.

Kings Bar
Cosmopolitan Hotel, 1 Sharia Ibn Taalab. Open 1000-0200.
A fairy salubrious, relaxing yet local-feeling choice, warmly lit by yellow lanterns, generally peopled with *pasha*-types shooting the breeze. It's a good place to snack or dine while you're drinking, with grills, salad, fish and steaks at quite reasonable prices.

Le Grillon
8 Sharia Qasr El-Nil, Downtown; T02-2576 4959.
Open 1100-0200.
Delightful covered garden, restaurant, bar and *ahwa*, very popular spot for local intellectuals and artists. Conversations about revolutions and poetry continue into the wee hours over *sheesha* and beer. The food is mid-priced and quite good, lots of meats, soups and salads, fairly standard Egyptian fare. It's a local place that is comfortable for single women.

Pub 28
28 Sharia Shagar Al-Durr.
One of the oldest pubs in Zamalek, it attracts a mature expat crowd as well as *pashas* quaffing large quantities of whisky in the smoky darkness. Cheap-ish beer and bar food (great French onion soup) means it's always crowded.

Purple
6 Imperial Boat, Saray El-Gezira, T02-2736 5796.
Highly expensive and plush club playing house and retro sounds. If you're planning on dropping a lot of cash, it's worth it to be in one of very few places where people really get dancing.

Nile Hilton
Corniche El-Nil, T02-2578 0444.
Three bar/clubs in one building, Jazz Up is a loungey vibe, with a bit of a mish-mash of decor but pleasant enough, open 1200-0200. A new addition, Mojito Sky Lounge is on the roof looking over the lights of the Nile and provides a Spanish mood and food, minimum charge E£100 at weekends, dancing gets going later on. Latex is more clubby and stays open until 0400, one of the better discos in Cairo for cutting loose. All are popular with sophisticated Cairenes.

Belly dancing
The Cairo Sheraton
Galae Square, T02-3336 9800.
Nightly shows.

Impress
Cairo Marriott, T02-2735 8888.
Shows on Monday and Thursday.

Semiramis Intercontinental
Corniche El-Nil, Garden City, T02-2795 7171.
At present hosts the most acclaimed dancer in town, every Thursday and Sunday night.

Casinos
Found in the following hotels: **Mena House Oberoi** (see page 104) and **Nile Hilton** (see opposite). Also in: **Semiramis Intercontinental** (Corniche El-Nil, Garden City, T02-2795 7171) and **Sofitel El Gezirah** (3 Sharia El Thawra Council, Gezira, T02-2737 3737, sofitel.com).

Sound & Light shows
Three performances daily at the Sphinx and the Pyramids, Giza. The voice of the Sphinx narrates the story of the pyramids in the following languages: Arabic, English, French, German, Italian, Japanese, Russian and Spanish. At 1830, 1930 and 2030 in winter; 2030, 2130, 2230 in summer. E£75, no student discounts. Call for specific schedules, T02-3383 2880/ 3587 6767, soundandlight. com.eg.

Theatre, music & dance
Arab Music Institute
22 Sharia Ramses, Downtown, T02-2574 3373.
Classical Arabic music performances, twice a week.

Beit Al-Suhaymi
Darb Al-Asfar, Al-Hussein, Islamic Cairo, T02-2591 3391.
Folk music and songs by El-Nil Troupe every Sunday at 2000, and occasional special events and performances, particularly during Ramadan.

Shopping

El-Genena Theatre
Al-Azhar Park, Salah Salem, T02-2362 5057.
Great venue to hear music, sometimes international.

El-Sawy Culture Wheel
Sharia 26 July, Zamalek, T02-2736 8881, culture wheel.com.
Bands and concerts most nights in a great venue under 15th May bridge, varying from Bedouin folk, to Arab rap, to Ghanaian flutes.

Makan
1 Sharia Saad Zaghloul, Al-Mounira, T02-2792 0878.
Zar dance performance by the Mazaher band every Wednesday and Tuesday at 2000, an essential night out and best on Wednesday.

Opera House
Gezira, info T02-339 8144, box office T02-2739 0132.
Has a hall with 1200 seats for opera, ballet and classical music

performances, a second hall with 500 seats for films and conferences and an open-air theatre. For grandeur, get tickets to the main hall show, advance booking recommended. Men must wear jacket and tie.

Whirling dervishes
On Wednesday and Saturday, 2030, during Ramadan 2100, in Wikala El-Ghoriyya, near Midan Hussein, Islamic Cairo. It's wise to arrive one hour early to ensure you get a good seat. Free. Cameras (but not video) permitted. Sponsored by the Ministry of Culture, the El-Tannoura Dance Troupe puts on a spectacular show in the restored *wikala*, which makes a great setting.

Books

American University in Cairo (AUC) Bookstore
1st floor, Hill House, 113 Sharia Kasr El-Aini, Downtown, on the old main campus, T02-2797 5900.
Open Sat-Thu 0900-1800 (-1500 during Ramadan).
Has the biggest and best collection of fiction and books on Egypt (and everywhere else).

Lehnert & Landrock
44 Sharia Sherif, T02-392 7606.
Open 0930-1330 and 1530-1930, and at the Nile Hilton near the entrance to the Egyptian Museum, closed Sat afternoon and Sun.
Books in German and English, but best known for the black and white prints by Lehnert & Landrock who documented the Middle East in the early 20th century.

Crafts & souvenirs
Al-Khatoun
3 Sharia Mohamed Abdou, Islamic Cairo, T02-2514 7164, alkhatoun.com.
Open 1100-2100 (1200-2300 during Ramadan).
Fabulous swathes of cloth, pots, beaten copperware, iron lamps, old film posters and other items of homeware that can make a dent in your wallet.

And Company
3 Sharia Bagat Ali, Zamalek, T02-2736 5689.
This is where to come for high quality Egyptian cotton,

Cairo Opera House.

Activities & tours

specializing in clothing, sheets, etc of a contemporary rather than ethnic bent. Also sells pottery, candles and the like, plus works by local artists.

Egypt Crafts
1st Floor, 27 Sharia Yahia Ibrahim, Zamalek, T02-2736 5123, fairtradeegypt.org.
Sat-Thu 0900-2000, Fri 1000-1800.
Helping to revive traditional crafts throughout Egypt, this non-profit fairtrade shop has a good selection of pottery, basketry, hand-woven scarves and rugs, jewellery and much more.

Loft
12 Sharia Sayed El-Bakri, Zamalek, T02-27366931, loftegypt.com.
Open 1000-1500.
An eclectic selection of oriental furniture, metalwork, friezes, over-the-top lighting, icons and antiques are displayed in a boudoir-like setting.

Souk Al-Fustat
Sharia Saydi Hassan Al-Anwar, Old Cairo.
Open 1000-2200.
Overpriced, but showcases traditional crafts (some made in the workshops of the complex). It doesn't have the air of being the commercial success that was hoped for, but it's a good place for handmade metal lanterns with arabesque motifs in all sizes and designs, curios, and such like. Haggling is possible in many shops.

Diving
Maadi Divers
18 Road 218, Maadi, T02-2519 8644, maadi-divers.com.
The first PADI dive centre in Cairo, they arrange live-abroad trips to the Red Sea.

Seascapes Diving and Safari
1/2 Sharia Lasilky, New Maadi, T02-2519 4930.
Mon-Fri 0900-1700.
PADI courses, diving trips and desert safaris.

Golf
Katameya Heights Golf Course
23 km southeast of Cairo, katameya heights.com.
27 holes across two courses.

Mena House Oberoi
Gezira Sporting Club and the Marriott Hotel at Mirage City also have 18-hole courses.

Horse riding
It's fun to ride in the desert by the pyramids, particularly for sunrise or sunset but avoid the sad-looking horses lined up for tourists by the pyramid's gate and head for the stables in Kafr El-Gabal (straight on past the entrance to Sound and Light show).

AA Stables, T012-153 4142, and MG Stables are recommended, have regular Western clients, and offer a variety of excursions from the standard hour-long ride around the pyramids (E£40) to a trip to

Saqqara. More elaborate excursions and night rides need to be booked in advance.

Swimming
Hotels with good pools include: **Grand Hyatt**, Garden City for E£200 per day 0700-1900; **Marriott**, Zamalek Sunday-Wednesday E£240, or Thursday-Saturday E£305; **Semiramis Intercontinental** is good for E£137 per day.

Tour operators
Egypt Rays
18 Sharia Hassan Shawi, Nasr City, egyptrays.com.
Can cut your costs by booking budget accommodation, entry tickets to all sites included.

See Real Egypt
El Obour Building, Sharia Salah Salem, Nasr City, T018-305 0677, seerealegypt.com.
For tailor-made or standard tours of the big sights in Cairo and the Nile Valley.

Spring Tours
11 Sharia Talaat Harb, T02-392 2627, and 3 Sharia Sayyid El-Bakry, Zamalek, T02-2393 2573, (0900-1800), springtours.com.

Thomas Cook
7 Sharia Baghdad, El-Korba, Heliopolis, T02-2416 4000; 17 Sharia Mahmoud.

Transport

Air
EgyptAir (egyptair.com) fly to these domestic destinations: Abu Simbel, Aswan, Hurghada, Luxor and Sharm El-Sheikh. Their office is at 9 Sharia Talaat Harb, T02-2393 2836, 6 Sharia Adly, T02-2392 7649, or Nile Hilton, T02-2579 9443.

Bus
It's wise to buy tickets in advance. Buy them at the bus station; phone reservations are still not possible. Do not rely too heavily on the following schedules as times and prices change constantly depending on the number of tourists and a million other variables.

The following services depart from Turgoman terminal: **Superjet**, T02-2579 8181, to Hurghada at 0730, 1430, 2315 (6 hrs); Sharm El-Sheikh at 0730, 1515, 2345 (6 hrs); Luxor at 2345 (9-10 hrs). **East Delta**, T02-2577 8347, to Sharm El-Sheikh 0630, 0715, 1030, 1330, 1630, 1930, 2300, 2415, 0100, 0145 (8-9 hrs); Dahab, 0715, 1330, 1930 (8 hrs); Taba, then on to Nuweiba 0600, 0930, 2215 (7 hrs); St Catherine 1100 (8 hrs). **Upper Egypt Travel**, T02-2576 0261, to Hurghada at 0800, 1200, 2000, 2200, 0100 (6 hrs) and on to Safaga; El-Quseir at 2000 (8 hrs) and Marsa Alam at 1330, 1830, 2300 (11 hrs); Luxor 2100 (11 hrs); Aswan at 1700 (14 hrs).

The **El-Gouna Transportation Company** operates several buses between El-Gouna and Cairo each day. Buses bound for El-Gouna leave from the Hilton Ramsis in central Cairo at 0730, 1345 and 0045. Three companies also operate daily services (0600-2000) from Aboud Station, including buses Luxor and Aswan, although you may want to opt for the comparably cheap and significantly more comfortable and convenient train.

Trains
Three trains per day depart for Luxor and Aswan at 0740, 2200 and 0030, for which tourists are sold advance tickets. Tickets can be booked up to one week in advance. It's recommended not to leave it any later than 48 hours in advance. See egypttrail.gov.eg for timetables and fares.

Abela Egypt Sleeping Cars
T02-2574 9474, F02-2574 9074, sleepingtrains.com.
Open 0900-2000.
This French company run daily sleeping cars to Luxor and Aswan (departing 2030). Claiming four-star status, the sleepers are a clean, comfortable way to travel. You can get off the train for 48 hours in Luxor and get back on to Aswan with the same ticket. During peak season it's best to buy your ticket in advance. Each train has a 'club' area (a very smoky but kitsch bar) and restaurant. Prices (US$60/person in double; US$80 for single; US$45 for children aged 4-9 years) – include dinner and breakfast. Credit cards and Egyptian pounds are not accepted, so have enough foreign currency to buy your ticket.

Tip...
Ramses Station is a bit confusing, with several different ticket counters selling tickets for different destinations. If you face the main platforms, tickets to Middle and Upper Egypt can be bought from the counters by platform 11 outside to the left, via the underpass. The tourist office, an information booth in the middle of the station or the tourist police can guide you in the right direction.

Contents

Luxor Temple at night.

Introduction

What to see in...

...one day
Spend the first couple of hours of the day at **Karnak**, before touring the West Bank's major sites, hitting the **Valley of Kings** before lunchtime (the earlier the better in summer). Afternoon at the **Luxor Museum** leads neatly on to an hour on a *felucca* for sunset, then an aperitif at the Winter Palace before dinner. After which meander through the *souk* en route to an illuminated **Luxor Temple**, rounding off the day with *sheesha* or a coffee.

...a weekend or more
Add in a sunrise balloon flight over the Valley of the Kings before exploring the above sights at a more leisurely pace, dedicating a day to each bank of the river. Pop into the **Mummification Museum** and plump for a longer *felucca* trip, perhaps to **Banana Island**, before catching some belly dancing and/or **Karnak's Sound and Light show**. Day trips to **Dendara** and **Abydos** also come into the equation.

With an overwhelming number of well-preserved sandstone temples and elaborate tombs, many deem Luxor the world's greatest open-air museum. The remains of Karnak Temple, a vast and beautifully preserved temple complex built over the span of more than 1000 years, are a highlight of any trip. Luxor Temple, once a refuge for every great religion that thrived in ancient Egypt, rises gracefully alongside the Nile and at night is splendidly lit and open to visitors. Across the river is the ancient capital of Thebes (1567-1085 BC), second only to the pyramids as Egypt's most visited attraction, where the Valley of the Kings yields a taste of the profound and vital journey to the next life.

A sunset *felucca* ride or sailing to nearby Banana Island, a meander through the colourful *souk* in the centre of town, or just an exploration of the West Bank villages are all vital ingredients for a rewarding experience of this tourist-trap town. Luxor also serves as a convenient base for day trips to the temples of Dendara and Abydos to the north, and the temples of Esna and Edfu, to the south.

Luxor Temple.

Essentials

❶ Getting around The East Bank is small enough to walk around (depending on how you tolerate the heat and the hassle). Walking around the Theban Necropolis is also just about feasible, but given the heat and the distances involved it's certainly easier to use taxis and pick-ups or hire a bike. If someone doesn't offer you one on exiting the ferry head to the couple of hire places on the left of the road after the taxi park, E£15-20 per day.

Buses Microbuses are a cheap (40 pt) and easy way to get around town and to the Karnak Temple. When they get close, call out your destination. A popular route around the East Bank, Sharia Karnak–Sharia Mahatta–Sharia Televizion, includes the train station to Karnak temple.

Ferries Depart for the West Bank from the Corniche in front of the Luxor temple. E£1 for foreigners, 25 pt for Egyptians; private motorboats or *feluccas* are also available for around E£5-10.

Taxis They congregate around the train station and can be hailed from all major thoroughfares; E£5-10 around town. If you want to see the West Bank at your own pace and have a ride, take the public ferry across the Nile and hire a taxi (from the landing) for a few hours. Expect to pay about E£120 to be shuttled around the major sights for three to four hours.

Calèches Horse-drawn carriages are all over the place, often in queues. E£10 should be enough to get you across town; the official rate is E£30 for an hour's ride. If all you want is to get from A to B, don't let the driver coerce you into stopping at any shops or taking a sightseeing diversion through the *souk*.

Feluccas These traditional wooden sailing boats are numerous on this most beautiful stretch of the Nile. Travel is limited to the southward direction, but this also has the most attractive scenery. Sunset is the best time to ride but bring a sweater and protection against mosquitoes (E£50/hr if you're a hard bargainer). It is a lovely journey to nearby Banana Island, where you can stroll through the papaya and orange plantations, it's about a 2-hr round trip. Longer *felucca* trips start from Aswan and head north with the current, see page 181.

❺ Bus station A fair trek out of town, close to the airport. Taxis charge E£40 for a ride into the centre; microbuses (40 pt).

❻ Train station On Sharia al-Mahatta in the centre of town and close to the *souk*.

❼ ATMs Five-star hotels and numerous banks have ATMs.

❽ Hospital Luxor International Hospital, Sharia Televizion, T095-238 7192-4.

❾ Pharmacies Maged Pharmacy, Sharia Aly Ibn Abi Taleb, T095-237 0524, open 24 hrs and can deliver.

❿ Post office The main post office is on Sharia El-Mahata.

⓫ Tourist information The Egyptian Tourist Authority (ETA), T095-928 0004, and the **The Tourist Police**, T095-237 3845, are based in an office on the Corniche, in front of Luxor Museum.

The East Bank

On Luxor's East Bank the ancient exists amid the contemporary like nowhere else. Evident in the architecture, the food, the clothes people wear, the things they sell and the games they play, Luxorians are remarkably capable of integrating layers of history with the present and future.

The town and the surrounding limestone hills had been settled for many centuries but during the Old Kingdom it was little more than a small provincial town called Waset. It first assumed importance under Menutuhotep II who reunited Egypt and made it his capital, but it was during the 18th-20th Dynasty of the New Kingdom that Thebes really reached its zenith. It was the capital of an Egyptian Empire that stretched from Palestine to Nubia for nearly 500 years, and at its peak the population reached almost one million. Besides being the site of the largest and greatest concentration of monuments in the world it was, for the ancient Egyptians, the prototype for all future cities.

Karnak Temple's ancient decoration.

Temple: daily 0600-1730, buy your ticket by 1600; E£50, E£25 for students. Sound and Light show (E£75, E£60 for students): daily 1830, 1945, 2100 in winter; 2000, 2115, 2230 in summer, with a fourth late-night slot to accommodate large tour groups, check the tourist office or T095-237 1229 for latest schedules. Walk or bike; microbus (yell out 'Karnak'); *calèches* and private taxis (bargain for E£15-20; E£35 plus *baksheesh* if they wait – 2 hrs – and bring you back). Map: Luxor, p120.

Karnak Temple, the largest pharaonic monument in the country after the Giza Pyramids covering almost half a square kilometre, is a rambling complex of towering pillars and mighty pylons. Known in earlier times as Iput-Isut 'the most esteemed of places', the extent, scale and quality of the remains is astonishing. As Flaubert said, Karnak gives 'the impression of a life of giants', and as you stand dwarfed by the massive masonry it becomes easy to believe in the vastness of the ancient city of Thebes. The complex's temples vary greatly in style because they were constructed over 1300 years and every great pharaoh made his mark. Their only common theme is worship of Amun, Mut and Khonsu who make up the Theban Triad of gods.

Visiting Karnak at dawn is undoubtedly the best plan, but in the thick of summer the mid-afternoon heat, if you can bear it, does wonders to drive away the hordes of tourists and touts. Large tour parties tend to arrive at 1100-1230 and 1600-1730, so these times are definitely best avoided.

Central Enclosure or Temple of Amun

The enormous Temple of Amun, which was altered, extended and added to by successive rulers, is approached via the Avenue of Ram-Headed Sphinxes.

Arriving through the First Pylon, you come to the Great Forecourt, begun in the 20th Dynasty but completed some time later. Immediately on the left is the very thick-walled rose-coloured granite and sandstone Shrine of Seti II (1216-1210 BC) which was

It's a fact...

An ambitious scheme is in full swing to reconnect Luxor and Karnak temples via the Avenue of the Sphinxes, which involves demolishing every building and home that stands in the way. It's hoped that by 2030 the two temples will be linked.

Five of the best

Jaw-dropping architectural features

❶ The imposing **First Pylon** is 130 m wide and each of the two unfinished towers are 43 m high. Although incomplete, nothing else quite matches its enormous scale.

❷ The **Hypostyle Hall** overwhelms with its 134 giant columns that were once topped by sandstone roof slabs, the 12 largest are a gigantic 23 m high and 15 m round. Another 122 smaller columns covering the rest of the hall are decorated by dedications to the gods and the cartouches of the pharaohs who contributed to the hall.

❸ Be they decapitated, truncated or broken right down to the feet, the scale of Karnak's assorted **Colossi** make an impact on every visitor. Which is just what the pharaohs they were modelled on would have intended.

❹ Hatshepsut's erect **obelisk** is decorated along its whole length with the inscription, "O ye people who see this monument in years to come and speak of that which I have made, beware lest you say, 'I know not why it was done'. I did it because I wished to make a gift for my father Amun, and to gild them with electrum."

❺ The **Avenue of Ram-Headed Sphinxes** once linked the entrance of Karnak to Luxor Temple across town – knowledge of which amplifies their collective grandeur.

a way-station for the sacred barques of Amun, Mut and Khonsu as they were taken on ritual processions. The outer façade portrays Seti II making offerings to various deities. In the middle of the Great Forecourt are the 10 columns of Taharga, which once supported a 26.5 m-high kiosk or small open temple.

Around the region

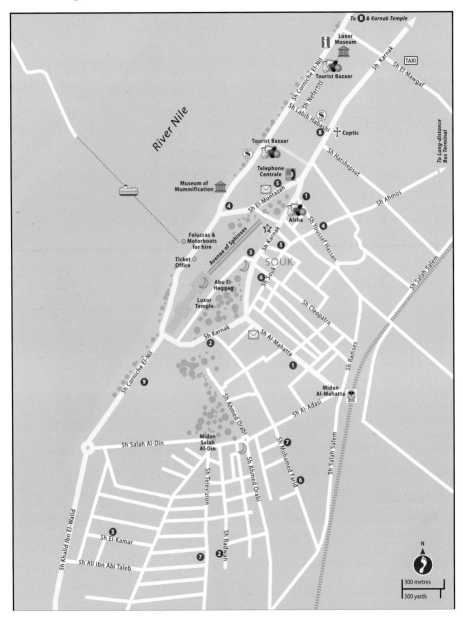

Luxor listings

Ancient hieroglyphics and cartouches.

To the left of the Second Pylon is the 15 m-high Colossus of Ramses II with his daughter Benta-anta standing in front of his legs. Passing through this Second Pylon brings you to the immense and spectacular Hypostyle Hall. Ramses is shown, on the south side of the internal wall of the Second Pylon, making offerings before the gods and seeking their guidance, while on the left is a beautiful representation of Thoth inscribing Seti's name on a holy tree.

The Third Pylon was constructed by Amenhotep III who also built a small court to enclose four Tuthmosid Obelisks in the narrow gap between the Third and Fourth Pylon. Only one pink granite obelisk (23 m high, weighing 143 tonnes and originally tipped with electrum) remains. Moving towards the earlier centre of the temple is the limestone-faced sandstone Fourth Pylon. Just inside is a small Transverse Hall where only 12 of the original papyrus bud columns and one of two 27 m and 340 tonne rose-granite

It's a fact...

Hatshepsut's long-frustrated and usurped infant stepson Tuthmosis III, who had plotted against her during her reign, took his revenge by hiding her obelisks behind walls almost to the ceiling, which actually preserved them from later graffiti.

Top: Karnak's towering pillars. Above: Colossus of Ramses II, Karnak.

Obelisk of Hatshepsut now remain. The tip of the fallen obelisk lies near the Sacred Lake.

The east wall of the Transverse Hall is the Fifth Pylon, beyond which is another hall and then the badly damaged sandstone Sixth Pylon. The world's first imperialist, Tuthmosis III, inscribed it on both sides with details of his vanquished enemies. Past the pylon is a Vestibule that leads to a Granite Sanctuary which has a star-covered ceiling. To the east is Tuthmosis III's Festival Hall which, with its central tentpole-style columns symbolising the tents used during his campaigns, is unlike any other Egyptian building; to the south is the Sacred Lake which has the Sound and Light Show grandstand at the far end. Beside the lake there is a statue of a giant scarab beetle that childless women circle five times in the hope that they will fall pregnant.

Luxor Temple

Corniche El-Nile.
Daily 0600-2100 in winter, 0600-2200 in summer. E£40, E£20 for students, camera tripods E£20. Map: Luxor, p120.

While dedicated to the same trio of Theban gods (Amun, Mut and Khonsu) as Karnak, fewer pharaohs were involved in Luxor Temple's construction, which makes for a simpler and more coherent visit. A couple of hours will be sufficient to tour this temple. It is particularly striking at night; your ticket permits re-entry on the day of purchase.

Begun in the 18th-Dynasty by pharaoh Amenhotep III, his son Akhenaten concentrated instead on building a shrine to Aten adjacent to the site. However, Tutankhamen (1361-1352 BC) and Horemheb (1348-1320 BC) later resumed the work. Ramses II (1304-1237 BC) can be credited with completing most of the building by adding a second colonnade and pylon as well as a multitude of colossi.

The Avenue of Sphinxes lines the approach, a 30th-Dynasty (380- 343 BC) addition. At first glance each statue in the Avenue of Sphinxes seems identical though actually each face (that

Ancient hierolglyphics and cartouches.

of Amenhotep III) is subtly different, some a little plump and others very serious, but all with the mysterious secret smile of the sphinx.

In front of the gigantic First Pylon are the three remaining colossi of Ramses II and to the left stands an obelisk towering 25 m high. A 22.8-m-high second obelisk was given to France by Mohammed Ali Pasha in 1819 and re-erected in the Place de la Concorde in Paris, where it stands today.

Pass through the pylon into the Peristyle Court. It is surrounded by a double row of columns which are shaped into the classic representation of papyrus reeds bound together to form a bud at the top. The east end of the court has not been fully excavated because it is the site of the Mosque of Abu El-Haggag, the patron saint of Luxor. At the south end of the court, the portal flanking the entrance to the colonnade supports two black granite statues bearing the name of Ramses II, but the feathers of Tutankhamen.

The daunting Colonnade of 14 columns leads to the older part of the temple where the walls are detailed with the procession of the Opet Festival. Beyond it is the Court of Amenhotep III, a second sweeping court with double rows of columns flanking three of the sides, which leads in turn to the Hypostyle Hall. Look out for the chamber that was converted into a Coptic church during the fourth century. The pharaonic reliefs were plastered over and early Christian paintings covered the whitewash, their colour and detail just recently exposed by a restoration project. Beyond is a smaller second vestibule, the Offerings Chamber, with its four columns still in place. Further on, in the Sanctuary of the Sacred Barque, the doors were made of acacia and inlaid with gold. Alexander the Great (332-323 BC) rebuilt the shrine in accordance with Amenhotep III's original plans. The east passage leads to the Birth Room built because of Amenhotep's claim that he was the son

What the locals say

Every day there are new discoveries for visitors to see. Keep looking! Our ancient monuments are like schools that Egyptologists must keep on studying. We must carry on researching from multiple sources for a variety of theories about the ancient civilization and continually excavating the foundation deposits for more evidence.

Shaimaa, *Tour guide, Luxor.*

Depictions of the Pharoahs, Luxor Temple.

of the god Amun, who is depicted as entering the queen's chamber disguised as Tuthmosis IV and breathing the child into her nostrils. The furthest hall has 12 poorly maintained papyrus-bud columns and leads on to the small Sanctuary of Amenhotep III where the combined god Amun-Min is represented.

Luxor Museum

Corniche El-Nil, halfway between Luxor and Karnak temples.
Daily 0900-1500/1600-2100 (last tickets 1230/2030) winter; 0900-1500 and 1700-2000 summer. Ramadan: 1300-1600 only. E£70, E£35 for students. Map: Luxor, p120.

The museum's well-displayed exhibits, set over two floors, range from pharaonic treasures to the Mamluk period. The most important and interesting are the New Kingdom statues found in a cache at Karnak in 1989. A newer wing presents 'Thebes Glory', the centrepieces of which are the unwrapped mummies of Ahmosis I and (possibly) Ramses I. A few choice exhibits from Tutankhamen's tomb are also displayed including a gold-inlaid cow's head of the goddess

> ## Tip…
>
> Don't bypass the documentary playing in the small cinema, as it's a quality production that puts the artefacts in context.

Mehit-Wehit, a funerary bed and two model barques. The prints showing how the sites looked in the 19th century are also interesting.

Museum of Mummification

Corniche El-Nil.
Daily 0900-2100 winter, 0900-2200 summer. Ramadan: 1300-1600 only. E£30, E£15 for students. Map: Luxor, p120.

Right on the banks of the Nile, down the steps from the Corniche, this museum illustrates the story of mummification. The museum, considered to be the first of its kind in the world, contains a small but very varied display. Exhibits include several human, reptile and bird mummies as well as stone and metal tools used in the mummification process. It is well set out and definitely worth a short visit.

The West Bank

The ancient Egyptians believed that the underworld was located in the west where the sun died each day, and so it was in the terrestrial west that they chose to bury their dead. Depending on your interest, it takes a day to cover the major highlights or up to two full days to explore it in its entirety.

Although the West Bank is dominated by the Theban Necropolis and the Valley of the Kings, there are also some fascinating temples and monuments above ground worth exploring, in particular the Ramesseum and Medinat Habu, which are not on the standard itineraries of large tour companies. In addition, the Tombs of the Nobles have few visitors but some of the most colourful and interesting paintings – they really shouldn't be missed.

Sites open 0500-1700 winter, 0600-1800 summer. Tickets to the Valley of the Kings (including Tutankhamen's tomb), the Valley of the Queens and Deir El-Bahri (Hatshepsut Temple) can all be bought at their sites. Tickets to everything else must be bought in advance at the old ticket booths (open from 0600-1600), 200 m after the Colossi of Memnon. Photography of all sorts is prohibited inside all tombs. Resist all temptation.

Expecting to see every single tomb and temple on the West Bank is impractical unless you intend to visit every day for a week. There is also a system in place to reduce wear and tear on the more popular tombs – by closing them at intervals. The changes happen so often that the guards who work in the Valleys have a hard time keeping up. A list of open tombs is displayed by the ticket booths. There are always at least 12 tombs open in the Valley of the Kings and three open in the Valley of the Queens. The Ministry of Tourism tries to ensure at least a few of the more remarkable tombs are always open.

Valley of the Kings

E£70, E£35 for students, to 3 tombs of your choosing, except for Tutankhamen's which costs E£80/40 extra and Ramses VI's, E£50/25. The visitors' centre has film footage, running on a loop, showing the emptying of Tutankhamen's tomb and a scale model of the valley, which is brilliant for getting your bearings and the depth and breadth of the site into perspective. Attendants inside the tombs will offer to point out details or lend you a torch, in return for *baksheesh*.

Also known as Wadi Biban El-Muluk, the Valley of the Kings is one of many necropoli in the limestone hills on the West Bank. The area first became a burial site during the New Kingdom rule of Tuthmosis I (1525-1512 BC) in the hope that the tombs would be safe from looters. The kings' tombs are not actually confined to the single valley and it is believed that there may be others still waiting to be discovered. Those already

Tip...

Hiring a bike allows you to visit pretty much everything in a full day and have time to relax as well. Be aware that it's a steady uphill gradient all the way to the Valley of the Kings – a bit tough, especially in the thick of summer, but coming back down is a breeze. Guards at the various sights will keep an eye on your bike for you. You may want to offer a bit of *baksheesh*, but it's not strictly necessary.

Above: Deir El-Bahri. Below: Tomb of Tutankhamen.

discovered are numbered in the chronological order of their discovery rather than by location, below are some of the highlights.

Note that tourists from cruise ships tend to congregate at the Valley of the Kings between 0700-1000, so avoid these times if at all possible. Lunchtime is always a fairly safe bet. It can't be stressed enough that the difference between a magical experience and one where you don't notice any tomb art because you are trying to survive being jostled by bus-loads of people hangs on what time you go

Although some of the tombs are simple and comparatively crude, the best are incredibly well preserved, stunningly decorated and a testament to the intricate craftsmanship of the workers. For example, the colours inside the tomb of **Ramses IV** are truly fantastic. The first two corridors contain reliefs of the Litany of Re, while the Hall and Burial Chamber are decorated with parts of the Book of the Dead and Nut spans the ceiling.

Despite being the founder of the 19th Dynasty, **Ramses I**'s short reign meant that this Ramses did not merit a larger tomb, but its beautifully ornate and sophisticated designs are also well preserved on the blue-grey foundation. The granite sarcophagus in the burial chamber is decorated with yellow while the wall relief depicts scenes of the pharaoh with local deities and divisions from the Book of Gates. The eastern wall of the entrance corridor is decorated with 12 goddesses depicting the hours of the night.

Typical of the later long, deep style that became the established style by the end of the New Kingdom is that of **Ramses IX**. The reliefs on the corridor walls depict Ramses before the gods. A four pillared Offerings Chamber leads to the richly decorated Burial Room where the ceiling depicts a scene from the Book of the Night with jackals, watched by Nut, drawing the barque through the skies to the afterlife.

A remarkable 3.6-m-wide entrance leads into the tomb of **Prince Mentuherkhepshef**, Son of Ramses IX. Splendid mock doors are painted on the walls at the portico together with door jambs decorated with serpents. Paintings in the main corridor of the prince making offerings to the gods, although sadly now rather damaged, are renowned for being among the most technically excellent in the Valley of the Kings.

With a burial chamber crudely adapted from what was to have been a passage to a larger room that was never excavated, it's assumed that the tomb of **Seti II** was a hastily completed monument. That said, it is considered important for developing

several innovations that became standard practice in subsequent tomb building.

After the long, steep and undecorated descent is the Well Room where beautifully detailed reliefs begin.

Seti I's is regarded as the most developed form of the tomb chambers in the Valley of the Kings. At some 136 m it is the longest, but it is usually closed for conservation purposes since its decorations suffer from condensation produced by visitors.

Of course, the Valley's best known royal tomb is that of **Tutankhamen**. It owes its worldwide fame not to its size or decoration, being on the

Sunrise over the Valley of the Kings.

whole rather small and ordinary, but to the multitude of fabulous treasures that were revealed when Carter opened it up in November 1922. In fact, the scale of the discovery was so vast that it took 10 years to fully remove, catalogue and photograph all of the 1700 pieces. Considering that the boy king reigned for a mere nine-10 years and was a comparatively minor pharaoh, the lavish funeral objects found seem all the more extraordinary.

The tomb's short entrance corridor leads to four chambers, but only the Burial Chamber is decorated. The glassed-in murals display, amongst other things,

The curse of Tutankhamen

Tutankhamen's tomb's fame and mystery was enhanced by the fate of several of those who were directly connected with its discovery. The expedition's sponsor Lord Carnarvon, who had first opened the tomb with his chief archaeologist Howard Carter, died shortly afterwards in April 1923 from an infected mosquito bite. Howard Carter supposedly protected himself by not entering the tomb until he had performed an ancient ritual. A subsequent succession of bizarre deaths added weight to British novelist Marie Corelli's unproven claim that "dire punishment follows any intruder into the tomb". However, such alleged curses have done nothing to deter the tens of thousands of visitors who still visit the site despite the fact that most of the treasures are now in the Egyptian Museum.

It's a fact…

The tombs generally follow two designs. The early 18th-Dynasty (1567-1320 BC) tombs are a series of descending galleries followed by a well or rock pit that was intended both to collect any rain water and deter thieves. On the other side of the pit there were sealed offering chambers and then the rectangular burial chamber built at right angles to the descending galleries. The later tombs, from the late 18th to the 20th Dynasties (1360-1085 BC), were built in the same way but the galleries and burial chambers were on the same axis, being cut horizontally but deeper, straight into the rock face.

Tutankhamen's coffin being moved to the shrine by mourners, the ceremony of the Opening of the Mouth, Osiris embracing Tutankhamen and the pharaoh's solar boat. The quartzite sarcophagus is still in place, with its granite lid to one side. Inside a temperature-controlled glass display case contains his mummified remains.

Deir El-Bahri & Mortuary Temple of Hatshepsut

E£25, E£15 for students.

Meaning 'Northern Monastery' in Arabic, Deir El-Bahri derives its name from the fact that during the seventh century the Copts used the site as a monastery. It is now used as the name for both the magnificent Mortuary Temple of Hatshepsut and the surrounding area.

Hatshepsut's imposing temple, which was only dug out of the sand in 1905, is built against the rocky cliffs of the Theban hills. The clean planes of the terraces, surfaces and ramps appear as brand-new rather than just reconstructed – it is almost impossible to comprehend that it is 3500 years old. The temple's three rising terraces, the lower two of which were lined with fountains and myrrh trees, were originally linked to the Nile by an avenue of sphinxes that aligned exactly to Karnak.

Hatshepsut's famous voyage to Punt (believed to be modern-day Somalia) is depicted on the left-hand side of the second colonnade. Further to the left is the large Chapel of Hathor where the

goddess is depicted both as a cow and as a human with cow's ears suckling Hatshepsut. This area is badly damaged because a resentful Tuthmosis removed most traces of the queen.

In the middle at the back of the whole temple is the Sanctuary of Amun, which is dug into the cliff-face and aligned with Hatshepshut's tomb in the Valley of the Kings on the other side of the hill. A further burial chamber for Hatshepsut's lies underneath the Sanctuary, but it is unclear whether she was ever actually interred in either place.

Tombs of the Nobles

The tombs are divided into groups, a ticket to each group costs E£12. The most popular groups are Ramoza, Userhat and Khaemhet; Nakht and Mena; and Rekhmire and Sennofer. Further tombs belonging to nobles are open for viewing at El-Asasif, El-Khokhah and Dra'a Abul Naga. The tombs of Sennedjem, Peshdu and Inherkhau are just above Deir El-Medina (see page 132).

Nobles' tombs are found at a variety of sites throughout Egypt but none are better preserved than those on the West Bank. While the pharaoh's tombs were hidden away in the Valley of the Kings and dug deep into the valley rock, those of the most important nobles were ostentatiously built at surface level overlooking the temples of Luxor and Karnak across the river. Their shrines were highly decorated but the poor quality limestone made carved reliefs impossible so the façades were painted on plaster. Freed from the restricted subject matter of the royal tombs, the artists and craftsmen dedicated more space to representations of everyday life. However, unlike the royal tombs, they were exposed to the elements and many of the nobles' shrines have deteriorated badly over time. Although some were subsequently used as store rooms and even accommodation, others are still in relatively good condition and give a clear impression of how they must originally have looked.

Indiana Jones moments in the Valley of the Kings

❶ Creep down the ninety steep steps and descending corridor into a pillared chamber where the axis of **Amenhotep II's tomb** shifts 90° to the left. Descend deeper (the air getting hotter and thicker with each step) to a short passage leading to the cavenous two-level Burial Chamber itself where the sarcophagus rests. Victor Loret opened this tomb in 1898 and found a trove of grisly and invaluable treasure including the pharaoh's mummified body, along with another nine royal mummies that had been removed from their original tombs for safety's sake.

❷ Hidden away high up a side valley is the **Tomb of Tu**, one of oldest tombs you can experience. A long, stuffy and sweaty initial descent, followed by a second steep corridor that veers sharply to the left, leads to an antechamber lined with lists of 741 deities portrayed as tiny stick figures. A cartouche-shaped burial chamber lays ahead, down a set of oval shaped steps.

❸ Inside the long, steep 80-m **tomb of Meneptah**, set back against the cliff face, awaits a wonderfully preserved false Burial Chamber and ceilings decorated with flying vultures and other forbidding reliefs. Steep steps lead down to genuine Burial Chamber itself where remnants of the pink granite sarcophagus remain.

❹ Far more fascinating for Egyptologists than the shattered sarcophagus of **Ramses VI** are the reliefs that decorate the corridors of his tomb. Drawn from unknown and long since lost ancient books, they held the key to those puzzling pharaonic concepts of reincarnated birth into a new life.

❺ A collapsed ceiling thwarts exploration of the final section of this exceptionally large 'Tomb of the Harpists'. Built for **Ramses III**, it is considered particularly beautiful and unusual, because unlike those of most pharaohs, it contains scenes from everyday life.

Hieroglyphics inside the Tomb of Rameses VI.

Five of the best

Vernacular paintings – Tombs of the Nobles

❶ The **Tomb of Userhat** has interesting representations of rural life, including a realistic hunting scene in the desert.

❷ The **Tomb of Nakht** colourfully depicts the harvest, a funeral banquet, wine treading and the marshland. At the funeral, Nakht (the top half has been badly defaced) is shown seated beside his wife, a cat at his feet is eating a fish and he is being entertained by a blind harpist and beautiful dancing girls.

❸ **Tomb of Mena** On the adjacent wall is a fine painting of Mena and his wife giving flowers. Opposite is a vignette of the younger members of the family making gifts to their father. In the left-hand limb of the outer hall note the depiction of Mena's wife in an elegant dress and jewellery as she stands with her husband before Osiris. In the inner hall there is a niche for a statue of Mena and his wife. In the inner hall, look out for the finely executed paintings of hunting and fishing scenes on the right-hand wall, close to the statue niche, showing crocodiles, wild cats and fish. The brightly coloured ceilings represent woven cloth.

❹ Two decorative tombs of the 48 at Dra'a Abul Naga (about 1 km south of the El-Khokha tombs by road), are open – those of **Roy** and **Shuroy**. Roy's is one of the most beautiful of the all nobles' tombs with remarkable scenes and colouring still intact. The southern wall is decorated with ploughing scenes, flax-pulling and a funeral procession showing grieving friends and mourners led by Anubis.

Shuroy's entry chamber is brightly coloured with many scenes looking as bright as the day they were drawn. The first hall is decorated with sketches of the deceased and his wife adoring divinities, and look on the right side for the gates decorated with demons.

❺ The **Tomb of Neferrompet** (one of 60 tombs from the Ramessid period at El-Khokha, about 500 m south of the El-Asasif tombs) is small but famous for a representation of 14 scenes from the Book of the Gates. Neferrompet and his wife drink from the pool, there's a weighing scene led by Anubis, a harpist singing, and his wife playing draughts.

Valley of the Queens

E£25, E£15 for students. Nefertari's tomb has now been closed to the public, due to the disintegration of the paintings as a result of exposure. It can only be viewed these days by VIPs or corporate groups, at enormous expense.

The Valley of the Queens was originally known as the 'Place of Beauty' but is now called in Arabic the 'Gates of the Harem' (*Biban El-Harem*). It was used as a burial site for officials long before the queens and their offspring, who had previously been buried with their husbands, began to be buried here in the 19th Dynasty (1320-1200 BC). It contains more than 80 tombs but many are still unidentified. The tombs are generally quite simple with a long corridor, several antechambers branching off and the burial chamber at the end. The most famous tomb is that of Ramses II's wife Nefertari, but now that this is permanently closed the Valley of the Queens has become the sight to miss if you're short on time.

Deir El-Medina

E£25, students E£15 for 2 tombs, an additional E£10 for Peshedu.

The original occupants of this village were the workers who excavated and decorated the tombs in the Valley of the Kings. The neat remains are certainly worth exploration (no entrance fee) and beginning at the north end is recommended. A narrow street, in places little more than a metre wide, runs south with the houses tightly packed on either side. The foundations show how small these dwellings were, and often they were subdivided, but remains of stairs indicate an upper storey and sometimes a cellar. Some houses were a little larger and contained a kitchen. Further south the street turns to the left and right, marking the limit of the 18th-Dynasty town.

Above the site are the three open tombs: Sennedjem, Peshedu and Inherkhau, foreman of a construction team in the 20th Dynasty. All, but especially the tomb of Sennedjem, are beautifully preserved and have outstanding paintings.

Deir El-Medina

The female Pharaoh

Hatshepsut was the only female pharaoh to reign over ancient Egypt (1503-1482 BC). Daughter of Tuthmosis I and wife of Tuthmosis II, she was widowed before she could bear a son. Rather than give up power to the son of one of her husband's minor wives she assumed the throne, first as regent for the infant Tuthmosis III but then as queen. Tuthmosis III was only able to assume office when Hatshepsut died 21 years later. As a woman she legitimised her rule by being depicted with the short kilt and the false beard worn by the male pharaohs.

Colossi of Memnon

On the main road 1.6 km from the river. No charge.

These two gigantic sandstone colossi represent Amenhotep III (1417-1379 BC). They once stood in front of his mortuary temple, which collapsed and was plundered for stone long ago. Although the faces and crowns have been eroded the two colossi make a strange spectacle seated in splendour on the edge of the fields and it's worth stopping on your way past.

The Ramesseum

Near the Tombs of the Nobles, on the opposite side of the road.
E£25, E£15 for students.

Ramses II's (1304-1237 BC) mortuary temple, or 'Ramesseum', a 19th-century name for what was effectively a state cult-temple is an extremely worthwhile stop. On its south side is a palace where Ramses stayed when he attended religious festivals on the West Bank.

The temple structure was built on Seti I's (1318-04 BC) much smaller but collapsing temple, in order to impress his subjects. However Ramses II failed to take into account the annual flooding of the Nile. The result was that this enormous tribute to Amun and himself was less eternal than he expected. The first two pylons collapsed and only a single colonnade remains of what would have been the First Courtyard.

In front of the ruins of the Second Pylon is the base of the enormous colossus of Ramses, which was originally over 17 m high but it is now much eroded and various parts of his anatomy are scattered throughout the world's museums. The forefinger alone measures more than 1 m in length. The upper part of the body crashed into the second court where the head and torso remain.

Although it is now roofless, 29 of the original 48 columns still loom tall in the Hypostyle Hall.

Colossi of Memnon, West Bank.

To the left of the entrance is the famous relief of the Egyptian victory over the Hittite city of Dapur during the Battle of Kadesh. Around the base of the west walls some of Ramses' many sons are depicted. At the far end of the hall a central door leads into the Astronomical Room, renowned for its ceiling illustrated with the oldest-known 12-month calendar. Because the temple was dedicated to Amun it is thought to represent a solar year.

Medinat Habu

E£25, E£15 for students.

The Mortuary Temple of Ramses III (1198-1166 BC), which lies west of the Colossi of Memnon at a place known in Arabic as Medinat Habu, was modelled on that built by his forefather Ramses II nearby. The immensity of the structures that remain are still quite overwhelming and the temple is a true highlight, uncluttered by visitors and a good place to finish a day on the West Bank as the sun sets.

The First Pylon would have been larger than the one at Luxor, standing 27 m high and 65 m long, but now the north corner and cornice are missing. On the left of the entrance way through the First Pylon, before arriving in the great First Court, Ramses III is shown worshipping the deities Ptah, Osiris and Sokar. The west of the court is flanked by eight columns and the east by seven Osiride pillars. On the Second Pylon the pharaoh is depicted marching rows of prisoners towards Amun and Mut. In the Second Court the intensity of the colours on pillars and on ceiling slabs are especially breathtaking and well-preserved.

It's a fact...

Second only to Karnak in terms of its size, the enclosing walls of the Medinat Habu complex were large enough to shelter the entire population of Thebes.

Easy side trips from Luxor

Dendara & Abydos

A s if Luxor itself doesn't boast enough archaeological wonders to make planning your sightseeing priorities a challenge! North of Luxor – a day trip away – are the magnificent temples of Abydos and Dendara, the unquestionable highlights of Middle Egypt, containing the most perfectly preserved and perfectly executed reliefs of any pharaonic structure in the land. Making these trips from Luxor normally involves taking the daily convoy and sharing space with coach-loads of others, but it's undoubtedly worth it.

From Luxor, a convoy for Dendara leaves daily, at 0800, carrying on to Abydos, before returning in the afternoon. Expect delays from the additional security procedures associated with visiting this area – the intervention of the tourist police can result in a lengthy wait (30 minutes or more) at both ends of the journey.

Dendara

Daily 0600-1700, last admission 1600.
E£30, E£15 for students.

Dendara was the cult centre of Hathor. The Temple of Hathor, built between 125 BC and AD 60 by the Ptolemies and the Romans, is the latest temple on a site begun by Pepi I in the Sixth Dynasty (2345-2181 BC). The enclosing wall of the temple is of unbaked bricks laid alternately convex and

concave, like waves of a primeval ocean – perhaps this had some religious significance. The huge, well-preserved temple dominates the walled Dendara complex which also includes a number of smaller buildings.

At the front, the pylon-shaped façade is supported by six huge Hathor-headed columns. Through in the Hypostyle Hall there are 18 Hathor-headed columns. The magnificent ceiling, which is illustrated with an astronomical theme, has retained much of its original colour. It is divided between day and night and illustrates the 14-day moon cycle, the gods of the four cardinal points, the constellations, the zodiac, and the elongated goddess Nut who swallows the sun at sunset and gives birth to it at dawn.

The next room, the Hall of Appearances, is where the goddess appeared from the depths of the temple as she was transported on her ritual barque for the annual voyage to Edfu. The second room, called the Nile Room, has river scenes and an exit to the back corridor and the well outside. Next is the first vestibule, which was known as the Hall of Offerings because it was there that the priests displayed the offerings for the goddess on large tables. The food and drink was then divided among the priests once the gods had savoured them.

The walls of the stairway from the left of the Hall of Offerings to the Roof Sanctuaries (which, unlike anywhere else, have been completely preserved), depict the New Year ceremony when the statue of Hathor was carried up to the roof to await the sunrise. The scenes on the left of the stairs represent Hathor going up while those on the right show her returning down.

The views from the uppermost level of the roof terrace are superb and provide an excellent opportunity to appreciate the overall scale and layout of the temple buildings, the extensive outer walls and the cultivated countryside surrounding Dendara.

At the front of the main temple to the right is the Roman Birth House, or Mammisi, which has some interesting carvings on its façade and south walls. The Sanatorium, between the Mammisi and the main temple, was where pilgrims who came to Dendara to be healed by Hathor were treated and washed in water from the stone-lined Sacred Lake, now drained of water. Between the two birth-houses is a ruined fifth-century Coptic Basilica, one

It's a fact…

Hathor, represented as a cow or cow-headed woman, was the goddess associated with love, joy, music, protection of the dead and, above all, of nurturing. Her great popularity was demonstrated by the huge festival held at Edfu, south of Aswan, when her barque symbolically sailed upstream on her annual visit to Horus. As they reconsummated their union the population indulged in the Festival of Drunkenness, which led the Greeks to identify Hathor with Aphrodite who was their own goddess of love and joy.

of the earliest Coptic buildings in Egypt, which was built using stone from the adjacent buildings.

On the exterior south wall of the temple there are two damaged reliefs depicting Cleopatra (the only surviving relief depicting Cleopatra in the whole of Egypt) and her son Caesarion.

Lotus flowers, Abydos temple.

Abydos

Daily 0800-1700, E£30, E£15 for students.

There are cemeteries and tombs scattered over a very wide area in Abydos but there are only a few buildings left standing that aren't too far apart: the Temple of Seti I, the Osirieon (Cenotaph) and the Temple of Ramses II.

The stunning Temple of Seti I was constructed in fine white marble by Seti I (1318-1304 BC) as an offering, in the same way that lesser mortals would come on a pilgrimage and make a gift of a stela. It contains some of the most exquisitely carved reliefs of any monument in Egypt, and the detail in faces, jewellery and hairstyles can be utterly transfixing, particularly on the unpainted reliefs. Meanwhile, blocks of white light coming through the holes in the ceiling allow you to admire the extensive colours of ochre, turquoise, umber and colbalt still clinging to the interior walls.

Carvings inside Seti I's temple, Abydos.

It's a fact...

The cult centre for Osiris, the god of the dead who was known as 'Lord of Abydos' because, according to legend, either his head or his whole body was buried at the site, Abydos was considered the door to the afterlife. Initially, in order to achieve resurrection burial at Abydos was necessary but the requirement was later changed to a simple pilgrimage and the gift of a commemorative stela (wood or stone slab). Pilgrims were making the journey to Abydos from the Seventh Dynasty (2181-2173 BC) until well into the Ptolemaic era (323-30 BC). And it is still a spiritual visit for many people.

It is unusual in being L-shaped rather than following the usual rectangle design and because it has seven separate sanctuaries rather than a single one behind the hypostyle halls. These seven rooms, dedicated to the deified Seti I, the Osiris triad of Osiris, Isis and Horus, and the Amun triad of Amun, Mut and Khonsu, would have contained the god's barque as well as his stela placed in front of a false door.

The Osirieon, built earlier than the main temple and at water level, which has led to severe flooding, is sometimes called the Cenotaph of Seti I because it contains a sarcophagus. Although it was never used by Seti I, who is actually buried in the Valley of the Kings in Luxor (see page 127), it was built as a symbol of his closeness to Osiris. Many other pharaohs built similar 'fake' tombs, which were modelled on the tombs at Luxor, in Abydos, but were eventually buried elsewhere.

The small Temple of Ramses II was erected in 1298 BC for Ramses' *Ka* or spirit in order to give him a close association with Osiris. Accessed via the track to the right of Seti I's temple (someone will fetch the key) it is naturally an anticlimax after the scale and sheer beauty of the Temple of Seti I. Although the temple was reportedly almost intact when first seen by Napoleon's archaeologists, it has since fallen into ruin except for the lower parts of the limestone walls which are still surprisingly brightly coloured. Ramses' chunky feet and calves are all that remain of the statutory in the main courtyard.

Paintings inside Seti I's temple, Abydos.

Listings

Sleeping

The East Bank

Sofitel Winter Palace Hotel €€€€

Corniche El-Nil, T095-238 0422/5, sofitel.com. Map: Luxor, p120.
The oldest and most famous luxury hotel in Luxor whose guests have included heads of state, Noel Coward and Agatha Christie. There are 110 small and rather basic (for the price) rooms

Tip...

Luxor has thousands of beds, therefore when tourism wanes due to the intense heat of summer or tension in the region, competition is fierce. Prices get sliced and bargaining is the norm. It's wise to book ahead for peak season (November-February); otherwise, shop around.
Virtually all budget hotels in Luxor include breakfast and virtually all breakfasts consist of bread, jam, cheese, tea or coffee, and a boiled egg.

in the old building, either overlooking the Nile or the verdant garden full of towering old palms. You're really paying for the history and the exquisite public spaces, such as the Victorian lounge with its creaky parquet floor, chandeliers and Orientalist art. Pavilion rooms by the luxuriant garden are cheaper while the New Winter Palace (which had significantly cheaper rooms in an adjacent tower block) is being rebuilt at the time of writing. Terrace bar in splendid position overlooking Corniche and river, and an unheated but chic pool. Breakfast is an extra E£15. The terrace bar (where a beer costs E£40) is classic sundowner territory.

Sonesta St George Hotel €€€€

Corniche El-Nil, T095-238 2575, sonesta.com.
A modern seven-storey building, the interior is all marble and glittering lights, generally bustling and busy. The lower level terrace overlooks the Nile and there's a fabulous pool for guests' use only. Ten restaurants and bars to choose from, of which the Mikado Japanese restaurant comes highly recommended for its food if not its atmosphere. Quality sport and fitness centre and all the five-star amenities you desire.

Domina Inn Emilio Hotel €€€

Sharia Youssef Hassan, T095-237 6666, F095-237 0000. Map: Luxor, p120.
The Emilio has gone up a notch and recently refurbished rooms all have satellite TV, air conditioning, minibar and inoffensive furnishings. There's a small bar in the foyer, two restaurants, a nightly disco (2100-2400), and a real bonus is the clean and popular pool on the roof. In winter, it's wise to make reservations as the place swarms with European groups.

Mina Palace Hotel €€

Corniche El-Nil, T095-237 2074, F095-238 2194. Map: Luxor, p120.
Rooms have been refurbished in this old stalwart, relatively sensitively, thus a sense of the past remains. There's a roof garden for beer, though sadly the street-level outside terrace has now been closed off to the elements. It's the only hotel with a view of the Nile unimpeded by cruise ships and it's one of the best choices in town in terms of location, quality and price at E£115 for a double.

Fontana €

Sharia Radwan, off Sharia Televizion, T095-228 0663. Map: Luxor, p120.
Rooms are simple and clean, ones at the front have balconies, all have air conditioning. Spacious bathrooms include toilet paper

and towels. Loquacious Mr Magdy and his staff are helpful, there's free use of the washing machine and an information board. Breakfast is served as early as 0500 or as late as 1200.

Happyland €
Sharia El-Kamar, near Sharia Televizion, T095-227 1828, luxorhappyland.com.
Map: Luxor, p120.
A bit of a victim of its own success, Happyland prices are not so budget these days. However, rooms remain spotlessly clean and bathrooms include towels and toilet paper.

Bikes for rent (E£10 per day), internet (E£8 per hour), Wi-Fi, laundry service, nice rooftop terrace, even a whirlpool. Luggage storage and use of facilities for guests after check-out.

Nefertiti €
Sharia El-Sahaby, look for a huge painted sign off Sharia Karnak, T/F095-2372386, nefertitihotel.com.
Map: Luxor, p120.
This comfortable, centrally located hotel offers the best budget roof terrace in town and has been a firm favourite with travellers for years. Doubles with

air conditioning and private bath (E£100) are clean, with towels and linens replaced daily. Games room has billiards, *tawla* (backgammon), TV, internet and free Wi-Fi. Outgoing owner Aladin Al-Sahaby has plans for a revamp sometime in the near future.

Nubian Oasis Hotel €
Sharia Mohamed Farid, T095-236 2671.
Map: Luxor, p120.
All rooms have private bath and the price is right (negotiation always possible). The rooftop terrace is a good spot to hang out and films are shown here in the evening, use of the washing machine is E£10, breakfast is generous, and there's no hassle. Good for meeting other travellers and well worth walking the extra 100 m down the street passed its rival, the Oasis Hotel, who have been siphoning off much of their custom.

Oasis Hotel €
Sharia Mohamed Farid, T010-380 5882.
Map: Luxor, p120.
Blue is the theme throughout this reasonably priced option, which has a lovely rooftop, perfect for a relaxing breakfast. Unfortunately, rooms are rather cell-like (particularly the singles) but it's clean and cheap and they're willing to bargain. Rooms come with or without private bath and air conditioning.

Below: Shabby-chic accommodation on Luxor's East Bank.
Opposite page: Cool beers, sunset, refined ambiance.

What the locals say

When I'm asked what makes Luxor such a special place to visit, firstly I have to say that it's the city's amazing history. Secondly, there's the energy of the place. Luxor has such a special energy. There's always lots going on and the people here are very friendly.

Aladin Al-Sahaby, owner of Nefertiti Hotel, Luxor.

although they're not huge they are fresh and attractive with especially comfy beds and pillows. Go for a corner room at the front for great views of the fields stretching east and windows and balconies on two sides. The location near Medinat Habu is utterly peaceful and rural. They also have an apartment that sleeps four for E£300 per night.

Camping

Rezeiky Camp
Sharia Karnak, T095-338 1334, rezeikycamp.com.eg.
Offers tent sites (E£10), and not-so-cheap air-conditioned rooms (doubles E£100).
On site, there's a swimming pool, internet café, washing machine and garden with bar and restaurant, serving different Egyptian meals nightly at reasonable prices.Recommended, though it's a bit of a hike to town.

The West Bank

In recent years, several charming hotels have sprung up on the West Bank. Though the area has a lot less action than the East Bank, and fewer services, people in search of a tranquil, rural experience may find these options appealing.

Beit Sabee & Le Lotus Bleu €€€
Medinat Habu, T010-632 4926.
Two beautiful traditional adobe houses both with glorious views of the Theban mountains. The

eight-roomed Beit Sabee has an unobstructed outlook onto Medinat Habu while six-roomed Le Lotus Bleu is on the edge of fields and looks onto the Nobles' Tombs. Rooms of varying sizes are simple but chic, all en suite, breakfast is included and lunch/dinner can be arranged. These maison d'hotel are special places.

El-Nakhil Hotel €€€
Gezira El-Bairat, T095-231 3922, T012-382 1007.
Beautiful spacious rooms have brick-domed ceilings and quality furnishings, lit by filigree lanterns, plus high-spec bathrooms (some with tubs). There is an air of peace and refinement throughout, a pleasant garden and Luxor Temple is visible from the rooftop restaurant. There is a room with disabled facilities, the only one the West Bank.

Amenophis Hotel €€
Near Medinat Habu Temple, T095-206 0078.
A good choice in the mid-range category, doubles are E£150 and

El Gezira Hotel €
Gezira, T/F095-231 0034, el-gezira.com.
This appealing hotel is run by a German-Egyptian couple, and has excellent facilities for the price, rooms have fridges, air conditioning and balconies. The rooftop and flowery garden are a bonus, you can dine inside or out and they serve alcohol. They also own the Gezira Gardens nearer the river, with a pool where Gezira guests get discounts for day use.

Marsam Hotel €
Gurna, T095-237 2403, T010-3426471.
Popular with archaeologists during the season (Jan-Apr), austere rooms have reed furniture and are cool, calm, dark retreats. Smaller rooms without bath are the cheapest deal on the West Bank. The rooftop looks out over fields to the Colossi of Memnon or back to the hills and the garden is a shady relaxing place to be. Bikes are available for hire.

Eating & drinking

Kim's at the Grand €€€
Sharia Khalid Ibn El-Walid,
T095-238 6742.
An unprepossessing canteen environment, but chock-full of Koreans enjoying authentic dishes that really hit the mark. Go early as everyone clears out by 2100. Efficient service and generous portions, you will struggle to eat your main after snacking on all the *kimchee.*

Le Lotus Boat €€€
Iberotel, Sharia Khalid Ibn El-Walid, T095-238 0925,
iberotelegypt.com.
Well-organized dinner cruises every Thursday offering international cuisine and an Oriental show from 1930-2200 (E£200), book to get a good seat. Also day cruises with a high-quality lunch while travelling to Dendara for E£425 per person on Sunday, Tuesday and Friday (Tuesday is the quietest).

Ali Baba Café €€
Sharia Karnak, enter on side street.
Map: Luxor, p120.
Rooftop dining that offers a lovely view of Luxor temple, particularly at sunset and in the early evening when the temple is lit up. The food is standard Egyptian fare, but the servings are quite small. Stella E£12, local wine E£20/glass.

Amoun €€
Map: Luxor, p120.
The best of the touristy restaurants in a courtyard by the temple. Indoor and outdoor seating areas. Offers a variety of cheap, good food including pizza, seafood, and all the usuals. Excellent juice bar and ice cream. Friendly service that will keep the hustlers away as you watch the people go by.

Chez Omar €€
Midan Youssef Hassan, smack bang in the middle of the souk, T095-236 7678.
Open 0800-0300.
Map: Luxor, p120.
This place offers decent food and fast, friendly service alongside Bob Marley prints, air conditioning and tablecloths. Lit up with green lights at night, it's a good place to breathe after a long day. Considering the alternatives and the fact it is tourist-oriented, it's still pretty cheap, for example E£40 gets you a five-course dinner including soup, salad, rice, vegetable, dessert and a meat of your choice.

Jamboree €€
29 Sharia El-Montazah,
T012-241 5510.
Map: Luxor, p120.
A small generic restaurant, with British proprietors, that offers a daytime snack menu (1030-1430) featuring omelettes, soups, sandwiches and jacket potatoes. Dinner is served from 1800-2200.

Entrées include an excellent salad bar. The food is tasty and good for unsettled stomachs. Also on offer are milkshakes and Movenpick ice cream, but no alcohol.

Jems €€
Sharia Khalid Ibn El-Walid, T012-226 1697, on the 2nd floor.
The atmosphere isn't quite as quaint as neighbouring restaurants but guests love the food and keep coming back. The policy is, if you return more than once in the course of the week, you are offered a modest discount that gets bigger every time you return. There are set vegetarian meals, a hodgepodge of Middle Eastern and British fare and an extensive bar. The *shish tawook* comes highly recommended.

Lotus €€
In the heart of the souk on the 2nd floor.
Map: Luxor, p120.
Serves a selection of Middle Eastern and European dishes including spinach cannelloni, fish and chips and a variety of vegetarian options. Large windows look down on thriving alleyways. 15% discount for students. The service is good,

Tip...

The cheap public ferry makes transport across the Nile easy, but if you're planning on an exceptionally late night, you'll have to hire a motorboat (E£5-10).

but if the restaurant is full, it can take a while. The chocolate mousse is delicious.

Oasis Café €€
Sharia Dr Labib Al-Habashi, T095-237 2914.
Map: Luxor, p120.
A hip café and gallery is something you rarely find in Egypt, and this really feels more like Morocco. On the ground floor of a period building, high-ceilinged rooms have darkly-painted walls and antiquey tiled floors. Unfortunately the food is not quite as special as the surroundings, but if you crave Western-style sandwiches and salads it fits the bill. Otherwise just go for a coffee to absorb the refined yet casual ambiance.

Abu Ashraf €
Sharia Mahatta, halfway between the station and the souk.
Map: Luxor, p120.
Sells tasty *koshari*, *shish kebab*, roasted chicken, and lots of salads. Nothing exceeds E£15 and the place is clean.

Mish Mish €
Sharia Televizion.
Map: Luxor, p120.
Serves tasty, cheap pizza with fluffy crust (E£10-16), although the local cheese doesn't melt like mozzarella, a medium should fill you up unless you're famished. Also serves pastas, sandwiches and other standard Middle Eastern dishes. A longtime popular eatery among backpackers.

The West Bank

Africa Restaurant €€
Immediately opposite the ferry landing, T095-231 1488.
Open 0800-2400.
The standard Luxor menu of rice, salad, meat/fish and veg is served for E£35 in a delightful outside courtyard. Surrounded by fruit trees and mint that staff will pick to accompany your tea. As the menu differs somewhat for English speakers, if there's a local dish you want that you don't see, ask for it. Serves a good traditional Egyptian breakfast. Beer available.

Memnon Restaurant €€
Next to the Colossi of Memnon, T012-327 8747.
A good resting place for a chilled drink and the food comes highly recommended. All sorts on offer, from pasta to fish, plus great soups and salads, all reasonably priced. You can't fault the view or the tiny flowery garden.

Nour El Gourna Hotel & Restaurant €€
Old Gurna, opposite the ticket office, T095-231 1430.
Delicious tagines and stews come in substantial portions – in fact, it's a good idea to negotiate sharing a meal. They can accommodate vegetarians, while meat eaters will be treated to duck and pigeon delicacies. A lovely spot under shady reed awnings.

Tutankhamun €€
From the ferry landing, turn left on the main road and walk 200 m to the motorboat landing, then follow the signs, T095-231 0918.
One of the oldest on the scene, the well-trained chef turns out rice and hearty veg stews and excellent grilled meats. More food than you could possibly eat. The roof terrace is another selling point. No alcohol.

Ramesseum Resthouse €
By the entrance to the Ramesseum, is perfect for a post-temple drink either inside the cool interior or outside in the shade. They even have beer (E£10).

Entertainment

Bars & clubs

Combine sightseeing with drinks at the historic **Winter Palace**, the Royal Bar inside (minimum food and drink charge/entry for non-guests of E£100) or sunset on the terrace, see page 140. In the winter, all five-star and most four-star hotels have some kind of 'live' music or belly dance floor show. In the summer, they're less frequent, it depends how many people are in town. The Mercure (locally known as the Etap) offers belly-dance shows and DJs in the Sabil disco from 2300 and sells cheap beer.

Esquire
Sharia Ali Ibn Abi Taleb, T012-228 7130.
Handy for the centre of town. A huge bar serving beer and spirits, daily happy hour 1700-1900. The diverse menu includes English traditional.

King's Head Pub
Sharia Khalid Ibn El-Walid, T095-228 0489.
The most longstanding and happening pub in town stays open until people are ready to go home (at least until 0200). The extensive menu includes a wide variety of hot and cold *mezze* (E£15), curries, sandwiches and English standards (fish and chips E£47).

Murphy's Irish Bar
Sharia El-Gawazat, near the passport office off Sharia Khalid Ibn El- Walid, T095-238 8101. Open 1000-0230.
Huge two-floor pub with pool table and football on the TV upstairs, comfy chairs and lots of wood, not too pricey with Stellas at E£14. Pub menu includes a veggie burger, jacket potatoes and loads of soups, salads and pastas. The basement disco gets going at about 2230.

Saint Mina hotel bar
Sharia Cleopatra, T095-237 5409. Open 1500-0200.
Down in the dingy cellar of the Christian-run hotel, this functional bar has a very local vibe and the cheapest Stella in town (E£8).

Sinbad
Sharia Al-Karnak, in front of the Luxor Wena Hotel, T095-238 0018.
Great for an outdoor drink under the trees decked with fairy lights. The food is average but not too pricey and beer is cheap.

Sinouhe/Red Lion Pub
Sharia Khalid Ibn El-Walid, located on the 2nd floor.
Pub and disco with black lights, red walls, a disco ball and pumping 1990s music. The action doesn't get started until after midnight and lasts until 0300.

Shopping

The gritty old *souk* has been somewhat sanitized, but that said it still bombards the senses with spices and dried herbs and a palette of colourful scarves. Local alabaster vases, pots and tagins are also sold cheaply here. Independent travellers can choose from an abundance of fresh fruit and vegetables around the *souk* in the town centre and in the Sharia Televizion Market on Tuesdays.

Belly dance costumes.

Tip...

Foreign newspapers are sold in a kiosk in the middle of the street outside the Old Winter Palace Hotel. There is a good chance that these will also be offered for sale by street vendors along the Corniche where the cruise ships are moored.

Activities & tours

Books

Aboudi Books

Near the New Winter Palace on Corniche El-Nil.
Open Sat-Thu 0800-2000.
May be the best bookshop for non-Arabic readers outside Cairo, offering fiction and historical books in English, German and French, also lots of maps and guidebooks to specific areas in Egypt and a decent selection of second-hand paperbacks.

Gaddis Bookshop

By the New Winter Palace on Corniche El-Nil, T095-372142.
Open 0800-2130.
Books in English, French and German. Cheaper than Aboudi, with almost as wide a selection.

Souvenirs

Aisha

Sharia Youssef Hassan, opposite the Emilio Hotel.
Open daily 0930-2300.
Has a wide array of tasteful crafts, scarves, throws, pottery, lamps and glassware, as well as Bedouin jewellery. A good place to browse without any hassle and prices are fixed.

Organized tours are definitely worth investigating if your time in Luxor is tight. Air-conditioned transport and certified local guides are widely available. Aim to pay about E£120-150 per person (excluding enter tickets) to tour the highlights.

Local travel agencies and tour operators, concentrated on the Corniche around the Old Winter Palace and the tourist information office, are good starting points for tours of Luxor's East and West Banks, day cruises to Dendara and trips further afield, also Hurghada–Sharm ferry tickets.

Eastmar Travel

Corniche El-Nil, Old Winter Palace, T095-237 3513.

Nawas Tours

By the tourist office, T095-237 0701/2.

Thomas Cook

Corniche El-Nil, next to the Winter Palace Hotel, T095-237 2402, thomascookegypt.com.

Balloon flights

All companies pick up from hotels on the morning of your flight around 0500-0530, most include a basic breakfast (instant coffee and a snack) on the boat as you cross the Nile. It's always wise to check that the operating company has insurance, certification and offer a full refund if the flight is cancelled due to unsuitable weather conditions.

Hod Hod Soliman (Sharia Televizion, T095-237 0116) and Magic Horizon (Sharia Khalid Ibn Walid, T095-236 5060) are two of the most reputable companies.

Alaska Balloons

Sharia Televizion, T095-227 3777, freewebs.com/alaska-balloons
This is the company with the most balloons (the bright red ones) up in the air. Price includes a souvenir certificate and T-shirt.

Up, up and away above the Thebian Necropolis.

Tip...

Generally the further away from the river you go shopping, the lower the prices will be and the less the hassle you will receive.

Transport

Sindbad Balloons
37 Sharia Hamed El-Omda, off Sharia Televizion, T095-227 2960, sindbadballoons.com.
This reputable company ask E£300 for a flight, refreshments are included.

Viking Air
2 Sharia Ahmed Orabi, T016-883 3577, vikingairegypt.com.
A little cheaper – standard cost is E£400, but they have frequent special offers of E£300.

Feluccas
Ask at your hotel, with a tour operator or at the Corniche.

Horse riding
Nobi's Arabian Horse Stables
Al-Gezira, West Bank, T095-231 0024, T010-504 8558.
Horse riding on West Bank is popular, usually passing through villages and some monuments towards the mountains (E£25-30 per hour). Call in advance.

Swimming
Most hotels with pools offer day use for a fee. At the cheaper end of the spectrum, the pool on the roof of the **Emilio Hotel** is largest and cleanest with plenty of sunbathers, E£30. The best deal in town is at the **Mercure**, which has a splendid pool with lots of loungers in a palm garden, day use E£50 per person including a light lunch. The pool at the **Iberotel** (E£75) actually floats on the Nile.

Air
EgyptAir, has frequent daily flights, particularly in the winter high season, to Cairo, Aswan, and Abu Simbel via Aswan. Three flights a week go to Sharm El-Sheikh. Fares change depending on the season. Book your tickets well in advance. Egyptair offices: the Winter Palace Hotel (T095-238 0581/2, open 0800-2000); Luxor airport (T095-238 0588).

Bus
Long-distance buses leave from the bus station, a 40 pt micro ride from the town centre or E£20 in a taxi. Currently, there are daily buses to Cairo at 2000 (10 hrs), Dahab at 1700 (14-17 hrs) via Sharm El-Sheikh (13-16 hrs) and Hurghada at 2000 and 2030 (4 hrs). They won't sell tourists bus tickets to Aswan or the towns south of Luxor, you need to join the convoy.

There are three daily convoys from Luxor to Aswan leaving at 0700, 1100, 1500 (the first two via Esna, Edfu and Kom Ombo); to Abydos and Dendara at 0800 and returns at around 1730.

Taxi
Long-distance private taxis may be available direct to Aswan or with stops in Esna, Edfu and Kom Ombo; also round trips to Dendara and Abydos (requires convoy).

Service taxis leave from the terminal just off Sharia El-Karnak, halfway between Luxor town centre and Karnak temple, these

Calèche ride, Old Winter Palace.

are quicker and more convenient than trains or buses but they may be required to travel with convoys if carrying foreigners long distances.

Train
Foreigners are technically restricted in their choice of trains. To Cairo, there are three 'secure' trains per day, all with air conditioning and restaurants on board. It is essential, particularly in the high winter season, to reserve your seat at the station a few days before you travel. First/Second-class trains to Cairo (10 hrs) leave daily at 0930, 2115, 2310. The 0930 Cairo-bound First/Second-class train also stops at El-Balyana (Abydos, 3 hrs). The privately run sleeper trains (Abela Egypt, T02-3574 9474, book at sleepingtrains.com) depart daily to Cairo at 2010 and 2120.

For El-Quseir or Marsa Alam you can take a train to Qift from where buses leave for the East Coast at 1100, 1530 and 1800 (on to El-Quseir, 2 hrs; Marsa Alam, 3 hrs). There are also regular service taxis from Qift, which you will have no problem boarding if you miss the bus.

Contents

Aswan, Abu Simbel & Lake Nasser

Lake Nasser.

Introduction

The stretch of the River Nile between Luxor and Aswan is best explored by boat – from the deck of a cruiser or more intimately in a *felucca*, with the Nile so close you can feel it mumbling and sighing, still as glass in the morning and raging like a rough sea by midday. You will pass by or pause a while at the striking Graeco-Roman monuments of Edfu and Kom Ombo. Placed at strategic and commercial centres near the river, these temples are among the most colourful and complete pharaonic structures in the country.

Aswan, Egypt's southern frontier town, in its delightful river setting, is for many the highlight of a Nile cruise. With the outstanding Nubian museum, colourful west bank villages and islands to explore, as well as proximity to several notable temples and the nearby High Dam, the city is much more than a stopover en route to Abu Simbel.

And, should you have the opportunity, a night spent in laid-back Abu Simbel on the brim of Lake Nasser rewards travellers with a peaceful dawn at the temples, a memorable experience as profound as the monument themselves.

What to see in...

... one day
If you've the sightseeing stamina to set off from Aswan before dawn breaks, you can pack in **Abu Simbel**, the **Philae Temples**, the **High Dam** and the **Unfinished Obelisk** and make it back in time for a sunset *felucca* voyage alongside **Elephantine Island** and dinner Nubian-style.

... a weekend or more
With vessels to suit all budgets and itineraries for every interest, cruising to or from Luxor, and/or around Lake Nasser, is time superbly spent. With longer in Aswan itself, criss-cross the Nile to the **Tombs of Nobles**, **Elephantine** and **Kitchener Island**, traverse desert sand to **St Simon's Monastery**, then cool off after dark in one of the restaurants on Corniche.

The Sun Temple of Ramses II, Abu Simbel.

Luxor to Aswan

A voyage through Egypt's Nile Valley from ancient Thebes to Aswan is one of travel's classic itineraries. Proof of which are the strings of cruise ships, dahabiyas and fellucas that chart purposefully up and down river, bursting with travellers eager to explore eye-poppingly well preserved cult temples dedicated to deities such as Sobek the god of crocodiles and Horus the falcon-headed sky god.

Temple of Khnum, Esna.

Essentials

❶ Getting around Travelling across Upper Egypt, at present, is fairly straightforward. With no terrorist attacks since 1997, there is little to worry about. Nonetheless, outside of the 'bubble' of Aswan, local authorities like foreigners travelling overland to move in convoys between the major sights. As such, accompanying a tour (which is sometimes just a ride) is often the easiest and most hassle-free way to go. There are many options, catering to both piaster-pinching backpackers as well as tourists with more resources. The main road follows the Nile along its east bank from Luxor, past Edfu (115 km) on the west bank, before continuing via Kom Ombo (176 km) to Aswan (216 km). There is an alternative, less crowded and less scenic route along the west bank from the Valley of the Kings to Esna (55 km) and Edfu before having to cross the river to continue the journey along the east bank to Aswan.

Boats Egyptian village life, often obscured from the road and not easily appreciated from the window of a speeding car, can be seen on this relaxing journey that many have deemed the highlight of their trip though Egypt. Most visitors make this journey by river in floating accommodation that can moor at the sites along the way (see Nile Cruises page 156).

Due to the direction of the river's flow, wind conditions and the problematic locks at Esna, extended *feluca* trips start in Aswan and go north towards Luxor, see page 181. Most common are the 1-day/1-night trips to nearby Kom Ombo (where the *felucca* stops immediately in front of the temple) and the 3-day/2-night trips to Edfu. From there, it's possible to carry on overland to other significant sights between Aswan and Luxor.

❷ Bus station Buses arriving in Edfu will stop on the east bank opposite town; in Kom Ombo they stop on Sharia 26th July.

❸ Train station Esna's station is an awkward 5 km out of town; in Edfu it is 4 km from town, both on the opposite side of the Nile.

❹ ATMs Esna has one bank (Sat-Thu 0830-1400, Sun 1800-2100, and Wed 1700 -2000); Edfu's centrally located bank is on Sharia El-Gumhoriyya; the bank in Kom Ombo is next to the mosque (Sun-Thu 0830-1400 and 1000-1330 during Ramadan).

❺ Post office Kom Ombo has an office on Sharia Tahrir.

Esna

A small market town about 55 km south of Luxor on the west bank of the Nile, Esna is best known for the Temple of Khnum and its sandstone dam, built in 1906 at about the same time as the first Aswan dam. Cruise ships and barges usually have to queue a while for their turn to pass through the barrages, though waiting time has been considerably reduced by the building of a second lock. It's a typical dusty town, not geared towards tourists save for the souvenir-sellers, and there is nothing to keep you here once you've finished at the temple.

The Temple of Khnum

Partially exposed in a deep depression in the centre of Esna.
Daily 0700-1600 winter, 0700-1700 summer, E£15, E£10 for students. Service taxis and buses stop about 10 mins' walk from the temple, which is in the centre of town, walk to the river and then south along the Corniche to the ticket kiosk.

Over the centuries, the annual Nile flood has deposited 10 m of silt over the temple site so that in fact all that is visible today is the Hypostyle Hall. This definitely comes as a disappointment to some visitors, and consequently many tours no longer

Tip...

You can be in and out of the Temple of Khnum in under two hours, which will keep the local police force happy.

Carvings of prisoners on the Sun Temple, Abu Simbel.

include Esna on their itineraries. The only part of the temple that can be seen is Ptolemaic/Roman, built on the foundations of a much older shrine was also dedicated to the ram-headed deity Khnum.

The hypostyle hall's Outer Façade is decorated from left to right with the cartouches of the emperors Claudius, Titus and Vespasian. Inside the lofty hall 18 columns with capitals of varying floral designs support the Astronomical Ceiling which is barely visible today because it was blackened by the wood fires of a Coptic village once housed within the temple. In places various deities and animals, including winged dogs, two-headed snakes and the pregnant hippo-goddess Taweret can be seen intermingled with signs of the zodiac. The hall's columns are inscribed with texts detailing the temple's various festivals. On the lighter side, look out for the cross-legged pharaoh, frogs on top of a capital representing the goddess Heqet and a column engraved with countless crocodiles.

Edfu

Edfu Temple, or Temple of Horus

Inland along Sharia Al-Maglis.
0700-1600 winter, 0700-1700 summer, E£40, E£20 for students. Enter from the ticket office in the northwest corner at the rear of the main temple. *Calèche* ride (many of which are drawn by emaciated and badly treated horses) from the river; 20-min walk or short ride from the service taxi terminal at the west end of the Nile bridge; intercity buses drop off on Sharia Tahrir or the parallel Sharia El-Gumhoriyya halfway between the bridge and the temple.

Edfu, 60 km south along the west bank almost equidistant from Luxor (115 km) and Aswan (106 km), is the site of the huge, well-preserved

Ptolemaic cult Temple of Horus. The almost-intact ceilings and wealth of colours make it more immediately impressive than many older pharaonic cult temples and give a strong hint of what they would have looked like in their prime.

A huge Grand Pylon flanked by grey granite statues of the hawk-god Horus leads into the giant Court of Offerings, at the north end of which is the First Hypostyle Hall (180-145 BC). Its 18 once brightly painted columns support the roof.

Leading north from the hall is a smaller 12-columned hypostyle hall, known as the Festival Hall. The oldest part of the building dates back to Ptolemy III (246-222 BC), where offerings entered the temple and were prepared. These were then carried through into the Hall of Offerings where the daily offerings would have been made at the many altars and tables bearing incense, juices, fruit and meat. The stairs here, illustrated with pictures of the priests carrying the statues of the gods, were used for the procession up to the roof where a Chapel of the Disc once stood.

If you are staying overnight in Edfu, the temple is particularly attractive at dusk when it is floodlit and many of the beautiful reliefs are shown at their best, especially in the first and second hypostyle halls. Taking a torch with you at this time of day is wise.

Silsila

In between Edfu and Kom Ombo, as limestone gives way to sandstone and the river narrows, the ancient quarries of Silsila come into sight. In use from the 16th to the first century BC, the quarries were the source of tonnes of sandstone used in temple building. Convicts were used to cut the huge blocks from the cliffs which were then transported on the Nile to sacred sights around Egypt. You can still see holes carved into the rock where the ancient boats were moored. The cliffs are decorated with graffiti and stelae. Small temples and statues were also carved in the surrounding rock. The cliffs of Silsila are particularly beautiful around sunset. As the cruise boatscannot dock here, *felucca* travellers get the place to themselves.

Temple of Horemheb

Silsila, west bank.
0600-1600 winter, 0600-1700 summer. E£25, E£15 for students.

If you're on a boat and have the chance to stop, it's definitely worth exploring this colourful temple, even after hours. For a bit of *backsheesh*, the guard will show you around. Arriving by land is a bit more of a challenge, it's really only worth the trek if you have a lot of time and a lot of interest, the closest town is Faris, from there, you will need to take a ferry to west bank where you can hire a private taxi for E£20 to bring you to the temple.

Kom Ombo

Kom Ombo Temple, or Temple of Sobek and Horus

On the banks of the Nile, 4 km south of town.
Daily 0600-1600 winter, 0600-1700 summer, E£25, E£15 for students. Most visitors come by *felucca* or cruiser; if catching the Aswan-bound service taxi get off at the turn-off 2 km south of Kom Ombo from where the signposted 'tembel' is 1.5 km away; from the town itself catch buses, service taxis or pickups.

This small but beautiful temple faces the Nile at a bend in the river and is unusual because it is dedicated to two gods rather than a single deity. The left-hand side is devoted to a form of Horus the Elder or Haroeris known as the 'Good Doctor'. The right-hand side of the temple is dedicated to the crocodile-god Sobek-Re (here identified with the sun).

At the north end is the double entrance of the First Hypostyle Hall which has five entrance columns and 10 internal columns. Its wall reliefs are especially decorative. Part of the roof has survived on the east side of the Hall and flying vultures are clearly depicted on the ceiling. The rear walls leading to the older Inner Hypostyle Hall, which has two entrances, 15 columns and a striking relief that depicts Horus the Elder presenting the Hps, the curved sword of victory to Ptolemy VII.

This is followed by three double Entrance Vestibules, each smaller and higher than the last. The inner vestibule has two doors leading to the two separate Sanctuaries of Horus and Sobek. Beneath these are the crypts, which are empty but, unusually, open to the public. Visible is a small secret chamber, from where the priests spoke to the gods. It lies between the two sanctuaries, in what would have appeared as a very thick wall.

On the inner wall of the outer corridor is the first known illustration of medical instruments, including bone-saws, scalpels, suction caps and dental tools, which date from the second century AD. Guides sometimes say that complicated operations were carried out 1800 years ago, but it is most probable that these were instruments used in the mummification process.

It's a fact...

Kom Ombo is an ancient crossroads, where the Forty Days Road caravan route from western Sudan met the route from the eastern desert gold mines. It is also the place where African war elephants were trained up for use in the Ptolemaic army.

Nile Cruises

I t is easy to arrange a cruise – lasting either two to five days (standard tour) or seven days (extended tour) – on arrival in Luxor, if you don't like planning things too much in advance. Most cruises go from Luxor to Aswan, with the journey sometimes in reverse, or a trip both ways. Starting from Aswan you are travelling with the current so the trip will be shorter, and it has the disadvantage of being against the wind which can make relaxing on the top deck almost impossible.

The quality of operator and cruise ship will, of course, be largely dependent on the price paid. There are scores of agents along Luxor's Corniche. Enquire at a few, try to see the actual boat if possible, and check their programmes – bottom-end cruisers probably won't include all the sights.

Tip...

Cruises can be disrupted twice-yearly, in June and December, when Esna's lock closes for maintenance. When this happens ships moor up at Esna and passengers are bused to points on their itinerary, reducing the pleasure of a cruising holiday. Try to find out the closure dates before you book.

In terms of accommodation, cabins at water level offer only limited views and, depending on position, may be more affected by engine noise and fumes than others. A supplement can be paid for a cabin on an upper deck. Top-level cabins may have a sun deck as their roof. It's best to obtain a plan of the vessel before you book your cabin. Bear in mind that when the ship is moored there may not be a view from the cabin whatever its level. Ships can often be berthed six or seven abreast and access to the shore is gained by walking through one ship after another. Expect to be issued with a boarding pass when going ashore.

You can expect three good meals per day, often buffet style. Meal times are likely to operate to a fairly inflexible timetable and some could be

Typical cruise itineraries

Luxor The West Bank (Valley of the Kings, Valley of the Queens, Colossi of Memnon, Temple of Queen Hapshetsut), Luxor and Karnak Temples (plus at least one alabaster factory shop). Option of Sound and Light show at Karnak.

Esna Temple of Khnum.

Edfu Temple of Horus – access by *calèche*.

Kom Ombu Temple of Horus and Sobek.

Aswan *Felucca* boat outing to Kitchener Island, trip to Nubian village on Elephantine Island, Unfinished Obelisk, High Dam, Temple of Philae (plus at least one papyrus factory shop).

Option of Sound and Light show at Philae.

served on a covered deck. Free tea, coffee and soft drinks are available at any time and, because the most money is to be made from alcohol, the bar will be open most of day.

Almost inevitably, at some stage during the cruise there will be an evening dinner at which travellers will be encouraged to dress in local Egyptian costume – a *gallabiya* party. Other evening entertainment may include discos, live Egyptian/Nubian music and performances by belly dancers, jugglers and acrobats.

Dahabiya cruises

These traditional sailing boats, some of which are renovated original crafts, are a more boutique way to cruise the Nile. It's advisable to book before arriving in Egypt, as they are often chartered by private groups and spaces are in any case limited by the small size of the vessels, for recommended vessels see Sleeping, page 176.

Feluccas

If you're considering a *felucca* because you're on a budget and would rather be cruising down the Nile in more luxurious style, bear in mind that it's possible to get a four-star cruise ship for US$40-50 per night – even less in summer. Ask at the tourist information office if they have any leads or take a wander down the Corniche and speak to the managers of the boats. If there are spare berths it is possible to negotiate a decent rate and bypass the travel agents.

Aswan

Not only is Aswan stunningly beautiful and charmingly romantic, it is the sunniest city in Egypt, hence its popularity. Across the river from the Corniche, dramatic desert cliffs merge with palm-lined Nile waters, and huge apricot-coloured sandbanks appear startling against the cloudless blue sky. In the late evening you can watch the flocks of egrets skimming the surface of the Nile as they go to roost before you feast on freshly caught Nile fish. In the early morning you can watch the sun rise behind the city and hear the call of the *muezzin*.

Nubian village, south of Aswan.

Philae temples

Temple: 0700-1600 winter, 0700-1700 summer, E£40, E£20 for students, for commercial photography E£10. Sound and Light Show: usually daily at 1830, 1945 and 2100 in winter and 2000, 2115 and 2230 in summer, times change during Ramadan and shows can be booked up, so check with the tourist office or T097-230 5376. Tickets E£75 (no discount), Mon English/French; Tue French/English; Wed French/English; Thu French/Spanish/English; Fri English/French/Italian; Sat English/Arabic; Sun German/French/English. Give yourself at least 45 mins to get to Philae from Aswan. Taxis to the dock cost E£30 return. Motorboats to the temple seat 8 people and should cost E£5 per person (although the boat men will demand E£20) or E£40 per private boat for the return journey including 1-hr wait. Request a 2-way trip or you will have problems later when they try to charge double.

Few would dispute that among the most beautiful and romantic monuments in the whole of Egypt are the Philae temples, which were built on Philae Island in the Ptolemaic era (332-30 BC) as an offering to Isis. In addition to the Temple of Isis there are smaller shrines on the island dedicated to both Nubian and local deities.

Temple of Isis 'Great Mother of All Gods and Nature', 'Goddess of Ten Thousand Names', and a representation of women, purity and sexuality, Isis' temple steals the show, covering over a quarter of the island. Its different sections were constructed over an 800-year period. You enter the temple through the First Pylon of Ptolemy XIII Neos Dionysus with illustrations showing him slaying his enemies as Isis, Horus and Hathor look on. The pylon was originally flanked by two obelisks, since looted and transported to the UK, but today only two lions at the base guarding the entrance remain.

Arriving in a large forecourt to the left is the colonnaded Birth House, used for *mammisi* (birth) rituals. The inner sanctum of which has scenes of

Essentials

❶ Getting around The city itself is walkable in the cooler part of the day. For farther flung sights use a mixture of taxis and river craft, or join one of many organized tours.

Boats Public ferries (max E£1, from 0600-2200) leave from the EgyptAir office and near the station to the Tombs of the Nobles. Foreigners aren't supposed to use them after sunset; *feluccas* from the Corniche El-Nil; motorboats to Phailae Temples from the New Port beyond the Aswan Dam. Official prices for short *felucca* transfers, regulated by the government, are E£25 per hr though you may struggle to get this. For example, if you sail to Kitchener's Island, Agha Khan Mausoleum and Elephantine Island, and spend a couple of hours wandering around, a three hour trip with one hour of sailing time should cost around E£70. If there are more passengers, prices usually go up. Haggle hard. For extended *felucca* cruises up river, see page 181.

❷ Bus station 3.5 km north of the town centre. Upper Egypt buses, office open 0700-1600, T097-230 0454.

❸ Train station North end of town, 2 mins' walk from the Corniche.

❹ ATMs Banks are on Corniche or Sharia Abtal El-Tahrir.

❺ Hospital German Hospital, on the Corniche, T097-302176.

❻ Post office Corniche, Sat-Thu 0800-2100, although you can post mail from any major hotel.

Isis giving birth to Horus in the marshes and others of her suckling the child-pharaoh.

The axis of the temple is changed by the Second Pylon, set at an angle to the first, beyond which a court containing ten columns opens onto the Hypostyle Hall. The ceiling in the central aisle

Around the region

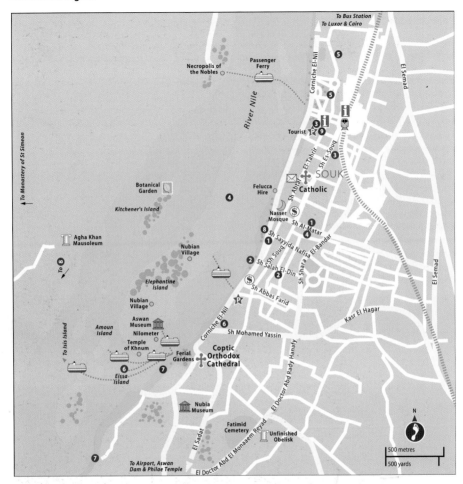

Aswan listings

❶ Sleeping

1 Hathor *Corniche El-Nil*
2 Keylany *25 Sharia Keylany*
3 Marhaba Palace *Corniche El-Nil*
4 Mövenpick *Elephantine Island*
5 New Abu Simbel *Sharia Abtal El-Tahrir*
6 Old Cataract *Sharia Abtal El-Tahrir*
7 Nile *15 Corniche El-Nil*
8 Pyramisa Isis *Corniche El-Nil*
9 Youth Hostel *96 Sharia Abtal El-Tahrir*

❶ Eating & drinking

1 Al Masry *Sharia Al-Matar*
2 Aswan Moon *Sharia Al-Matar*
3 El-Medina *In the souk*
4 Esmailya Sons *Sharia Al-Matar*

5 Kasr Elhoda *Sharia Abtal al Tahrir*
6 Nubian *Eissa Island*
7 Nubian House
On a hill behind the Basma Hotel
8 Pharaohs
South of Aga Khan's Mausoleum

Easily missed details

❶ The outer **western wall** of the **Birth House** carries a memorial tablet to the 101 men of the Heavy Camel Regiment who lost their lives in the Sudanese Campaign of 1884-1885.

❷ Look carefully at the Hathor-headed columns facing into the **Inner Court** from the walls of the **Birth House** – at the far end her face is straight but at the near end she is smiling.

❸ On either side of the wall, backing onto the **Second Pylon**, Ptolemy VII and Cleopatra II can be seen presenting offerings to Hathor and Khnum. Crosses carved on pillars and walls here provide evidence of the Coptic occupation.

❹ Interesting reliefs on **Hadrian's Gate** depict Isis, Nephthys, Horus and Amun in adoration before Osiris in the form of a bird. Behind is the source of the Nile emerging from a cavern while Hapy, a Nile god in human form, pours water from two jars, indicating the Egyptians' knowledge that the Nile had more than one source.

❺ Looking southeast from the Kiosk of Trajan towards the original Philae Island, it is possible to see the remains of a cofferdam that was built around it to reduce the water level and protect the temple ruins before they were moved to Agilkia.

Temple of Philae from the Nile.

has representations of vultures that were symbolic of the union of Lower and Upper Egypt. The rest of the ceilings have astronomical motifs and two representations of the goddess Nut. From the entrance at the far end of the Hypostyle Hall is a chamber that gives access to the roof.

The Temple of Isis and the rest of the monuments were moved to the neighbouring Agilkia Island by UNESCO in 1972-1980 when the construction of the High Dam threatened to submerge Philae forever. They were then reconstructed to imitate the original as closely as possible but the new position no longer faces neighbouring Bigah island, one of the burial sites of Osiris, which was the raison d'être for the location in the first place.

Sound and Light Show Like most big temples in Egypt, Philae has its own sound and light show. This one is an informative and melodramatic hour-long floodlit tour through the ruins. Some find it kitchy, others find it majestic. Arriving before sunset in time for the first show can be especially memorable. Travelling out from the harbour in a small flotilla of boats, watching the stars come out and tracing the dark shapes of the islands in the river silhouetted against the orange sunset sky is a stunning prelude to the beauty of the ancient floodlit ruins.

Aswan High Dam

Cross between 0700-1600 in winter, 0700-1700 in summer, E£20, E£10 for students. Taxi journeys here from Aswan (E£25 return) can also include stops at the Unfinished Obelisk (see page 167) and Philae temple (around a 3-hr trip) for around E£50 plus motorboat.

It is the so-called High Dam, just upstream from the original 1902 British-built Aswan Dam, that is Egypt's pride and joy and which created Lake

Below: Aswan High Dam. Opposite page: *Feluccas*, Elephantine Island.

David Roberts – painter of Egypt

David Roberts, born in 1796 in Edinburgh, arrived in Egypt in 1838 and spent 11 months travelling through the Nile Valley and visiting the Holy Land. He was a prolific sketcher of sites and left six volumes of lithographs of this visit, many of which were later translated into oil paintings full of atmosphere and wonderful colour.

In his absence, he was made an associate of the Royal Academy. He lived to the age of 69 years and produced many famous masterpieces based on his travels in Egypt, including the *Island of Philae, Temple of Dendara, Nubia* and *A Street in Cairo* together with his paintings of the Temple of Ramses II at Abu Simbel.

It is useful to pick up one of many inexpensive cards and books containing copies of his illustrations. They show very clearly parts that have disappeared and parts that are now too high to view and give an excellent idea of the colourful decorations.

It's a fact...

Nilometers measured the height of the annual Nile flood which enabled the coming season's potential crop yield to be estimated and the level of crop taxation to be fixed.

Nasser, the world's largest reservoir. The High Dam is so big (111 m high, 3830 m long, 980 m wide at its base and 40 m at its top) that it is almost impossible to realize its scale except from the observation deck of the lotus-shaped Soviet-Egyptian Friendship tower or from the air when landing at nearby Aswan airport. It is claimed that the structure of stones, sand, clay and facing concrete give it a volume 17 times that of the Pyramid of Cheops. To help appreciate the scale and consequences of the dam's construction, the visitors' pavilion, which includes a 15-m-high model of the dam and photographs of the relocation of the Abu Simbel temple, is worth a visit.

Elephantine Island

A local ferry (E£1) from 0600 until 2400, lands in front of the Aswan Museum; *feluccas* cost E£20 per hour as your captain waits; E£30/1 hr to sail around. Map: Aswan, p160.

Only a short ferry ride away in the middle of the Nile is sultry Elephantine Island. Measuring 2 km long and 500 m at its widest point, the island gets its name from the bulbous grey rocks off its south tip that resemble bathing elephants. Meandering

to the far side for an unimpeded vista of Agha Khan's Mausoleum and the amber sands of the west bank is a timeless interlude from life.

In addition to the museum, Nilometer and temple ruins, there are two small Nubian villages in the middle of Elephantine Island. A wander here gives a taste of contemporary life, albeit not much changed in centuries. The spirit and generosity of the Nubians becomes fast apparent. You may be invited into someone's home. And if not, you can always visit Mohammed at his beautiful Nubian House (the crocodile house) next to the museum. Decorated with traditional Nubian handicrafts, you can enjoy a cup of tea or a bite to eat on his colourful roof.

The Aswan Museum

On Elephantine Island.
Daily 0800-1600 winter, 0800-1700 summer, E£25 (E£15 for students) and E£10 for camera, includes the ruins of the Yebu and the Nilometer. Map: Aswan, p160.

This museum was established in order to display relics salvaged from the flooded areas behind the Aswan dams, which is ironic because the villa and its sub-tropical gardens originally belonged to Sir

Around the region

William Willcocks, designer of the first Aswan Dam. It offers a spread of pharaonic material, Roman and Islamic pottery, jewellery, and funerary artefacts. The ground floor is arranged in chronological order with items from the Middle and New Kingdoms while the basement displays a series of human and animal mummies and an impressive gold-sheathed statue of Khnum.

Take the pathway to the south of the museum entrance to see the Roman Nilometer, recovered in 1822. Besides Roman and very faint pharaonic numerals, there are also more recent tablets inscribed in both French and Arabic on the 90 walled stairs that lead down to a riverside shaft.

Temple of Khnum

At the south end of Elephantine Island.

Long before Aswan itself was occupied, Elephantine Island's fortress town of Yebu (the word for both elephant and ivory in ancient Egyptian) was the main trade and security border post between the Old Kingdom and Nubia. It was reputed to be the home of Hapy, the god of the Nile flood, and the goddess of fertility, Satet, both of whom were locally revered, and the regional god Khnum, who was represented by a ram's head. This ruined temple (30th Dynasty), at the south end of the island, offers a high viewpoint from which to enjoy the beautiful panorama of the Aswan Corniche to the east, including the picturesque Old Cataract Hotel, the islands and the Nile itself.

Kitchener's Island

Daily 0800 until sunset. E£10. Take a felucca.
Map: Aswan, p160.

Kitchener's Island lies north of the larger Elephantine Island. Originally known as the 'Island of Plants', it has a magnificent Botanical Garden. The beautiful island was presented to Lord Kitchener, who had a passion for exotic plants and flowers from around the world, in gratitude for his successful Sudan campaign and the gardens have been maintained in their original style. The atmosphere is very relaxed and its lush vegetation, animals and birds make it an ideal place to watch the sunset. There is an expensive café at the south end of the island.

Below: Elephantine Island. Opposite page: Bas-relief of the god Khnum with a ram's head.

Necropolis of the Nobles

0700-1600 winter, 0700-1700 summer.
E£20, E£10 for students. *Felucca* or ferry (50 pt-E£1).
Map: Aswan, p160.

The Necropolis of the Nobles at Qubbet Al-Hawwa (Dome of the Wind), a riverside cliff layered with tombs from various periods, is further north along the west bank of the Nile. It is illuminated at night by hidden spotlights – magnificent when viewed from the Aswan side of the Nile.

Just above the waterline are the Roman tombs, and higher up in the more durable rock are those of the Old and Middle Kingdoms. The majority of the dead are believed to have been priests or officials responsible for water transport between Egypt and Nubia. Sarenput II, Harkhuf, Pepinakht and Sarenput I are the more interesting tombs.

Agha Khan – worth his weight in jewels

This beautiful building (closed to the public) on a hill on the west bank of the Nile, was built of solid white marble for the third Agha Khan (1877-1957) who was the 48th Imam of the Ismaili sect of Shi'a Muslims. He was renowned for his wealth and was given his bodyweight in jewels by his followers for his 1945 diamond jubilee. As an adult he visited Aswan every winter for its therapeutic climate, having fallen in love with its beauty, and built a villa on the west bank. Until her death, his widow lived in the villa every winter, and erected Agha Khan's mausoleum on the barren hill above it.

To the north of these tombs is a separate tomb-temple, that of Ka-Gem-Em-Ahu, reached by a sandy path. Ka-Gem-Em-Ahu was the high priest of Khnum in the late New Empire. His tomb was discovered by Lady William Cecil in 1902. Enter the low entrance to the main tomb where the ceiling is quite ornately decorated with flowers, birds and geometric designs. Although the walls are quite plain, the left-hand side inner pillar carries painted plaster with a representation of the deceased and his wife.

Monastery of St Simon

Daily 0700-1600 winter, 0700-1700 summer, E£20, E£10 for students. Ferry from the Governorate building, then a 30-min walk through soft sand or a 10-min camel ride (which can carry 2, aim for E£40). Map: Aswan, p160.

This fortress monastery was founded and dedicated in the seventh century to a fourth-century monk Anba Hadra. Used by monks, including Saint Simeon about whom little is known, as a base for proselytizing expeditions, it stands at the head of a desert valley looking towards the River Nile.

Although uninhabitable, with its main feature the surrounding walls, the lower storeys of hewn stone and upper ones of mud-brick have been

> **Tip...**
>
> When visiting the Necropolis of the Nobles, wear a strong pair of shoes and take a torch. There is a guide on duty to show the way, unlock the tombs and turn on the electric lights, his services are part of the entry fee but a small tip is also a good idea.

preserved and the internal decorations are interesting. At intervals along the walls there are remains of towers. A cave chapel, richly painted with pictures of the Apostles, leads to the upper enclosure from which the living quarters can be entered. Up to 300 monks lived in simple cells with some hewn into the rock and others in the main building to the north of the enclosure, with kitchens and stables to the south.

Up to 300 monks lived in simple cells with some hewn into the rock and others in the main building to the north of the enclosure, with kitchens and stables to the south.

The Nubia Museum

On a granite hill to the south of the town, on the road past the Old Cataract Hotel.
0900-1500 winter, 1600-2100 summer, E£40, E£20 for students. Walk or taxi. Map: Aswan, p160.

Incorporating features of Nubian architecture and showcasing some 5000 artefacts tracing the area's culture from prehistoric to modern times, this UNESCO-sponsored museum is regarded as a great success. A colossal statue of Ramses dominates the entrance, a reminder of his positive presence in Nubia. There are sections devoted to Graeco-Roman, Coptic and Islamic influences in Nubia, and of course a section about the project to save the monuments threatened by the creation of Lake Nasser.

It's a fact...

Following an encounter with a funeral procession on the day after his own wedding, Anba Hadra (founder of St Simon's Monastery) decided, presumably without consulting his wife, to remain celibate. He became a student of St Balmar, rejected urban life and chose to become a desert hermit living in a cave.

Unfinished Obelisk

On the outskirts of Aswan about 2 km along the highway south.
Daily 0600-1600 winter, 0600-1700 summer, E£20, E£10 for students. Walk the 2 km, hire a bike, or take a taxi (E£20 return, or, combined with Philae and the High Dam, E£50). Map: Aswan, p160.

In the quarries that provided red granite for the ancient temples lies a huge, abandoned obelisk which would have weighed 1168 tonnes and stood over 41 m high. It was intended to form a pair with the Lateran Obelisk, the world's tallest obelisk that once stood in the Temple of Tuthmosis III at Karnak but is now in Rome. Unfortunately, a major flaw was discovered in the granite before any designs were carved. When it was discovered by Rex Engelbach in 1922 the Unfinished Obelisk shed light on pharaonic quarrying methods, including the soaking of wooden wedges to open fissures, but shaping and transporting them remains an astounding feat.

Left: Nubian art. Below: The Unfinished Obelisk.
Opposite page: Tomb of Sirenput II in the Temple of the Nobles.

Abu Simbel & Lake Nasser

Upon seeing the mighty statues of Abu Simbel, it's difficult to believe that they were buried for centuries by desert sands. Johann Burckhardt, geographer and explorer, finally happened upon them in 1813. Their grandiosity is surely the ultimate testimony to Ramses II's sense of self. The giant pharaonic statues are absolutely spectacular and well worth the detour south to the largest man-made lake in the world. The juxtaposition of crystalline blue water teeming with life and the harsh dry desert outlining it is striking and makes Lake Nasser a treat to explore. Besides the wide variety of migrating birds, there are fox, gazelle and huge crocodiles that live off the shallows and shores of the lake. Fishermen travel from afar to partake in extraordinary fishing (the rich silt that once nourished the riverbank of the Nile now nourishes the bellies of the lake's inhabitants). There is also a magnificent collection of Nubian temples scattered around Lake Nasser's shores and the Lake Nasser cruise, while expensive, is incredibly rewarding.

Some 280 km south of Aswan and 40 km north of the Sudanese border, this is the site of the magnificent Sun Temple of Ramses II and the smaller Temple of Queen Nefertari. With the exception of the temples, hotels and the homes of tourist industry employees, there is almost nothing else here. That is part of its charm, as is the immediate warmth of the locals that's so refreshing after the cut-and-thrust of Aswan. It is an attractive and sultry village, utterly sleepy except when the tours are passing through, where swathes of turban are de rigeur for men and you see women wearing traditional Nubian black net dresses decorated with weaving.

Interior of the Sun Temple, Abu Simbel.

Tip...

If you come here independently, go to the Sound and Light show for sunset. The next morning, head to the temples for dawn. It's almost certain that you will be alone for at least an hour – and as sunrise colours the colossi it takes your breath away.

Essentials

❶ **Getting around** Abu Simbel's cheapest hotels are within walking distance of the bus drop-off point; the temples are about a 20-min walk away, past the banks and post office.

Convoys New roads allow access to the Lake Nasser's temples, via organized convoy.

Buses Free buses run from Abu Simbel airport to the temples.

Boats You can tour Lower Nubian antiquities aboard elegant cruise boats (see page 181).

❷ **Bus station** Buses drop off in Abu Simbel village centre.

❸ **ATMs** Du Claire and Bank Misr, Sat-Thu 0830-1400.

❹ **Pharmacy** By the turning to the Mercure Seti Hotel, and in the village opposite the *souk*.

❺ **Post office** Sat-Thu 0730-1430, on the way to the temple, past the turning to the Mercure Seti.

❻ **Tours** Travel agencies and hotels in Aswan all run trips here, options include air conditioning coach with a tour guide, or day trips via plane. Budget hotels also offer 2 basic trips incorporating Abu Simbel (the short, E£40-50 and the long, E£60-70). The short trip picks you up from your hotel at 0330 in the morning, transports you to the temple and gets you back by 1300. The long trip stops at the High Dam, Unfinished Obelisk, and Philae Temple on the way back and finishes around 1530. Price usually only includes transport in a minivan, not admission. In summer, it is worth the extra few pounds for the air conditioning. You have about an 1½ hrs to look around before being bussed back to Aswan or on to the next stop on your tour. Bring the food and water you'll need for the morning and use the toilet before you get on the bus.

The Temples of Abu Simbel

Daily 0500–1700 winter, 0500-1800 summer, E£80, E£43.50 for students. Sound and Light show, E£75, no discount, lasts 35 mins, first show 2000 in winter (1-3 shows, or more on Fri), 1900 in summer (1-2 shows), headphones provide commentary in all languages. Free buses from the airport; public buses from Aswan's main station (three per day) – only take the bus if you intend to stay the night in Abu Simbel.

The two temples, which were rediscovered in 1813 completely buried by sand, were built by the most egotistical pharaoh of them all, Ramses II (1304-1237 BC) during the 19th Dynasty of the New Kingdom. Although he built a smaller temple for his queen, Nefertari, it is the four gigantic statues of himself carved out of the mountainside that dominate Abu Simbel. It was intended that his magnificent and unblinking stare would be the first thing that travellers, visitors and enemies alike, saw as they entered Egypt from the south. Behind

Burckhardt the Explorer

Anglo-Swiss Johann (John) Ludwig Burckhardt was born in Lausanne, Switzerland on 24 November 1784. He studied in London and Cambridge and between 1806 and 1809 lived in Syria, where he learnt Arabic and became a follower of Islam, taking the Muslim name Ibrahim Ibn Abd Allah. He left Syria, en route for Cairo and the Fezzan (Libya) from where he was to attempt to cross the Sahara. Local Bedouin spoke of the ruins of a 'lost city' in the mountains. Knowing that the legendary lost city of Petra was in the vicinity of Aaron's tomb on Jebel Harun he persuaded his guides of a desire to sacrifice a goat in honour of Aaron at his tomb. His scheme succeeded and on 22 August 1812 he was guided through the Siq and into the valley where he saw the Al-Khazneh and the Urn Tomb – enough to recognize the City of Petra. When he arrived in Cairo he could find no immediate transport to Fezzan so instead he journeyed up the Nile and discovered the Temple of Ramses II at Abu Simbel. He next travelled to Saudi Arabia, visiting Mecca. He returned to Cairo where he died on 15 October 1817, before he was able to complete his journey.

the statues is Ramses II's Temple of the Sun, which was originally built to venerate Amun and Re-Harakhte but really is dominated by, and dedicated to, the pharaoh-god Ramses II himself.

It was not until the monuments were threatened by the rising waters of Lake Nasser that international attention focused on Abu Simbel. UNESCO financed and organized the ambitious, costly (US$40 million) and ultimately successful 1964-1968 operation, to reassemble the monuments 61 m above and 210 m behind their original site.

Ramses II's Temple of the Sun Entrance steps lead up to a terrace where the imposing façade of the main temple (35 m wide by 30 m high) is dominated by the four-seated Colossi of Ramses II wearing the double crown. Each figure was originally 21 m high but the second from the left lost its top during an earthquake in 27 BC.

At the entrance into the temple's rock Hypostyle Hall is a door bearing Ramses II's cartouche, after which you are met by eight striking statues of Ramses, 10m high and clad in a short kilt typical of the Nubian Osiride form, carved into the eight enormous square pillars supporting the roof. The hall's ceiling is crowded with vultures in the central aisle and star spangled elsewhere.

The temple Sanctuary itself, which was originally cased in gold, has an altar to Ramses at its centre, behind which are now statues of Ptah, Amun-Re, Ramses II and Re-Harakhte, unfortunately mutilated.

Temple of Queen Nefertari Although dedicated to the goddess Hathor of Abshek, like that of her husband, the queen's temple virtually deifies the human queen Nefertari. Unsurprisingly it is much smaller than that of Ramses II but is nevertheless both imposing and extremely beautiful. It is cut entirely from the rock and penetrates about 24 m from the rock face. The external façade is 12 m high and lined with three colossi 11.5 m high on either side of the entrance. Nefertari stands with her husband while their children cluster in pairs at their knees.

Above: Sound and Light Show, Abu Simbel.

Five of the best

Abu Simbel's interesting details and depictions of pharaoh–god

❶ Below Ramses' thrones are reliefs showing Egypt's vanquished foes, the **Nine Bows of Bound Nubians** on the south side and **Bound Asiatics** to the north side. The colour and clarity of these larger-than-life fettered prisoners is quite confronting, their differing hairstyles and earrings denote their origins.

❷ The façade of the **Temple of the Sun** is lined, above the heads of Ramses, with a row of 22 baboons smiling at the sunrise.

❸ On the far left of the **Inner Hall**, Ramses can be seen before Amun – on the right he makes an offering of lettuces, considered an aphrodisiac.

❹ The north wall of the **Hypostyle Hall** is the most dramatic – four scenes depict the Battle of Kadesh against the Hittites in 1300 BC. Chariots and camps are particularly revealing of ancient battle methods (it seems lions were involved) but, more interestingly, Ramses' double arm lancing a Libyan may have been an ancient attempt at animation.

❺ Some of the reliefs in the hall of **Nefertari's Temple** are rather gruesome – the walls backing the entrance show the pharaoh slaying his Nubian and Libyan enemies, who beg for mercy while Nefertari and the god Amun look on.

Lake Nasser & its temples

Although it took a number of years to fill, the most visible effect of the Aswan High Dam was the creation of Lake Nasser. This has enabled Egypt, unlike Sudan or Ethiopia, to save water during times of plenty and have an adequate strategic reserve for times of shortage. The extra water from the dam significantly increased the area of land under permanent irrigation and allowed over 400,000 ha of desert to be reclaimed. In addition, the extra electric power facilitated the expansion of the industrial sector throughout the country.

There were, however, major implications of the dam's construction because the rise of Lake Nasser

Tip...

Short cruises on Lake Nasser pamper you with luxurious surroundings and service, and high-calibre guides, so you can sit back and appreciate the sheer vastness of desert and lake. Few more tranquil places exist and cruise guests have the monuments almost to themselves.

flooded the homeland of the Nubians who were forced to migrate north to other towns and cities such as Kom Ombo. Another drawback is that the lake accumulates the Nile's natural silt that used to fertilize the agricultural land downstream from Aswan. Consequently farmers in Lower Egypt now rely heavily on chemical fertilizers, destabilizing the whole food chain. In view of its expanding population, however, Egypt would be in an absolutely hopeless situation without the dams.

Originally spread along the length of the Nile, the important Nubian antiquities saved by UNESCO from the rising waters of Lake Nasser were clustered in groups of three to make for easier visiting. Many of the Nubian monuments do not have the magnificence of those north of the High Dam, although their new sites are more attractive.

Kalabsha

Daily 0800-1600 winter, 0800-1700 summer. Tickets E£25, E£15 for students. Taxi is easiest (E£30 round trip from Aswan) or possibly as part of a half-day tour including the Unfinished Obelisk, the Aswan Dams and Philae. Be firm in negotiations with the boatmen at the west end of the High Dam to get them to take you for E£40. Pay at the end of the return trip after about an hour on the site.

The Temple of Mandulis, built in the 18th Dynasty (1567-1320 BC) honours the Lower Nubian sun god of fertility equated with Horus/Isis/Osiris and usually shown in human form with an elaborate headdress of horns, cobras and plumes all topped off with a sun disc. It is the largest free-standing Nubian temple and was relocated by West German engineers in 1970 to now stand semi-marooned on an island or promontory (depending on the water level). It is rarely visited by tourists, although so easily accessible from Aswan, and the lake setting and harsh surrounds provide a good backdrop to the remains.

The Kiosk of Kertassi at Kalabsha, Nubia.

The Kiosk of Kertassi South of the Temple of Mandulis, near the lakeside, is the Ptolemaic-Roman Kiosk of Kertassi rescued by UNESCO from its original site 40 km south of Aswan. Described by the photographer Francis Frith in 1857 as a "bonnie little ruin", the single chamber has two Hathor-headed columns and other lotus-topped columns sharply decorated with foliage and flowers. Dedicated to Isis, the temple is undecorated except for one column in the northwest whose reliefs on the upper part depict the pharaoh standing before Isis and Horus the child.

Beit El-Walil In the hillside behind stands a small rock temple, Beit El-Wali (House of the Governor), again part of the UNESCO rescue mission. It was originally situated northwest of Kalabsha when it possessed a long causeway to the river. The reliefs and residual colours are well preserved and bright, making it worth the short walk. Built during Ramses II's youth by the Viceroy of Kush, it is believed to have been erected in honour of Amun-Re as he is depicted most frequently. The reliefs in the temple's narrow forecourt depict Ramses II victorious against the Nubians and Ethiopians (south wall) and defeating the Asiatics, Libyans and Syrians (north wall). In fact a great deal of smiting and defeating is illustrated.

Wadi El-Seboua

Daily 0800-1600 winter, 0800-1700 summer. Tickets E£25, E£15 for students.

Most people will be visiting as part of a Lake Nasser cruise, during which the boats moor to see the temples illuminated at night. Only recently made accessible by road, the temples are not on the programmes of most big tour operators so normal convoy is not an option. It is possible to take a private convoy with a police escort – the tourist office in Aswan can help with prices.

It's a fact...

The Christians who used the Temple of Wadi El-Seboua as a church covered the reliefs with plaster to permit their own decoration, thus preserving the earlier work.

Temple of Wadi El-Seboua 135 km from
the High Dam, are the Temple of Wadi El-Seboua,
the Temple of Dakka and the Temple of Maharakka.
The giant Temple of Wadi El-Seboua (Valley of
the Lion), built between 1279 BC and 1212 BC,
is dedicated to Amun, Re-Harakhte and the
deified Ramses II and is named after the two
rows of sphinxes that line its approach.
Unfortunately, a number of the sphinxes have
been decapitated and the heads illegally sold to
treasure hunters. Going some way to making up
for this is a huge statue of Ramses II and a sphinx,
guarding the entrance.

Temple of Dakka It's a painful 1500-m walk uphill
to this Ptolemaic-Roman site. Like many temples it
was used for a time by the Christians as a church
and in some places fragments of their decorations
remain. This is the only temple in Egypt facing
north, an orientation preserved by UNESCO,
pointing to the home of Thoth but more probably
an error by the foreign-born Ptolemaic builders.
The pylon is still in good condition, standing an
imposing 13 m in height, and houses stairs to
the roof, from which a fine view is obtained.
Look for the deep incisions in the inner pylon
wall, probably made by locals convinced that the
stone possessed healing properties. The main

**This is the only temple in Egypt
facing north, an orientation
preserved by UNESCO, pointing to
the home of Thoth but more
probably an error by the foreign-
born Ptolemaic builders.**

> ## It's a fact...
>
> Enter the Temple of Meharakka and go right for
> access to the roof. Not only are the views spectacular,
> but you will have just ascended the only known
> spiral staircase in an Egyptian building.

temple building is across an open courtyard
flanked by four interconnecting rooms where
deities are illustrated. A staircase leads off the
vestibule on the west side up to the roof –
again the views are staggering.

Temple of Meharakka The unfinished Roman
temple, dedicated to Isis and Serapis, is less
impressive. This stood on the southern border of
Egypt in Ptolemaic and Roman times, but is now a
short walk down the hill from the Temple of Dakka.
Rather plain inside, bar the Roman graffiti from
travellers and soldiers fighting Nubian troops in 23
BC, the temple illustrates the union of Egyptian and
Roman styles. Isis is depicted full frontal, instead of
the more common profile, while her son Horus
wears a toga.

Amada Some 40 km further south. Accessible to
cruise boats only, whose passengers are ferried to
the site on motor launches.

Temple of Amada Here in the Amada Oasis is the
oldest temple in Nubia, one dedicated to Amun-Re
and Re-Harakhte and built by Tuthmosis III and
Amenhotep II. A roofed pillared court was added
by Tuthmosis IV which accounts for the many
scenes of Tuthmosis IV with various gods and
goddesses on the walls and pillars. Inside, reliefs on
the right show the Pharaoh running the Heb-Sed
race and cattle being slaughtered and presented
as offerings as heads and haunches. Opposite are
the foundation ceremonies, an interesting
depiction of the way a site for a building was
marked out, foundations dug, bricks manufactured
and the construction eventually completed and
handed over to the owner. In the central section
are more offerings of pomegranates, very realistic
ducks and cakes:

The Rock Temple of Al-Derr The only temple on
the east bank of the Nile in Nubia, the Rock Temple
honours Amun-Re, Re-Harakhte and the divine
aspect of the pharaoh. It is notable for the excellent
colour and preservation of its reliefs. On the outer

the leaves of a tall acacia tree. Entering the sanctuary, on the left, Ramses is putting in a plea to live forever.

The Tomb of Pennout The rock-cut tomb of the Chief of the Quarry Service, Steward of Horus and viceroy of Wawat (northern Nubia) under Ramses VI, is a rare example of a high official buried south of Aswan. The ancient Egyptians believed that their souls were only secure if their bodies were carried back and buried in Egyptian soil. The tomb's wall paintings rather poignantly reflect this conviction, expressing Pennout's desire to be laid to rest in the hills of Thebes.

Qasr Ibrim

By cruise boat only.

The fortress, 40 km north of Abu Simbel, is the only Nubian monument to inhabit its original site, once a plateau but now an island. It is noted for an exceptional length of continuous occupation, from 1000 BC to AD 1812.

walls of the first Hypostyle Hall, for example, the majority of the reliefs boast of the pharaoh's (Ramses II) military triumphs and warn the Nubians that his might is unassailable. However, inside the second Hypostyle Hall, the pharaoh, depicted as a high priest, becomes a humble servant of the gods. On the right-hand wall he gives flowers, offers wine, escorts the barque, receives jubilees from Amun-Re and Mut and, further along, the Heb-Sed emblem is produced nine times. On the opposite wall he has his name recorded on

Sleeping

Luxor to Aswan

Esna is so close to Luxor, that most make the visit it on a day trip or on a cruise (see page 156). There are no good hotels in Edfu and most tourists are either only passing through or staying on cruise ships. For Kom Ombo it's best to stay in nearby Aswan. If you are desperate, Kom Ombo's best bet is Cleopatra Hotel (€), near the service taxi depot on Sharia 26th July.

Dahabiya cruise ships
Assouan, El-Nil, Meroe & Malouka
nourelnil.com.
Some of the largest *dahabiyas* on the Nile, these replica vessels are perfect down to the finest detail, while plumbing and conveniences are state of the art. Departing from Esna for Aswan on Mondays, for five nights, Assouan and El-Nil have a few standard rooms that are slightly more affordable.

El Bey, El Hanem, Zahra, Nesma, Amber and Musk
dahabiya.com.
Small boats measuring 38 m by 6 m, accommodating up to 12 people in two-person air-conditioned cabins. They moor on private landings where verdant gardens provide vegetables for dinner, and picnics and barbeques are organized here and on islands. Sailings are every Saturday from either Luxor or Aswan and last seven days.

Royal Cleopatra
nubiannile cruises.com.
Resembling a yacht, the Cleopatra is in fact a converted *sandale*, a *felucca* that used to carry cargo along the Nile. Sleeping up to six guests in two gorgeous wood and white staterooms, some meals are eaten al fresco on shore. An Egyptologist guides you through the sites between Esna and Aswan.

Vivant Denon
dahabeya.net.
Built in 1889, this vessel has been beautifully restored to sleep six passengers in four cabins. Cruises generally run between October and April, although it is possible to charter for summer sailings the fact there is no air conditioning on board has to be considered. In-depth tours are given of all the sites, with the itineraries tailored to group requests. Cabins are not sold separately, the boat is rented in its entirety, which costs €6000 for one week, departing on Saturdays.

Aswan

Movenpick €€€€
Elephantine Island, T097-230 3455, moevenpick-hotels.com.
Map: Aswan, p160.
Fabulous balconied rooms, excellent location in middle of river, reached by a free ferry, the hideous tower that spoils most views in Aswan is less of an obstruction from the confines of the hotel. Orangerie Restaurant and the Lounge Bar are chic, and the pool and grounds are superb. Recommended for pure luxury in Aswan.

Old Cataract Hotel €€€€
Sharia Abtal El-Tahrir, T097-231 6000, sofitel.com.
Map: Aswan, p160.
An Edwardian Moorish-style hotel, probably Egypt's most famous, the Old Cataract featured in Agatha Christie's *Death on the Nile* and has been the classic place to stay since it opened in 1899. Unfortunately, since May 2008 it has been closed for renovation and will remain so until late 2010 at the earliest. Minimum charges for non-residents taking drinks on terrace makes afternoon tea, which includes sandwiches and cakes, better value than morning coffee. Connected by a series of gardens is the cheaper, New Cataract, in an unfortunate slab of a building (also closed for refurbishment).

Tip...
It is possible to stay in houses on Elephantine Island – spend a few hours there and someone is sure to suggest it to you.

Marhaba Palace Hotel €€€
Corniche El-Nil, T097-233 0102-4,
marhaba-aswan.com.
Map: Aswan, p160.
Mingles contemporary Arabic
with faux Pharaonic style,
fortunately mainly in the public
areas. Rooms are spotless and
well furnished, some have huge
terraces, but bathrooms are a bit
squashed. The astro-turfed roof
cafeteria has a great view across
the river thick with *feluccas* to
the Tombs of the Nobles,
unblemished by the Movenpick
tower. Try to negotiate a discount.

Pyramisa Isis Hotel €€€
Corniche El-Nil, T097-231 5100,
F097-231 5500.
Map: Aswan, p160.
Chalet rooms are a bit overpriced
for the quality, but this is the only
hotel actually on the riverbank
facing Elephantine Island. Offers
air-conditioned bungalows in a
small garden with a pool and all
the usual four-star amenities,
riverside terrace and restaurant.
Look for a good deal online.

Nile Hotel €€
15 Corniche El-Nil, T/F097-
2314222, nilehotel-aswan.com.
Map: Aswan, p160.
A pleasant, bright hotel that is
deservedly popular. Rooms all
have Nile views, side view rooms
have balconies while front-facing
don't (though they are bigger).
Subtle decor, rag rugs, TV, fridge,
air conditioning, safety boxes
and the dining room is more

attractive than most. There are a
couple of suites, more expensive,
but very spacious and with
immense terraces.

Hathor €
On the Corniche El-Nil,
T097-231 4580, F097-230 3462.
Map: Aswan, p160.
Has an excellent location and
great rooftop with loungers,
though you probably won't
want to chance the teeny pool.
Decent rooms have air
conditioning (centrally
controlled) and baths are
clean and tiled, if a bit cramped.
Soft pillows rather than bolsters,
bigger than average beds and
a nice atmosphere make it the
best choice in this price bracket.

Keylany Hotel €
25 Sharia Keylany, at the
southern end of the souk,
T097-231 7332, keylanyhotel.com.
Map: Aswan, p160.
Spotless white painted rooms,
attractive tiled floors and a lovely
rag-rug-and-reeds chill-out café
on the roof make this a nice place
to be. Excellent reports about the
staff, the tours and the breakfasts.
Priced a bit more than budget.
Air conditioning, fridge, safety
box, and the rooftop pool is
a few weeks off completion.
The internet café in the basement
is effective but expensive, and
Wi-Fi is E£25 for 24 hours.

New Abu Simbel Hotel €
Sharia Abtal El-Tahrir,
T097-230 6096.
Map: Aswan, p160.
On the northern side of town, the
hotel's selling point is its pleasant
garden where breakfast is served.
Rooms are clean but getting jaded
with air conditioning and private
bath. Across the street from a few
local *ahwas*, it's still a good place
to escape any bustle and hassle.

Youth Hostel €
96 Sharia Abtal El-Tahrir,
entrance from the alley on the
right of the October Hotel,
T097-230 2313.
Map: Aswan, p160.
Dorms with fans, eight beds
(bunks) and nothing else cost
around €2. Usually empty, except
when universities let out and
then it becomes a popular spot
for Egyptian college students.
Open all year, midnight curfew
casually imposed. It's only really
worth staying here if you're on
the tightest of budgets, but the
sheets are clean and you won't
be pestered to go on a tour.

Abu Simbel

Eskaleh €€€€
T097-340 1288, T012-368 0521.
Built in the style of a traditional
Nubian house, with furniture
fashioned from date palms,
rough stone floors, domes and
terracotta-coloured walls, this
little guesthouse is a delight. And
though the bathrooms aren't in

Eating & drinking

keeping with the rustic building, they are modern and sparkling. Larger, more expensive rooms have more space and terraces surrounded by flowers, some have mud-brick lattice windows, all have mosquito nets, air conditioning, and free internet for guests.

Mercure Seti Abu Simbel €€€€
T097-340 0720-2, setifirst.com. Call the Cairo office, T02-2736 0890-5, for the best price.
The fanciest place to stay in Abu Simbel. There are all the five-star amenities although rooms are a little jaded, but splendid views of Lake Nasser go some way to compensate as do the two terraced pools set in verdant gardens. Upstairs rooms are better. Breakfast not included, discounts at the discretion of the general manager.

Abu Simbel Tourist Village €€
T097-340 0092, F097-340 0170.
The cheapest choice in town is still a little overpriced, although in summer and if tourism is in a slump, they're known to offer significant discounts. Homely salmon-pink rooms all have private bath, most have air conditioning. There's a good view of Lake Nasser from the little garden and management is kind and friendly. It's a 10-minute walk from the bus stop on the edge of the village, about 2 km from the temple.

Nobaleh Ramsis Hotel €€
T097-340 0106, F097-340 1118.
Huge high-ceilinged rooms are cool and comfortable if spartan, with TV, air conditioning and fridge. Cheap buffet breakfast but you'd expect a higher standard of bathroom for the price and there are no views. Some 2 km from the temples, but close to the bus stop, and big discounts negotiable if you call ahead. With prior warning, the manager Yassin may be able to arrange a boat to take you out on the lake.

Camping
Sometimes the Abu Simbel Village (opposite) permit camping on their grounds. Call ahead to be sure.

Cruise boats
For cruising Lake Nasser, see Activities and tours, page 180.

Luxor to Aswan

Esna has a few cafés and stalls sprinkled around its central square. Edfu has the standard food stalls, a pricey café by the temple, and **Zahrat El-Medina Restaurant** (€), on the Corniche across from El-Medina. A cheaper place to sit down for a bite to eat. In Kom Ombo, besides small stalls serving *fuul, taameyya* and kebab, there are a couple of cafés by the Nile serving meat standards.

Aswan

1902 Restaurant €€€
In the Old Cataract Hotel.
Map: Aswan, p160.
If the Cataract has opened again after refurbishments, the 1902 will be serving international food spiced with Nubian dancers in classic decor. Even budget-conscious visitors may want to indulge in a cup of tea or a glass of wine at sunset on the terrace. It really is an institution.

Nubian Restaurant €€€
Eissa Island south of Elephantine, T097-230 0307, T012-216 2379.
Map: Aswan, p160.
Offers set Nubian meals and a free boat to get there, leaving from the dock in front of EgyptAir. Wine and beer are available, but pricey. The setting is romantic, but the folkloric show is clichéd and doesn't happen if tour groups aren't around.

Al Masry Restaurant €€

Sharia Al-Matar.
Map: Aswan, p160.
Spotless air-conditioned restaurant popular with both locals and tourists. Offers huge portions of fish, chicken, kebab and pigeon.

Aswan Moon €€

On the Corniche.
Map: Aswan, p160.
The most acclaimed of the floating restaurants, the food is OK, but it's better to come here for the Nile-side setting and colourful atmosphere plus it's 10°C cooler by the river than on the street. More lively at night, sometimes there's entertainment in the summer and it's a good place to meet other travellers.

El-Medina €€

In the heart of the souk.
Map: Aswan, p160.
Clean, renowned local joint that serves up good homemade cooking. Mostly meat dishes, but they will prepare you a vegetarian meal.

Esmailya Sons Restaurant €€

Sharia Al-Matar.
Map: Aswan, p160.
Has standard meat, soup, rice, salad and veg meals, though the fish option is most popular. It's opposite Al Masry restaurant and is significantly cheaper, there's a menu displayed outside in Arabic and English.

Nubian House €€

On a hill behind the Basma Hotel, T097-232 6226.
Map: Aswan, p160.
A popular, intimate restaurant serving authentic and delicious Nubian food. *Sheesha* also on offer, but no alcohol. Outdoor seating with stunning panoramic views over all of Aswan make it worth the trek from the centre of town, especially around sunset. When there are groups in for dinner a Nubian troupe provides music, so call ahead if you'd rather avoid this.

Pharaohs €€

On the west bank south of the Aga Khan's Mausoleum, T012-791 9895.
Map: Aswan, p160.
Accessible only by boat, good Nubian home cooking, something a bit different and beautiful boat trip to get there. Call ahead, don't just turn up.

Kasr Elhoda €

Sharia Abtal al Tahrir, north of the station.
Open 1000-0200.
Map: Aswan, p160.
Has cheap and delicious *fatir* and is always packed with Egyptians. It's a typical marble interior with air conditioning and no English menu. There's also a good bakery next door.

Abu Simbel

Despite Abu Simbel's position in the middle of the desert and the fact most supplies come from Aswan, there is no problem getting a good meal. Good felafel is served in the market, from a stall down the street to the right of Restaurant Al-Horya.

Restaurant Al-Horya €

Does a mean lentil soup – one of the best you'll have in Egypt – plus simply served fish, freshly plucked from the lake. No need to quibble about prices.

Wadi El Nil €

Serves your basic stewed veg, meat, rice and salad. Ask the price first, as it is very much negotiable (E£10 or above, depending if you eat meat) and veggies should be wary of scraps of meat in the potato stews. But the freshly painted seating area under the rustling trees is a good spot from which to watch life.

Listings

Entertainment

Aswan

An evening is well spent wandering through the *souk*, puffing on a *sheesha* in a local *ahwa*, or strolling by the Nile. Families tend to congregate in the *midan* across from the train station, where there are plenty of cafés. A night time *felucca* sail is always a romantic way to spend an evening. There are nightclubs in the big hotels that offer Nubian and Western floorshows when enough tourists are in town. During the winter, except on Friday, there are nightly performances (from 2130-2300) by the **Nubian Folk Troupe** at the **Cultural Palace**, T097-232 3344, at the north end of the Corniche.

Emy, next to Aswan Moon, the best place for an evening drink. The top floor of the floating restaurant picks up a nice breeze and most of the clientele wear *galabiyas* and turbans.

The Horus Hotel
89 Corniche El-Nil, T097-230 3323.
Has female singers accompanied by *oud* and *tabla* on the rooftop every night from 2200. Beer is E£12 and *sheesha* E£4. The distant west bank lights glow orange while city minarets glow green helping to set the atmosphere.

Shopping

Luxor to Aswan

There is a main tourist bazaar next to the Edfu temple complex, offering a colourful selection of cheap goods, particularly *gallabiyas*, scarves and other local souvenirs. Kom Ombo's small but colourful tourist bazaar in the street below the entrance to the temple.

Aswan

Books
Nubia Tourist Book Center
The rowing club building (El Nadi el-Tagdeef) on the Corniche, T097-231 9777.
Open 0800-2300.
Regarded as Aswan's best bookshop, stocking AUC titles and books in different European languages, as well as good postcards and Lenhert & Landrock prints.

Souvenirs
As santitized as it may be these days, Aswan's pedestrianized thoroughfare, the Sharia Souk, still has good tourist shopping. There is also a duty-free shop on the Corniche (near the EgyptAir office), as well as a large departmental store on Sharia Abtal El-Tahrir.

Activities & tours

Aswan

Boat trips
Names of *feluccas* that have been recommended include: **Nubia Museum, Nile Majesty, Sheraton, Lucky** and **Elizabeth**; and captains to trust are Zayna, T012-485 8340, and Gamal T012-415 4902.

Swimming
Basma Hotel
Basma Hotel, Sharia El-Fanadek, T097-231 0900/1, basmahotel.com.
The best and biggest pool in town available to outside guests, day use costs E£25.

Cash back

When the cruise ships reach Esna locks the traders appear in a flotilla of small rowing boats and attempt to sell a wide variety of clothing, etc. Goods are hurled from the boats in a polythene bag onto the top deck of the ship for the purchaser to examine and then barter over the price. Rejected goods are thrown back (although these are not always dispatched with the same accuracy as they were received). If a price is agreed and a purchase made, a small garment to act as ballast, again in a bag, is then thrown up on deck with the expectation that payment will be placed inside the package and returned to the sender.

Tip...

Keep your ears open for celebratory sounds as you may well run into a wedding party – which you will very likely be invited to join.

Pyramisa Isis Hotel
Corniche El-Nil, T097-231 5100,
F097-231 5500.
A conveniently located (and right
on the Nile) pool for E£30.

Tour operators
All hotels organize transport to
Abu Simbel and other sites. Be
aware that most hotels pool their
guests. What that means is one
person may pay E£50 for a ride to
Abu Simbel in one hotel and
someone else may pay E£70 in
another to wind up on the exact
same bus. Shop around a bit and
bargain hard, especially when
the season is low. Cheaper places
tend to book cheaper trips.

Numerous travel agencies
and guide companies around
town are also touting for your
booking. Half-day tours usually
include a trip to the Unfinished
Obelisk, the High Dam and the
Temple of Philae (E£180). Travel
agencies can also organize
felucca trips to the nearby islands
if you have a group of at least
three (E£50-80 per person).

Try **Eastmar Travel**, Corniche
El-Nil, T097-232 3787; **Misr Travel**,
one block behind Corniche on
way to railway station, adjacent
to Tourist Information; or
Thomas Cook, Corniche El-Nil,
T097-230 4011, daily 0800-1400
and 1700-2000.

Abu Simbel & Lake Nasser

Boat trips
If there are quite a few of you,
hire a boat to visit some of the
many mesmerizing islands, see
part of Lake Nasser's 8000 km
stretch of shore and, of course,
view the temple from the water.

Yassin at the **Nobaleh Ramsis
Hotel**, T097-340 0106, can
arrange a boat for a half-day
holding up to 20 people
for E£500; he needs a day's
advance warning in order to get
permission from the authorities.

Cruises
Since the construction of the
High Dam the upper part of the
Nile has been effectively cut off to
navigation from the lower reaches.
The solution? Set up a shipyard
and build a vessel designed for
these deeper waters. Cruises
usually last three nights/four days
or four nights/five days starting
either in Aswan or Abu Simbel.
Some boats have seven-day
itineraries going from Aswan
to Abu Simbel and back again.

Cruise boats on Lake Nasser
with five-star rating:

Felucca cruises

With more than 500 *feluccas* and at least that many sailors based in
Aswan, it can be a stressful experience choosing a captain, but incredibly
worthwhile once you're lazily meandering down the Nile. If you're having
a hard time finding someone that feels good, check in with the tourist
office for a lead. If you're looking for other passengers to share a boat
with, you can leave a note at the tourist office.

Feluccas don't go all the way to Luxor and you will have to take a
microbus or taxi the final leg of the journey. It's easy to hire a taxi back to
Aswan or north to Luxor from your destination and captains will be keen
to arrange it for you (bear in mind it will be more expensive than what
you could find on your own). This is where you are often at the mercy of
unscrupulous drivers (probably related to your *felucca* captain) who insist
that there is no way of travelling on by public transport, and won't rush
to help you find the bus stop.

The standard number of passengers is between six and eight. Aim
for six if you want a bit of space to move about. The government has
established fixed prices for *felucca* trips: with at least six passengers,
about E£45 per person to Kom Ombo, E£70 to Edfu Temple (E£85 to the
town itself); in addition are 'permission' (E£5), food and bottled water
(E£35-40, per day for three meals). Whether or not demand for *felucca*
cruises is high, captains will ask for more; bargaining is the norm. Beware
of a captain who accepts a price lower than the ones cited, chances are
the money you save is coming out of the amount allotted for your food
or you run the risk of being deposited somewhere south of your desired
destination. If there are fewer than six people in your group, pay more to
accommodate for the captain's loss.

MS Eugenie
Bookings through Belle Epoque Travel, 17 Sharia Tunis, New Maadi, Cairo, T02-2516 9653, eugenie.com.eg.
Constructed in 1993 in the style of a Mississippi paddle steamer, 52 air-conditioned cabins with balcony, two suites, excellent food and no enforced entertainment. Memorable features include a private sunset tour of Abu Simbel followed by a candlelit dinner on board for which the temples are specially lit.

Kasr Ibrim
Also owned by Belle Epoque, kasribrim.com.eg, see above.
Some 65 rooms of an equally excellent standard but this time with 1930s art deco styling.

MS Nubian Sea
T02-2738 3384.
Seventy cabins and suites, and serves excellent food.

MS Prince Abbas
movenpick-hotels.com.
Owned by Movenpick hotels and fully refitted to a high spec, 65 standard cabins, 18 junior suites and 4 royal suites.

Fishing

The African Angler
T097-230 9748, african-angler.co.uk
A good company to go with. They have highly trained local staff and boats specifically designed for fishing on Lake Nasser. Check their website for the latest prices.

Lake Nasser Adventure
lakenasseradventure.com.
Offer fishing trips sleeping in small boats for one-three people, for freedom from any schedule, or via fast boats from a central mother ship. They also organize desert cruises, visiting not only temples but allowing time for treks and swimming on two boats sleeping up to 14. However, for complete luxury, their Nubiana takes a maximum of eight people on either fishing or desert adventures. Discounts between June and September.

Transport

Air

There are regular daily flights both to Luxor (30 mins) and Cairo (1 hr). There are 3 daily flights to Abu Simbel – often booked out by tour groups. EgyptAir is located at the southern end of the Corniche, T097-23315000-5, egyptair.com.

Bus

With the authority's attempt to 'protect' foreign visitors, the unwritten rule decrees that any bus leaving Aswan can only carry up to four foreigners, or they must join a convoy. The fact that bus tickets cannot be purchased in advance makes it a frustrating proposition for the traveller – arrive early enough and you may be a lucky one.

It's a fact...

Lake Nasser is the result of flooding 496 km of the Nile Valley with the construction of the Aswan Dam. The extraordinarily rich silt that once coated the valley during the seasonal flood is now at the bottom of the lake, sustaining the marine environment. As a result of the extreme nourishment, the fish have grown to huge sizes (record catch of Nile perch is 176 kg; catfish 34 kg). There are over 6000 sq km to fish in and 32 species to catch, all on a catch-and-release policy unless needed for the evening meal.

Currently, buses for Abu Simbel depart at 0800, 1100 and 1700 (4 hrs). Don't take the later buses unless you intend to stay the night. There are two Cairo buses, the 1530 takes 12-14 hrs, and stops at Hurghada (6-7 hrs) and 1700, a bit cheaper, that stops in Suez; both should have air conditioning and TV. If the 1530 bus to Hurghada is leaving too late for you, take an early train to Luxor where you can change to a bus (0815, 1030, 1430, 4 hrs). The Marsa Alam bus leaves at 0700 daily (4-5 hrs) and you should have no problems boarding. Hourly buses head north to Kom Ombo (1 hr), Edfu (2 hrs) and Esna (3 hrs), ending in Luxor (4 hrs). Be prepared for stops at several checkpoints, have your passport ready and don't worry, it's standard procedure.

Taxi

Service taxis have security restrictions and are presently not permitted to carry foreigners from Aswan. They get stopped and fined at the police checkpoint on the way out. It is possible to hire a private taxi and join a convoy. For a trip to Luxor, stopping at all the major sights along the way, expect to pay E£300.

Train

Given the bus situation, trains are definitely the easiest option, though there are still restrictions. Technically, foreigners are only permitted to travel on three

Tip...

Seats on the left-hand side of the aircraft usually offer the best views as it circles the temples before landing at Abu Simbel.

'secure' trains bound for Cairo (0600, 1800, 2000, 12-14 hrs). All have air conditioning and a restaurant on board. There is also a private company that runs sleeper cars to Cairo (1700, 1820). For all trains to Cairo, it's wise to book your tickets at least one day in advance.

Air

EgyptAir runs daily flights during the winter high season from Cairo via Luxor to Abu Simbel. Direct from Aswan during the summer when the season slumps there are still at least two flights per day and three during the high season. Most tickets are sold on the assumption that you will return the same day but it is possible to include overnight stopovers. Free buses from Abu Simbel airport to the temples.

Bus

For Aswan (from Wadi El-Nil Restaurant) at 0700, 1300 and sometimes 1600 (4 hrs). Microbuses are marginally quicker. Ask people hanging around Wadi El-Nil to point you in the right direction, you might have to wait a while and scout for passengers.

Contents

The Red Sea

El-Gouna, Red Sea.

Introduction

Start exploring what Egypt's Red Sea region has to offer and you'll soon find that shoehorning even modest plans into just a couple of weeks away from home becomes a delightful puzzle. For that, you can thank the region's climatic consistency – year-round sunshine and gusty cross-shore winds – coupled with the topographical diversity of its two coastlines; both strung with blooming coral reef, expansive deserts and mountainous interiors.

The 'first' Red Sea coast stretches south from Suez to the Sudanese border, backed by the arid sands of the Eastern Desert. The 'second', across the water, is the Sinai Peninsula, a mysterious land: utterly stark, wildly beautiful and intensely dramatic. Here, formed by a literal collision of continents, austere and unforgiving mountains plummet down from the interior to meet golden beaches, before melting into the coral gardens off the southern headland and the fringing reef that lines the Gulf of Aquaba.

What to see in...

... one day
Take a short camel ride into the desert, an excursion to the **Red Sea Monasteries** or trek to the summit of **Mount Sinai** in time for sunset; sail and snorkel around the islands off Hurgahda or take the plunge with a 'try dive' in **Sharm El-Sheikh**, before hitting a handful of bars and a club. A day is also long enough for a couple of shore dives or a kite surfing lesson in Dahab, before dinner and *sheesha*, Bedouin-style, beneath the stars.

... a weekend or more
Depending on your inclination and sporting proficiency you can mesh together desert safaris, diving beneath or/and riding the waves, and reclining in the sun; popular two-day/one-night desert safaris include camping in **St Catherine's National Park**, the **Ras Abu Gallum** experience or heading inland from Marsa Alam to a nearby **wadi**.

Street vendors in El Quseir, Red Sea coast.

El-Gouna & Hurghada

Within this section of Red Sea coastline plush El-Gouna tempts wealthy Cairenes and Western package tourists with its luxurious accommodation and high-class dining. All of the hotel developments and villas have been constructed in a Nubian/Arabesque style and are dotted across a series of beautiful islands interlinked by sea-water lagoons. There are also many uninhabited islands and coral reefs that are exposed only at low tide.

Hurghada (in Arabic, *Al-Ghardaka*) lures visitors with the promise of clear skies, water-sports facilities and easy access to diving. A few hotels have coral gardens actually on their site and there are plenty of coral islands offshore from which to study the hidden life below the warm blue waters. Travellers merely passing through between the Nile Valley and the Sinai will easily be able to fill time, find a cheap hotel with use of a pool, and have a big night out for not too much money.

Giftun Island.

Essentials

❶ Getting around Getting around from one end of these resorts to the other, and to and from the airport, calls for a mixture of taxis, shuttle buses or micro-buses, whichever suits your budget and inclination.

In Hurghada, although it is easy to walk around the relatively compact town of Dahar, you will need transport to the port or the holiday villages in the south of town.

Buses In El-Gouna, if your hotel doesn't offer a free shuttle bus, tickets cost E£5 daily, E£15 weekly. In Hurghada minibus and microbuses make circuits of Dahar, Sigala and the resorts (E£1).

Taxis Hurghada's taxis are among the most expensive in the country, and before getting in, check that the diver knows where your destination is and agree a fare.

Tuk tuks Jump on one of El-Gouna's recently imported tuk-tuks that run around town for E£5. Hailing from Pakistan they inject some colour into the transport system.

❷ Bus station Hurghada's main station, **Sharia El-Nassr** in Dahar, T065-354 7582, is for Upper Egypt buses; El-Gouna (T065-355 6199) and Superjet are located further down the street.

❸ ATMs El-Gouna has 7 banks (open Sun-Thu 0900-1400). Hurghada's resort hotels normally have them, or there are the following banks: **Banque Misr**, Sharia El-Nasr, T065-354 7512; **HSBC**, Sharia Sheraton, T065-345 0105.

❹ Hospital The best is **El-Gouna Hospital**, T065-3580 0127, hyperbaric chamber, T012-218 7550. In Hurghada there is the **International Hospital**, El-Ahya, T065-355 3785, **El-Salam hospital**, Sigala, T065-354 8785, and the **General Hospital** on Sharia Aziz Mostafa, T065-354; decompression chamber at the **Naval Hospital**, T065-344 9150.

❺ Pharmacies El-Gouna has 3 pharmacies, open 0900-2100.

❻ Post office El-Gouna, central office, Sat-Thu 0900-2200; Sharia El-Nasr, Hurghada, open Sat-Thu 0800-2100.

❼ Tourist information El-Gouna, open 0900-2300, or check elgouna.com; Sharia Bank Misr, Hurghada Resort Strip, T065-346 3221, open daily 0830-2000. Tourist Police, T065-344 7774.

El-Gouna

This up-market resort is just 25 km (30 minutes in a taxi) north of Hurghada but a million miles away in terms of ambiance and aesthetics. It attracts a far more sedate foreign crowd, mainly families and couples, plus wealthy Egyptians who come to their private villas on weekends and public holidays. With its collection of chic restaurants and cosy inns overlooking a harbour brimming with colourful sails, a stroll down the boardwalk is a delight. The resort centres around an immaculate square surrounded by tasteful shops and sophisticated restaurants and cobbled streets lit by pottery lanterns. It doesn't look or feel like anywhere else in Egypt, and for many travellers the effect is too plastic and surreal to warrant an extended stay, but for a special evening out away from the tacky bustle of Hurghada, El-Gouna certainly delivers quality and class. For listings, see page 220.

Tip...

Pick up useful free publications, including the *Red Sea Bulletin* and *In My Pocket Hurghada*, available in hotels and restaurants.

Around the region

People generally end up in Hurghada, 506 km southeast of Cairo, 395 km south of Suez and 269 km northeast of Luxor, for one of three reasons: they've landed an absurdly cheap package tour, they're a diver, or they're stopping off en route between the Sinai and the Nile Valley. In fact, the city is viewed in an ever more disparaging light as increasing numbers of Eastern European package tourists swamp it year-round. Hotel developments stretch for 25 km down the coast and the booming real-estate business means there is furious construction of apartment blocks inland.

The area has been developed too quickly since the first constructions in 1992 and frequently without adequate planning controls. All of this said, the beauty of the sea and surrounding mountains is indisputable, and some parts of town feel Egyptian in a way sanitized Na'ama Bay, for example, fails to. Despite the heavy tourist presence plenty of folk are genuinely friendly and anything goes.

If you want to observe a bit of the real life of Hurghada residents, take a stroll around the 'Egyptian areas' in Dahar behind the Three Corners Empire Hotel or near 'Ugly Mountain' behind Sharia Abdel Aziz (from which there are great views, sunsets are especially spectacular in the autumn). The housing is pretty crumbly and the streets strewn with litter. Here you will find traditionally dressed women staying at home and scruffy children playing in the streets, boys are bold and loud and girls in higabs wander from school in demure, giggly groups.

The old harbour area is an interesting stroll as well, with brightly coloured fishing vessels, a vibrant dry dock and small shops catering to locals. There's been a bit of a move to clean up these areas because of the tourists but you can still get a glance of life as it really is in the rest of Egypt. For dive sites see page 221.

Tip...

Rather than feeling uncomfortable on the less than pristine public beach (where bathing costumes are unacceptable), you can pay to use one of the resort hotels' beach and pools. Entry as a day visitor costs between E£20-60 daily. Ask the hotel's reception for details.

The Marine Museum and Aquarium

Sharia El-Corniche, 6 km to the north of the town centre.
Museum: daily 0800-2000; Aquarium: daily 0900-2200. E£5 for entry to both.

The museum is associated with the National Institute of Oceanography and Fisheries and is a good place to begin learning about the marine life of the area with stuffed examples of coral reef fish, shark, manta rays and associated birdlife as well as samples of coral and shells. The adjacent Aquarium is quite small but has live specimens in well-marked tanks. It may be worth a visit if you are not a diver, though a glass-bottomed boat or snorkelling might be more fun.

Clown Fish.

South of Hurghada

Until the 1980s, the coast south of Hurghada was virtually untouched by tourism and a wealth of coral reefs and islands lay undisturbed but by the adventurous few. Recent years have seen a boom in hotel building, and large resorts now pepper the coast between El-Quseir and Marsa Alam as an airport brings in package tourists. Yet the port of El-Quseir remains a peaceful little place, with accommodation suiting backpackers and an atmosphere that's quite unique, while south of Marsa Alam restrictions imposed to protect the environment mean that new hotels have to be eco-friendly and hence there are some truly stunning getaways if you have the time and the money.

Marsa Alam at sunset.

Safaga

567 km from Cairo, 65 km (45 minutes by taxi) south of Hurghada's airport, where the coastal road meets the main road across the Eastern Desert to Qena.

Though the town isn't particularly beautiful, it has this stretch of the Red Sea's usual attractions: diving, snorkelling and perhaps the most famous wind on the coast. The stiff breezes that favoured the trading vessels along these shores now provide excellent conditions for windsurfing and kitesurfers, generally cross-shore in the morning and side-shore in the early afternoon.

Soma Bay

North of Safaga.

Soma Bay was borne of a masterplan to cocoon package holiday makers in blissful luxury on a peaceful peninsula surrounded by coral-rich waters. Cosseted guests are treated to 360° views of the Red Sea, top-class golf courses, spa treatments, scuba-diving and wind- and kitesurfing. Just north of Safaga, it takes a 45 minute transfer from Hurghada, plus a gated 7 km private road, to reach these five resort hotels: **Sheraton Soma Bay**, sheraton-somabay.com; **Robinson Club**, robinson.com; **La Résidence des Cascades**, residencedescascades.com; **The Breakers Diving & Surfing Lodge**; **Kempinski Soma Bay**, kempinski-somabay.com.

El-Quseir

650 km from Cairo and 80 km south of Hurghada.

Further south is El-Quseir, an old Roman encampment and busy port. Far enough away from the hoards of package tourists in Hurghada, and without any mega-resorts, this small, sleepy town has managed to retain a lot of its ancient charm. The surroundings are still pristine and the nearby diving superb, but the town's real charm lies in the unspoilt continuity of real life – something that's missing from other more user-friendly beach retreats in Sinai and the Red Sea.

Essentials

❶ Getting around Buses, service taxis and Peugeot-style taxis run up and down the coast, so ease and speed of your travels depends on your budget.

❷ Bus station El-Quesir's bus station is 2 km west of the seafront.

❸ ATMs There are branches of **Banque Misr** in Safaga (El-Quseir-Hurghada Road) and El-Quseir (Sharia 10th Ramadan); mini-banks in all resort hotels.

❹ Post office El-Quseir has a post office on the main road out of town (open Sat-Thu 0830-2000).

❺ Tourist information Safaga, T065-345 1785.

The partly ruined 16th-century **Fortress of Sultan Selim** (daily 0800-1700, except during Fri prayers, E10, E5 for students), dominates El-Queseirs town centre and creates a sort of mystique that no other Red Sea village quite has. The central watchtower affords good views of the mountain ranges to the south, which contain the mineral wealth of the area, and it was from here that the sea and mountains were surveyed for invaders.

Marsa Shagra

113 km south of El-Quseir, 13 km north of Marsa Alam.

This remote bay has transformed into a small village celebrated by divers.

Marsa Alam

130 km south of El-Quseir.

A tiny fishing village, Marsa Alam is a gem of the southern coast. The village is also a way station between the Nile Valley and the Red Sea since a road through the Eastern desert connects it to Edfu, 250 km to the west. The small harbour is nestled in a beautiful area where the coast is lined

Around the region

with rich mangrove swamps that encourage rich bird and marine life. These mangroves are protected and all new developments are supposed to be eco-conscious in order to ensure the preservation of the fragile environment. There is nowhere to stay in the town itself, and the coast north to El-Quseir is dotted resorts that make an astonishing spectacle lit up at night. For local dive sites see page 223.

Berenice

160 km south of Marsa Alam.

A very ancient city – named by Ptolemy II, Berenice became a trading port around 275 BC. The ruined temple of Semiramis is near the modern town. Inland there are remains of the emerald mines of Wadi Sakait that were worked from pharaonic to Roman times. Berenice is noted for both quantity and quality of fish and for having a climate reputed to promote good health. The coast is lined with mangrove swamps and there are some beautiful coves that are completely isolated.

Offshore is the Zabargad, a most unusual volcanic island. Declared a Protected Marine Park, it's a wonderful place to watch the dolphins and, in season, the migrating birds.

Tip...

Sometimes a permit is required for Zabargad, though a bit of *baksheesh* to the right people can often grant access. It is still relatively untouristed and safari boats spend three-four days exploring the dive sites and surrounds.

Protected Marine Park Zabargd.

Easy side trips into the Eastern Desert

Although sightseeing is usually the last thing on the minds of most visitors to the coast, whose major focus is maximising their exposure to Egypt's abundant sunshine, wind and underwater wonders, a trip to these isolated mountain monasteries is recommended. St Anthony's and St Paul's are Egypt's oldest monasteries, attracting thousands of Coptic pilgrims to the desert hinterland.

Day tours for non-Coptics are offered by a number of travel agents or you could negotiate a price with a local taxi. Be aware that trying to visit either of the monasteries in one day by public transport and walking is a tall order, and it would be foolish to attempt both unless you are intending (and allowed) to stay in one at the end of the day. It's a tough 30-km trek over a plateau between the two monasteries, and this should never be embarked upon without a guide.

St Anthony's Monastery

Daily 0700-1700, except during Lent and between 25 Nov-7 Jan.

Known locally as Deir Amba Antonyus this is the more important of the two monasteries for Coptic pilgrims, and attracts more foreign visitors than St Paul's to its bright wall paintings. St Anthony (AD 251-356) was the 'father of monasticism' and the Christian monastic tradition has its origin in the community that established itself here in the fourth century. Daily rituals still observed have hardly changed in the last 16 centuries. St Anthony's has undergone attack, ruin and rebuilding. What survives today is a five-church monastery that has developed into an enormous complex containing all the commodities of a village.

The oldest church, St Anthony's, has fabulously vivid wall paintings and icons that were previously preserved under centuries of soot and grime. The Cave of St Anthony, 276 m above and 2 km northeast of the monastery, is a steep 45-minute walk but the view alone from the cave, 690 m above the Red Sea, justifies the climb. The cave, where St Anthony is supposed to have spent the last 25 years of his life, consists of a terrace, chamber and tunnel – all of which are a tight squeeze.

Tip...

Male visitors can apply for permission to spend a night at the monasteries by contacting Cairo's Coptic residence, Kineesa El-Morqosiyya (T02-2590 0218). The monks at St Anthony's are less inclined than St Paul's to welcome visitors who are not Coptic pilgrims, though neither monastery is likely to leave you bed-less in the desert if you make the trek without a reservation.

St Paul's Monastery

Daily 0900-1700 except during Lent and between 25 Nov-7 Jan.

The smaller Monastery of St Paul was built around the cave where St Paul the Theban (AD 228-348) spent his life. He is the earliest hermit on record and was visited by St Anthony to whom he gave a tunic of palm leaves. St Paul apparently acknowledged him as his spiritual superior and St Anthony's monastery has always overshadowed that of St Paul's both theologically and architecturally.

The larger of the two churches is dedicated to St Michael and there are two sanctuaries. The south one is dedicated to St John the Baptist where a strange 18th-century gilded icon depicts the saint's head on a dish. The Church of St Paul contains the actual cave where he lived and what are claimed to be his relics, which were preserved during the many raids on the monastery. The worst of these was in 1484, when Bedouin tribes massacred the entire population of monks and occupied the monastery for the following 80 years.

Sharm El–Sheikh & Dahab

On the eastern coast of the Sinai Peninsula there's a way of life to suit everyone, from high-class resorts to backpacker havens and off-grid Bedouin camps. Ras Mohammed National Park, at the peninsula's southern tip, is a sanctuary to every species of life that thrives in the Red Sea and is a fascinating underwater world for divers and snorkellers. From Ras Mohammed to Taba at the very top of the Gulf of Aqaba, runs one of the most attractive shoreline coral reefs in the northern hemisphere, with dive sites suited to every level of experience and confidence. Above the surface, the climate, tempered by the sea, varies from pleasant in winter to hot but bearable in summer.

A resort at Sharm El-Sheik.

Known by locals and regulars simply as 'Sharm', this name misleadingly encompasses both the town of Sharm El-Sheikh and the resort of Na'ama Bay (6 km further north). The area has developed very rapidly becoming an international resort destination, equally glamorous and gaudy. Besides the wide sandy beaches (made private to each resort hotel) and pristine blue sea, Sharm offers a spectacular and exceedingly popular diving area. There is over 60 km of rainbow-coloured vibrant reef teeming with hundreds of different underwater species, dramatic drop-offs and breathtaking formations unparalleled anywhere else in the diving world, see page 224.

As the region brims over with Western tourists, local people are accustomed to their ways; and, as a result, there is significantly less hassle on the beaches.

Sharm Town

The small community, still dubbed by some 'Old' Sharm, is rapidly shedding its dilapidated image while managing to retain a relatively authentic Egyptian vibe. These days you can snack cheaply on a kebab or be refreshed at a local juice stall, yet rest assured every tourist requirement will be met at a modern, attractively landscaped hotel. In the Old Market there are still scars from the decimation caused by the bombs that killed 17 people in July 2005, but the area has bounced back and souvenir stalls, supermarkets and unpretentious restaurants teem day and night with a mix of Egyptians and foreigners. Cushions and rag-rugs festoon the cafés and fairy lighting is de rigeur along the pedestrianized strip. However, it is possible to feel disillusioned by the soulless air and obvious construction close by, and by every second sign being in Russian.

Hadaba is a hilltop neighbourhood between the town and resort area where high-quality hotels are now springing up and the international community of dive instructors is based, attracted by cheaper property prices and the proximity to

Essentials

❶ Getting around Free or cheap shuttle buses from major hotels in Sharm to Na'ama Bay; microbuses also link the two areas, and run to Hadaba. Walking around Na'ama is possible. Independent travellers need taxis or microbuses to/from the bus station or airport. Taxis are everywhere. Check that drivers know where they are going and agree fares in advance.

❷ Bus station Behind the Mobil petrol station, between Sharm El-Sheikh and Na'ama Bay.

❸ ATMs Dotted around the tourist thoroughfares; also in various resort hotels including Hilton Dreams and the Sonesta, Na'ama Bay.

❹ Hospital International Hospital, Main Road, T0696-366 60893/5; **Sharm Specialized Hospital**, Peace Road, T069 366 1745/6; **Ambulance**, T069-360 0554; **Search and Rescue**, T012-313 4158.

❺ Pharmacies Dr. Hany, El Salam Rd (opposite Sonesta Beach), Naama Bay, T012-1613379; **El-Ezaby Pharmacy**, Il Mercato centre.

❻ Tourist information Hadaba tourist office is barren. Major hotels provide detailed information. Tourist Police, T069-3660311.

Ras Um Sidd, a spectacular shore diving spot. While friendly communities form around the clusters of mini- markets, coffee shops and dive centres, the Il Mercato centre – a grandiose Italianate mega-mall selling every brand of coffee and training shoe imaginable – is a surreal reminder of the aspirations at work in Sharm.

Around the region

Na'ama Bay

Purely a tourist resort, Na'ama Bay, or 'God's blessing' in Arabic, is generally considered to be more attractive than Sharm town and Egyptians are immensely proud of their 'Riviera'. Famed for its smooth sandy beach (mostly private for hotel guests or day visitors) and peaceful Corniche, huge choice of international hotels and some of the best diving opportunities in the world, Na'ama is rivalling the ancient wonders of the Nile to be the leading tourist attraction in Egypt. You don't have to be interested in diving but it helps, as outside of the sea and surrounding desert peaks, there is very little to see.

Nabq Managed Resource Protected Area

35 km north of Sharm El-Sheikh.
Entrance €5. Most hotels organize day trips; taxis from Sharm are E£100 for 1-way but it is advisable to keep the taxi for the day at around E£200.

Nabq Managed Resource Protected Area is an outstanding area (designated in 1992) of dense mangroves – not only the largest mangrove forest in Sinai but the most northerly in the world. The area covers over 600 sq km around Wadi Kid, at the edge of which are rare sand dune habitats and a swathe of arak bushes, still sold in bundles in the village markets and used for brushing teeth. The presence of the mangroves has allowed multiple ecosystems to develop, sheltering more than 130 plant species and a diverse selection of wildlife. Storks, herons, ospreys and raptors are quite common; mammals like foxes, ibex and gazelles are more rare. The area's sandy bottom make it a great place for swimming and the diving is good although there is risk of sediment and the reefs lie at some distance. Though popular with safari groups, Nabq is significantly less crowded than Ras Mohammed, but the beaches are decidedly inferior.

A small Bedouin settlement, Ghargana, lies on the coast where the tribesmen continue to fish in a traditional manner. Another Bedouin village, Kherieza, is inland from the main coastal valley

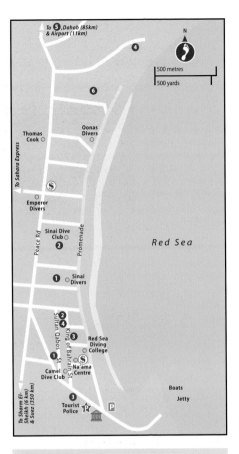

Na'ama Bay listings

● Sleeping
1 Ghazala Beach
2 Hilton Fayrouz Village
3 Kanabesh
4 Sanafir
5 Sharks Bay Umbi
6 Sonesta Beach Resort

● Eating & drinking
1 Abou El Sid
2 Inuka-Ya
3 Little Buddha
4 Rangol

It's a fact...

Since the beginning of civilization, the Sinai has been one of the most important crossroads to human expansion. For the Pharaohs, Sinai served as an easily protected barrier allowing ancient Egypt to blossom unthreatened; they also created a path through the peninsula connecting Egypt to Jerusalem. Later in the third century BC, it was the stage for the Israelites' exodus out of Egypt.

Entrance to Ras Mohammed National Park.

Wadi Kid. The parks make a sincere effort to involve the Bedouin in their work and to protect their traditional lifestyle, currently under much pressure from the rapid development in the area.

Ras Mohammed National Park

Open from sunrise to sunset, as is the visitors' centre, which includes a restaurant, audio-visual presentations, first aid, shops and toilets. Entry is €5 per person plus €5 per car. Taxis from Sharm El-Sheikh cost E£100 1-way, but as there are no taxis at Ras Mohammed it's advisable to keep the taxi for the day (E£150-200).

Jutting out from Sinai's most southerly tip is a terrestrial and marine area covering 480 sq km. Just 30 minutes from the mania of Sharm, the park offers an underwater spectacle unsurpassed anywhere on the planet (see Diving in the Red Sea, page 66).

Tip...

Ras Mohammed is beyond the Sinai-only visa jurisdiction, so you will need a full Egyptian tourist visa to enter. Vehicles pass through UN checkposts and passports are scrutinized at the Egyptian checkpoint where Israelis or any non-Egyptians who come in through Taba may experience delays.

Ras Mohammed is remarkable too for its rare northerly mangroves that lie in a shallow channel at the tip of the peninsula, in an area with many rock pools and crevices in the fossil reef that shelter shrimp, among other stranger creatures. The famous Hidden Bay confuses visitors, because it appears and disappears with the changing tide. The Saline or Solar Lake is interesting for its range of salt-loving plants and birdwatchers will also find this a delightful spot. The park is also an important area for four heron species – grey, goliath, reef and greenback – as well as gulls, terns and ospreys. Although much of the land appears to be barren and hostile it is in fact home to a variety of life, from insects to small mammals, Nubian ibex and desert fox.

Dahab

Dahab, meaning 'gold' in Arabic, still manages to shimmer despite the march of progress. Known for its cheap accommodation and food, and a super-chilled backpacker vibe, people used to come here to get stoned, go diving, and kick back. Although this Dahab remains, things are changing.

Sinai's tourist authority initiated a 'Sharm-ifying' of the area, and so the sandy walkway along the beachfront has been replaced with a paved promenade and the wooden stalls have turned into marble-fronted shops as prices are hiked. Newcomers and old-timers will still find beach cafés, bazaars and mosques amid Bedouin huts, crumbling concrete

Essentials

❶ Getting around Most walk, but there is no shortage of pickups and taxis (E£10) from one section of town to the other. To the Blue Hole, E£50 – the driver will wait and bring you back.

❷ Bus station East Delta bus station, T069-364 0250, is on the northern side of Dahab City; pickup taxis (which will be waiting) will transport you to Assalah for E£3-5.

❸ ATMs There's a handy one in the bay on the promenade, between the bridge and Desert Divers.

⊕ Hospital Dahab-Clinic, Sharia Al-Mashraba.

✛ Pharmacies Dr Ahmed, Mashraba Road.

☏ Post office Dahab town centre (Sat-Thu 0830-1500). In Masbat, a phone and post shop is signposted near the bridge that sells stamps and delivers mail.

camps, and palm trees. Local Bedouin girls sell bracelets, while their fathers and brothers hawk camel rides and invite visitors for tea in the desert. The magic of the sea, sun and stars remains unsoiled.

Assalah

3 km north of Dahab City.

The Bedouin village and its nearby surroundings remain a good place to experience the richness and beauty of Bedouin culture and to take time out for as long as life allows. With more bona fide safari companies emerging, Dahab serves as a notable set-off point for serious desert trekking to explore Sinai's mystical oases and exquisite rock formations, but it's primarily a chill out and diving zone (for dive schools and sites, see page 227). Local Bedouin offer camel trips into their nearby villages; lucky visitors may be invited for a cup of spiced Bedouin tea in their homes. The protected area of Ras Abu Gallum (see below) lies to the north and Nabq (see page 200) to the south. Both are easily accessible and offer enchanting tastes of Sinai's terrestrial and aquatic wilderness.

Ras Abu Gallum

East coast north of Dahab.

In addition to pristine marine gardens Ras Abu Gallum, another protectorate area designated in 1992, the coast between Dahab and Nuweiba holds some of the most striking above-ground scenery in Sinai. High mountains and long winding valleys run right down to the sea. From the Blue Hole (see page 67) you can hire a camel for E£60, or better still, walk the magical 7 km to a nearby village only accessible on foot (you are strongly recommended not to leave the marked trails). Although the Protectorate is valued mainly for its rare plant life, the diving here is also superb (see also page 227).

As the Gulf of Aqaba narrows, sprawling coastal resorts are replaced by intimate camps and the mountains of Saudi Arabia loom ever closer across the tranquil sea. Nuweiba, from where ferries leave for Jordan, has plenty of mellow places that provide a real escape from humanity while still having all amenities to hand. Venturing further north, civilization peters out and simple Bedouin getaways mingle with the occasional tourist village along a dazzling stretch of coast. The road leads to the border town of Taba, in Egyptian hands since 1989, and chiefly of interest as an entry point to Israel.

Along the striking stretch of shore between Nuweiba and Taba where rugged red mountains twist and turn and pour down to the sea, there is a scattering of Bedouin camps and tourist villages that offer respite and serenity away from the more trafficky resorts of the south. Some are dilapidated forgone attempts falling apart at the seams, others are gems and sensitive to their environs.

Nuweiba

67 km north of Dahab, 64 km south of Israeli border.

Nuweiba's Moshav, or co-operative village, used to be a major destination for Israeli tourists during the occupation but has long since been surpassed by

Sinai's protected areas

Although tourism generates jobs and brings in lots of foreign currency, the hasty pace of development in Sinai is of great concern to many. Since the peninsula was returned to Egypt in the early 1980s, South Sinai alone has seen the onslaught of almost 25,000 hotel rooms. The waste of perpetual construction coupled with the overload of tourists and careless divers is resulting in the rapid deterioration of Sinai's main tourist asset: the rich life of the surrounding seas.

The authorities are, thankfully, taking measures to protect the asset that is at the heart of the industry. This protection has taken the form of a network of protected areas along the coast from Ras Mohammed National Park (see page 201), Nabq Managed Resource Protected area (page 200), Ras Abu Gallum Managed Resource Protected Area (see opposite) to the Taba Managed Resource Protected Area (page 204), and St Catherine's National Park, which covers a huge swathe of the southern mountains.

Tip...

If you travel to Taba via Israel's Eilat airport, which is only 15 km across the border, guests of the Taba Hilton and Nelson Village (page 214) do not have to pay Israeli departure tax. These hotels will provide a pass to allow free movement through the border during your time of stay. Taxis and buses run to the border and the hotel is just a few steps on.

Morning at Nuweiba in Sinai.

Around the region

Na'ama Bay as the Sinai's primary resort destination. It is divided into three distinct areas: the 'city', the port to the south, and the Bedouin village of Tarabeen to the north. Sadly, all three areas (and indeed most of the hotels and small camps along the coast up to Taba) have an eerie ghost-town feel since the Ali Baba Shopping Center, Masbat uprising, and, at the time of writing, border tensions between Rafah and Gaza means the absence of Israeli tourists is complete.

Neglect and dereliction are much in evidence, as the skeletons of unfinished bungalows and old bamboo huts disintegrate and plastic bags wash up on stretches of Nuweiba's gorgeous coast. But if complete peace and freedom from hassle are what you desire, there are still plenty of cosy camps on clean white sand to be found, and Nuweiba has a natural advantage over most of Dahab in that you can swim straight off the beach and snorkel out to some colourful reefs.

Tarabeen

A 20-min walk along the beach north of Nuweiba city.

Tarabeen, a Bedouin settlement, lies sprawled along a stunningly beautiful sandy bay. Reminiscent of Dahab a decade back, there are traditional 'camps', Bedouin-style restaurants and a couple of hotels scattered about a dirt road alongside mini bazaars where shopping is relaxed and easy. Notable differences are the white sandy beaches and a distinct lack of tourist police.

Trash is washing up on the shores, huts are collapsing and there is a tangible air of sadness and despair. Yet several camps in 'central' Tarabeen are keeping standards up and it's easy to fall in love with the place. From the shore you can see the mountains of Saudi Arabia painted pink on the near horizon as the Gulf of Aqaba narrows towards the north, and as night falls tiny clusters of lights come on in villages across the water – it is utterly magical.

Taba

70 km north of Nuweiba.

This international border town between an empty desert and the bright lights of Eilat is an unusual place. The coastline is beautiful but exceedingly windy. Besides hotels there is little else in the tiny enclave except barracks and facilities for the border guards and customs officials. Having won Taba back from Israel, the government is now concentrating on development of the tourist industry in the region and is building power stations and other infrastructural facilities to support the planned influx. Taba Heights, a new tourist development just 9 km southwest of Taba, is just such an attempt. The vision is to build a 'village' comprising of hotels, cafés, shops, casinos, and a dive centre, with the hope of attracting European visitors. To date, a few high-end huge hotels with hundreds of rooms, private beach, pools, restaurants, shops, water sports, health clubs and all the other usual five-star amenities are open, and more are under construction.

Salah Al-Din's fortress (Pharoah's Island, a short boat ride, 400 m, from the Salah-el-Din Hotel), the most important Islamic remains in Sinai. It was originally built in 1115 by the crusaders to guard the head of the Gulf of Aqaba and protect pilgrims travelling between Jerusalem and St Catherine's monastery. It was also used to levy taxes on Arab merchants travelling to and from Aqaba. Salah Al-Din took it over in 1171 but abandoned it in the face of European attacks 12 years later. There is a café here but it is absurdly expensive and not always open. The hotel also organizes snorkelling trips around the island's surrounding reefs, but beware – the currents can be strong.

The newest and largest in the network of coastal and inland protected areas (designated in January 1998), **Taba Managed Resource Protected Area**, it lies south and west of Taba and includes the Coloured Canyon. There is a wealth of ancient writings and carvings on rock walls in the area that span the history of Sinai, the crossroads between Asia and Africa. The scripts include Arabic, Semitic, Greek, Nabatean and other, unknown, languages.

Easy side trips into the Sinai Interior

Sinai is a diving paradise but its rugged interior, too, is magical: where sun and wind and water have converged to paint pictures in the rock and carve jagged peaks that fade endlessly into the horizon in a million shades of pink. Trekkers and pilgrims journey from afar to scramble up the splendid face of Mount Sinai, gaze at the rising sun and marvel at the sacred spot where Moses received the Ten Commandments. Before ascending the mount many will visit St Catherine's Monastery, built as a sanctuary for the Burning Bush, through which God is said to have spoken to Moses. Organized tours are readily available. Alternatively, a safari through this relatively untouched region; across the desert plateaux, past dusty acacias and dry riverbeds; can be done by foot, camel or jeep. Staying overnight in a simple campsite or at the summit of Mount Sinai makes the trip even more magical.

Tip...

Scuba-divers must remember that St Catherine's Monastery and Mount Sinai are both located at high altitude. After your last dive, apply the current recommended guidelines for flying before attempting to visit these sites.

St Catherine's Monastery

Mon-Thu and Sat 0900-1145, Fri 1100-1200, closed Sun and public holidays, free. (Only Orthodox Christians are allowed to attend the long Sun service.) The local bus stops in the village of St Catherine, 2 km away.

The supposed site of the Burning Bush was developed into a monastery and in the 10th century named after Saint Catherine, who was a Christian convert martyred in the early fourth century for refusing to renounce her faith. After her execution her body vanished and according to legend was transported by angels to the top of Egypt's highest mountain, now named after her. Three centuries later her body was 'discovered', brought down from the mountain and placed in a golden casket in the church where it remains to this day. The highlight of the walled monastery, which includes the monks' quarters, refectory, library and gardens (not open to the public), is the highly decorative and incense-perfumed St Catherine's Church. Hanging oil lanterns and swinging incense burners, plus Greek monks lit by shafts of sunlight, do something to detract from the camera-wielding masses shuffling through (even though photography is forbidden). Dress modestly inside the monastery.

St Catherine's Monastery, Sinai.

An overgrown evergreen bush, which is claimed to be a transplanted descendant of the Burning Bush, grows in the courtyard inside the monastery, and there is an almost continual photo-call going on beneath its thorny branches.

Mount Sinai

According to Christian tradition, Moses received the tablets of Law known as the Ten Commandments at the summit of Mount Sinai (Jebel Musa), 2285m. The view from this revered place is particularly spectacular at sunset and sunrise. However, the vast majority traipse up for sunrise, setting off at an ungodly hour in the cold and dark to find it all but impossible to secure a good spot amidst the mass of huddled forms at the summit. It is better to start the ascent at about 1600 (earlier in winter) in order to arrive at sunset. And, if you walk up via the more challenging steps, frequent solitary interludes can indeed feel spiritual and the passionate pilgrims met on the way only serve to intensify the experience.

The 3700 steps, accessed from immediately behind the Monastery, are the shortest route

Tip...

Stout shoes and warm clothing are essential for the stiff walk up. There are refreshment stalls on the way up, getting more expensive nearer the summit, but take at least two litres of water per person if making the ascent during the day.

(maximum 1½ hours), tough going and very difficult in the dark. The path is less crowded and dirty than the other route, which is easier but indirect (about 2½ hours) and can be done on camel – there are plenty for hire behind the monastery for about E£50. Either way, the last 700 steps have to be done on foot and take another 30 minutes. On Mount Sinai is a chapel where services are performed on some Sundays by the monks and a mosque where a sheep is sacrificed once a year. Blankets and mattresses are available for hire (E£10) around the summit. The altitude makes for sub-zero night-time temperatures for much of the year – a torch, good sleeping bag and warm clothing are absolutely essential.

Listings
Sleeping

El-Gouna

Movenpick €€€€
T065-354 4501, F065-545160.
Built from terracotta, in gardens
with tropical plants and palms
framed by the desert behind and
the lagoon in front. There are
four pools, a health club, a
Turkish bath, a disco, a selection
of bars and restaurants including
El-Sayadin on the beach, plus a
children's club.

Captain's Inn €€€
T065-358 0170.
Cosy and comfy rooms,
overlooking Abu Tig Marina; some
of the cheapest beds in El-Gouna.

Hurghada

Except perhaps during the
winter high season, independent
travellers should be able to find a
room, usually in the Dahar area.
Single female travellers should
be on guard when staying at
budget hotels.

Hilton Hurghada Plaza €€€€
*Gabal El Hareem Street, T065-354
9745, hiltonworldresorts.com.*
Everything you would expect of
a hotel in this category, including
private beach, pool with
swim-up bar, three restaurants
and expansive lobby with ATM.
A private marina offers
glass-bottom boat trips and
excursions to Giftun Island.
Day guests welcome.

Oberoi Sahl Hasheesh €€€€
*Sahl Hasheesh, T065-344 0777,
oberoisahlhasheesh.com.*
Truly luxurious and utterly
exclusive, miles away from the
mass tourism of Hurghada in
both mood and geography, this
is the top choice for those who
can afford it. An all-suite resort,
built in the domed Moorish style,
all columns, arches and striped
facades, from the sunken marble
baths you can see the sea or the
walled gardens. The pools are
sublime as is the private beach,
and the spa receives high praise.

Royal Palace Hotel €€€€
*Sigala, T065-346 3660,
royalpalacehotel.com.*
120 rooms, private beach, three
restaurants, good food. With its
Sonesta Diving Centre and easy
access to the beach for disabled
people, this is one of the best
hotels in Hurghada.

Giftun Village €€€
*Sigala, T065-344 2665,
F065-344 2666.*
Comfortable bungalows set in a
vast private sandy beach a little
out of town. Pool, squash, tennis
and all water sports are free
except diving, windsurfing and
tennis lessons. Main restaurant
provides buffet meals and there
are bars and discos. Barakuda
Dive Centre within the hotel.

Sindbad El-Mashrabiya €€€
*Resort Strip, T065-344 3330/2,
sindbad-group.com.*
A pleasant Moorish-style hotel
with three pools, plenty of
water-sport facilities and a
private beach. This is where
the yellow Sindbad Submarine
trips are based.

Zak Royal Wings Hotel €€
*Sigala, T065-344 6012,
zakhotel.com.*
All rooms have views on to the
small central swimming pool
and the standard amenities
you would expect for the price.
Everything is painted white
giving an almost Mediterranean
air, the restaurant serves Italian
food, and the location set back
from the road is in its favour.

4 Seasons Hotel €
*Off Sharia Sayed al-Korayem,
Dahar, T065-354 5456.*
Rooms are clean, all with
balconies, and staff are
pleasant and helpful. Use of the
pool at the Geisum Village is a
bonus, as is the roof terrace.
Recommended among others in
the budget category, breakfast
included.

White House €
*Sharia Sheraton, near old
harbour, Sigala, T065-344 3688.*
Very clean, up-market budget
hotel, German-owned,
45 comfortable air-conditioned
rooms with bath and balconies,
decent restaurant, TV lounge,

guests can use facilities of Giftun Village which is a short taxi ride away, for divers this transfer is free.

Camping
There are so many cheap hotels that camping is unnecessary. If you are still considering camping on the coast, enter fenced-off areas at your peril – large areas of shoreline are still mined.

National Youth Camp, 5-6 km north of town, E£10 per night, is the site most recommended.

Safaga

Menaville Village €€€€
5 km north of Safaga port, T/F065-326 0060.
A good four-star choice. Chalets and villas in gardens, by pool or adjacent to the very good beach, all rooms air-conditioned, telephone, minibar and terrace or balcony. Shops, bank, laundry, clinic. 24-hour café, cycle hire, table tennis. Has own dive centre, menadive.com, with private jetty.

Cleopatra Hotel €
Safaga Street, T/F065-253 3926.
An adequate hotel in the town centre near the port. The 48 rooms all have private baths that are clean enough, and there's a bar in the hotel and pizza restaurant next door.

Hotels in town don't have pools, but the beach at Rocky Valley Beach Camp, 14 km north, for E£20 per day, is an option.

Movenpick Resort €€€€
El-Quadim Bay, T065-332100, movenpick-hotels.com.
Unbeatable value and one of the coastline's most stunning hotels with a coral reef running the entire length of the private beach. You can almost snorkel from your room. Moorish style, environmentally conscious, lovely gardens and beach, large pool, three restaurants of which Orangerie is recommended. Masses of activities on offer and Subex Dive Centre.

Al Quseir Hotel €€
Sharia Port Said, T065-333 2301.
At the northern end of the harbour, this hotel of just six rooms in an old merchant's house is atmospheric and unusual. Large rooms have little furniture (bed, wardrobe, sink, fan and air conditioning) but the wooden floors and ceilings, old doors with Islamic details, and exposed brick walls make them special. Although expensive for a budget traveller, it's a place you won't forget.

Rocky Valley Beach Camp €€
T065-333 5247, T010-653 2964, rockyvalleydiverscamp.com.
Possibly the best camp on the entire stretch of eastern coast,

pristine, tasteful huts with comfy beds are dotted up the hillside. It's candlelit at night (the generator is on for a few hours every day) and they throw a great party by firelight. Has its own dive centre, and perfect host Hassan El Assy runs trips to the Eastern desert.

Marsa Shagra

Ecolodge Shagra Village €€€
Reservations in Cairo T02-2337 1833, in Shagra, T012-398 9682, redseadivingsafari.com.
Extensive diving day-long safaris can be organized from this hotel. It's owned by Hossam Helmi, a pioneer in the area, and one of the foremost environmentalists on the coast; he's a diving enthusiast and knows the surrounding seas better than most. Two offshore dives cost E35/person all inclusive. A central domed area containing all the main facilities is surrounded by chalets, huts and tents with lots of space. All are spotlessly clean and very comfortable but only the chalets have private bath. There is no pool or bar, but the bay boasts a stunning beach with a fantastic house reef, good for shore dives and snorkelling.

Marsa Alam

The owner of the **Ecolodge Shagra Village**, Hossam Helmi, (see Marsa Shagra, above) has two other high-end camps, each with their own bay and diving live-aboards.

Marsa Nakari (€€€), 18 km south of Marsa Alam. Offers chalets, huts and tents.

Wadi Lahami (€€€), 142 km south of Marsa Alam, has chalets and tents. Diving safaris are organized with a three-day live-aboard programme at E85 per person per day, all inclusive (food and dive gear). Wadi Lahami also has kite- and windsurfing facilities. Reservations for all three through the Cairo office, T02-2337 1833.

Aquarius €€€
T010-646 0408, aquariusredsea.com.
The 18 circular rush peaked huts all have white linen, draped sail-effect interiors, camel wool blankets and rugs (but no fan, windows, or en suite). Larger bungalows have bathrooms and fans. Either way, the rooms on higher ground are breezier and the best choice. Electricity switched off 2400-0600 and 0900-1600. Fullboard is the only option. Their Aquarius Dive Centre is fully equipped.

Tip...
Even if you're not into diving, the old-style camps in Tondoba Bay, 14 km south of Marsa Alam, offer a peaceful, friendly place to hang for a couple of days. Taxis from Marsa Alam bus station should cost E£25, ask for 'Kilo Arbatarsha' if the driver seems unsure where Tondoba is.

Bedouin Valley €€€
T02-2635 2406, southredsea.net.
Cobbled stone chalets have wooden floors, proper furniture and tiled bathrooms with towels, plus there are standing fans. In landscaped rockery gardens, there's a *sheesha* corner for starlit chilling and in- and outdoor restaurants, but no alcohol. South Red Sea dive centre on the beach.

Shams Alam €€€
50km south of Marsa Alam, reservation office in Cairo, T02-2417 0046.
A comfortable resort, though the food is not highly rated. Accommodation is in white two-storey bungalow-like complexes with domed roofs. There's a private sandy beach with a bar as well as a freshwater pool with a bar. The Wadi Gamal Dive Centre nearby specializes in diving safaris to more remote reefs in the south and is recommended. Price includes halfboard.

Deep South €€
T012-450 1296.
Best views as on the highest ground and there's a cute wicker pub on site. Rooms are quite basic with twin beds and wardrobes being the only furniture, no fans, and all decorated with murals. Clean, tiled shared bathrooms adjoin the open-air restaurant. New larger chalets are near completion and will have private baths.

Fustat Wadi El Gemal €€€
Inland from the coast by 6 km, T012-240 5132, wadielgemal.com.
These striking tents inside one of Egypt's most beautiful and culturally fascinating national parks make a great base for anyone who has seen enough of the beach and wants to get back to nature. The tent accommodation is attractive, shared bathrooms positively chic, and the main dining tent stylishly lit by a chandelier with huge cushions to recline on.

Iberotel Grand Sharm €€€
1 km from Ras Um Sidd, T069-366 3800, iberotel- eg.com.
On a coral beach equipped with floating jetty to facilitate entry into water. Pools, restaurants, disco and athletic facilities. Good snorkelling, dive centre, and beautiful views of the sea and Tiran Island.

Ritz Carlton €€€
Ras Um Sidd, T069-366 1919, ritzcarlton.com.
The first Ritz on the continent is the most de luxe hotel in Sharm and has every amenity imaginable and then some. Sea and garden views, beach access, award-winning restaurants – each with a different theme – athletic facilities, diving centre, luxurious spa and candle-lit evenings gazing out to sea.

Sun Rise Hotel €
*Hadaba, Motels Rd,
T/F069-366 1725.*
The best mid-range option, so book ahead as it gets busy. Clean, fresh rooms and a decent-sized pool surrounded by flowers. Restaurants, shuttle bus to beach and Sinai Rose diving centre is adjacent.

Youth Hostel €
*Hadaba, near the police station,
T069-366 0317.*
Eighty beds in air-conditioned dorms, family rooms (three beds per room, E£55 per person), doubles available. Additional 80 beds in men-only dormitory. Open to non-members for modest extra charge, open 24 hours. Kitchen or meals available. The only really cheap option in Sharm, but often full and a bit wary of single women travellers. Breakfast included in price.

Na'ama Bay

Ghazala Beach €€€€
*Centrally located on the bay, sister hotel is across the highway,
T069-360 0150, redseahotels.com.
Map: Na'ama Bay, p220.*
This old-timer in Na'ama was the tragic scene of one of the 2005 bombs; after renovations, no physical scars remain save for strong security. An assortment of restaurants indoors and out represent different cuisines, bars in lobby and next to huge pool,

easy access to beach and all facilities, helpful tourist office offering maps of the area and access to sports equipment, diving and desert tours.

Hilton Fayrouz Village €€€€
*Centrally located, T069-600136,
hilton.co.uk /fayrouz.
Map: Na'ama Bay, p220.*
One of the oldest and most picturesque hotels in Na'ama Bay, it offers double bungalow rooms in delightfully lush gardens, with the largest private beach, a playground for children, several outdoor bars with happy hours, excellent food and Wi-Fi, first-class water sports (and dive centre), yacht, glass-bottom boat, pool, tennis, mini-golf, beach volleyball, horse riding, massage, aerobics, disco, games room.

Sonesta Beach Resort €€€€
*Northern edge of Na'ama Bay,
T069-360 0725, sonesta.com/
SharmResort.
Map: Na'ama Bay, p220.*
Overlooking the bay, it's a good place to enjoy an evening drink or stay in one of the cool collection of white domes in extensive gardens. Attractive and spacious, the hotel has seven pools (some heated and some not), dive centre, shops and boutique. The 520 split-level rooms are decorated in Bedouin style with either balcony or patio.

Camel Hotel €€€
*King of Bahrain St, T069-360 0700,
cameldive.com.*
Comfortable and convenient, book ahead as space is limited. The Roof bar is the place for late-night drinking among the diving fraternity.

Sanafir €€€
*King of Bahrain St, T069-360 0197.
Map: Na'ama Bay, p220.*
A block from the beach and right in the action on the main drag, the Sanafir retains a bit of flavour. Highly recommended by guests, relaxed, friendly authentic Egyptian atmosphere, funky courtyard area with pools and bridges. Home to the hippest club in Na'ama Bay, Pacha, and to Bus Stop bar, which is a social hub. A good place to mingle and meet people, but not recommended for the tranquillity-seeker.

Kanabesh Hotel €€
*On the bay, T069-360 0184,
F069-600185.
Map: Na'ama Bay, p220.*
A more modest option with air-conditioned rooms in attractive grounds. Generally in the thick of things, with a beach (E£30 for non-guests) that stands out for having more character than others in the vicinity.

Sharks Bay Umbi €€
*6 km north of Na'ama Bay
(E£20 from airport by taxi),
T069-360 0942, sharksbay.com.
Map: Na'ama Bay, p220.*

Three levels of accommodation, ranging from basic bamboo huts with clean communal showers (hot water) to the domed Bedouin-style chalets on the hillside. There's an excellent restaurant in a tent by the beach where the speciality is, unsurprisingly, seafood. Coral garden for snorkelling is directly off the beach and the very popular dive centre offers courses and equipment.

Camping

It is possible to camp inside Ras Mohammed National Park, at designated sites. It is camping of the rugged sort, with no showers. It costs about E£100 to be dropped off from Sharm by taxi and there is an entrance fee of E5 per person with an additional E5 fee for cars. Bring everything you will need including water, as it may not be available.

Dahab

Accor Coralia Club €€€€
Laguna, T069-364 0301, accorhotels.com.
Attractive bungalow rooms spaced out among lush gardens, good for kite- and windsurfers (there are both German and

> ## Tip...
>
> Prices in Dahab for everything are always negotiable and better deals can be made in the low season.

British schools operating from the beach). Superior rooms have kitsch Moroccan style with huge sea-facing balconies, the cheaper garden-view rooms get booked up fast. Two restaurants, bar, pool, ATM, tennis courts, volley ball, horse riding, safari and desert trips, diving centre, non-residents can enjoy the pool (but not other facilities) for E£40.

Hilton Dahab Resort €€€€
Laguna, T069-364 0310, hilton worldresorts.com
A fully self-contained resort of whitewashed dome-shaped rooms with seductive hammocks on their terraces. Large diving centre (see sinaidivers.com), wind- and kitesurfing and aquasports centre, however the pool is nothing special and swimming is not permitted in the lower level. Three good restaurants and Coconut Bar on the rooftop. It's the snazziest hotel around Dahab though quite isolated from the pulse of Assalah. Off-season, there are bargains to be had.

Alf Leila €€€
Masbat, El Fanar St, T069-364 0595, alfleila.com.
Dahab goes boutique in this Arabic-style B&B. The eight rooms are individually designed and themed, using rich colours and Islamic motifs. It's 10 minutes walk from the seafront, which some might feel is a good thing. Fabulous German bakery attached.

El Dorado €€€
Assalah, T069-364 1027, eldoradodahab.com.
An intimate place painted dusky Marrakesh orange, with extremely well-maintained rooms and helpful staff. The beach area has attractively laid-out loungers beneath woven parasols, with great access to the Eel Garden. Italian-managed hence the good Italian restaurant.

Nesima Hotel €€€
Mashraba, T069-364 0320, nesima-resort.com.
One of the nicest places to stay in Assalah, and certainly in Mashraba. Rooms are classy yet cosy, with domed ceilings, some with wheelchair access and some with breathtaking views across the Gulf. There's an elegant restaurant, poolside bar and a popular night-time bar with happy hours and live football.

Bedouin Moon €€
Assalah, T069-364 0695.
Beautiful Bedouin-owned and run hotel situated solemnly amid mountains and sandy beach. Rooms have private bath and domed ceilings, three-person dorms available. Prices vary depending on extras, which may include air conditioning or fan, sea view. There are dorm beds for US$14. Highly acclaimed dive centre, Reef 2000, attached. Excellent restaurant. A few kilometres north of Masbat – a

good place to stay if you're here for the diving and peace.

Inmo Hotel €€
Mashraba, T069-364 0370-1, inmodivers.de.
One of the first hotels in Dahab, this is a quality place owned by a German-Egyptian couple. Four categories of room, range from chic and luxy with private terrace to clean backpacker-basic. Has a little pool area, all-round good atmosphere and fills up fast (particularly rooms with balconies on the seafront) so book ahead. Primarily known as a divers' hotel, they also organize desert safaris with local Bedouin guides.

Sphinx and New Sphinx €€
Mashraba, sphinxdahab.com.
Two hotels next door to each other with the same owner, they are fairly similar but one is – obviously – newer, and thus higher-spec and with a pool. But both are very acceptable, and the original Sphinx offers value for money at E£70-80 for a decent room (without breakfast). The beach-side restaurant, Funny Mummy, is surrounded by palms and is a very popular hang-out for groups of travellers.

Sunsplash Camp €€
Mashraba, T010-6183 5501, sunsplash-divers.com.
This long-standing camp, chiefly catering to divers from Germany, is moving with the times – the

wicker huts are spotless and most now have bathrooms, air conditioning and heat, and there are some chalet-style rooms at the front. Peacefully located on the edge of Mashraba you can, with just a few strides, snorkel the house reef.

Bedouin Lodge €
Mashraba, T069-364 1125, bedouin-lodge-dahab.com.
Popular, well-established camp with subtly decorated rooms and an unpretentious atmosphere. Bedouin-run and family-friendly. Good views of the sea from the pricier rooms, but no breakfast included. Camel, snorkelling and jeep trips arranged; bike rental is possible.

Bishbishi €
Mashraba, T069-364 0727, bishbishi.com.
Although located on the roadside away from the beach, this camp has become a mecca for backpackers as the owner, 'King' Jimmy, succeeds in reviving some of the essence of old Dahab. The courtyard is attractively planted with date palms and has cushioned seating areas.

Dolphin €
Mashraba, T069-364 0018.
An older camp with a reputation for cleanliness, this is one of few places that still has some huts made of bamboo as well as concrete options. Conveniently located for the centre while

maintaining a peaceful air, there's a good restaurant and cushioned seating areas.

Ras Abu Gallum
In recent years, a group of Bedouin have built about 15 modest huts on the beach that can be rented for E£15-25 per night. There are a few clean squat toilets but no cars, running water or electricity. Water and other basic necessities are available at inflated prices and there are a couple of restaurants.

Nuweiba to Taba

Nuweiba Hilton Coral Village €€€€
On the beach just north of the port, Nuweiba, T069-352 0320, hilton.com.
A stylish resort, very relaxing if rather isolated from rest of Sinai resorts. Has a choice of restaurants, camel and horse riding, safaris, bicycles, squash, tennis, children's facilities, two heated pools, bank, internet access, travel agency, disco Excellent snorkelling just 30 m offshore where there is a coral garden. Aquasport Dive and Watersport Centre on the beach.

Nuweiba Village €€€
On shoreline near police station, Nuweiba, T069-350 04013, nuweibaresort.com.
Cosy rooms with all the extras, private beach, dive centre, beach volleyball and pool. It's worth

shelling out that bit extra for well-kept grounds, comfy loungers under wicker parasols, and to be somewhere that's fairly bustling (by Nuweiban standards). US$60 with breakfast or US$80 half board.

Basata Ecolodge €€
23 km north of Nuweiba, T069-350 0480/1, basata.com.
Basata (meaning 'simplicity' in Arabic) has become one of Sinai's most appealing getaways where an off-grid, communal vibe rules. Candlelight illuminates the simple, beachfront huts, there's no drugs or alcohol (in public) and no late-night noise, and the kitchen runs on an honour system. The beach is perfect and there's a good reef for snorkelling offshore. Book ahead.

Nakhil Inn €€
Tarabeen, T069-350 0879.
A tasteful well-run hotel at the northern tip of the bay, on a spotless private beach with direct access to snorkelling on the reef. Rooms are spacious with huge windows (the nicest have a mezzanine with views of the sea from the bed) bar, free Wi-Fi, indoor (with fireplace) and outdoor restaurant, dive centre (closed in off-season).

Sally Land Tourist Village €€
A few km north of Basata, T069-353 0380, F069-353 0381.
In a Bedouin settlement called Bir Zuir, tastefully planned attractive chalets enjoy a beautiful white sandy beach, courteous and efficient staff, mainly European guests, restaurant, café, bar, shop and beach snack bar, snorkelling and windsurfing equipment for hire.

Ayaash's Camp €
The first camp from Nuweiba; and lies directly in front of the 'head'. Also known as Ras Shitan, T010-525 9109.
Accommodation is extremely simple, open huts are scattered about the hills and shore, some are only a few metres from the waterline. There is no hot water or electricity. Desert safaris are available and it's possible to rent snorkel and fins to explore the reef offshore. There's also a busy restaurant that often is the gathering spot for late-night jam sessions.

Taba Hilton and Nelson Village €€€€
Taba, T069-353 0140, hiltonworldresorts.com.
The reliable, high-rise Hilton has dominated the area for years, right on the Israeli border. Private beach looks onto the tip of the Gulf of Aqaba, two pools, tennis courts, acceptable restaurants and bars, plus a nightclub and casino. Nelson Village is an

extension of the hotel and they share facilities. It's more sensitively designed using natural materials and set in pleasing gardens.

Tobya Boutique Hotel €€€€
Taba, T069-353 0275, tobyaboutiquehotel.com.
Though having an on-site casino rather ruins its credentials as a boutique retreat, it is the most quirky choice in town, 2 km south of the border. It is worth knowing that outside guests can use the pool and private beach for the day, should you be stranded for a few hours in Taba.

St Catherine's National Park

Camping
Desert Fox Camp
Between St Catherine's monastery and town centre, T069-347 0344, T010-698 7807, desertfoxcamp.com.
Nestling by an olive orchard, clean, attractive huts with plenty of blankets are E£25 per person and decent shared baths have hot water. You can camp down here for E£10 per tent, or there are a couple of stone-walled gardens 20 minutes' walk up the valley, with freshwater supply, for a night under the stars. Run by two local Bedouin brothers who also organize trips through the desert plateaux (as opposed to trekking in the high mountains).

Eating & drinking

El-Gouna

Bleu Bleu €€€
Abu Tig Marina, T065-549702-4.
Unquestionably El-Gouna's most elegant restaurant, the French cuisine is superb and set in lovely environs.

Club House €€€
Opposite Dawar El-Omda, elgounaclub house.com.
Try the lunch selection of Italian-inspired food, freshly prepared. As the population of El-Gouna is largely Coptic, they have developed a good range of vegetarian dishes to fit in with the frequent fasting. It's also a friendly and bustling place for a drink by the pool.

Tamr Henna €€
Outdoors only. Mixture of Turkish, Egyptian and Italian dishes. Something for everyone, it's also the best place to have a *sheesha* and people-watch in the main square.

Hurghada

Little Buddha €€€€
Next to Sindbad Resort, Village Rd, Resort Strip, T065-345 0120, littlebuddha-hurghada.com.
Cocktails, great sushi and Pacific cuisine can be sampled on the first-floor seating area under the gaze of a giant gold Buddha. Food served from 1600.

Red Sea Reunion €€€
Sharia Sayed al-Korayem, Dahar, T012-719 6267.
In its heyday, this was about the only restaurant with a rooftop terrace and hence always packed out. Not so now, but the rooftop remains relaxing and pleasant both day and night, offering Italian, Indian, fish and steaks. They have Nubian music on Wednesday nights and the staff are genuinely friendly.

Shade €€€
Marina Blvd, Sigala.
Swedish-owned, this restaurant-bar has a Norwegian chef and everything on the menu is grilled and fresh. The salmon steak is tremendous. Frequented by Hurghada's expats.

Amon Grill €€
Sharia Sayyed, Dahar.
Has the cheapest burgers and *shish tawook*, takeaway available.

Pizza Tarboush €€
Opposite Restaurant Bella Riviera, Dahar, T065-354 8456.
Student discount, over 20 types of pizza generously and cheaply served, plus salads, seafood and standard grilled fare, nice little place.

Star Fish Seafood Restaurant €€
Sharia Sheraton, Sigala, T065-344 3751.
Excellent value for grilled, fried or baked fish, fabulous shrimps and the salads are some of the best around for only E£3. A large clean functional place, busy at all hours, also home deliver.

Young Kang €€
Sharia El-Sheikh Sabak, Dahar.
This little hideaway doesn't look like much, but it's the place to go for authentic Asian dishes, it's been run by a Korean lady for years. Recommended.

Ahwas & cafés
Coppa Cabana
Sharia Sheraton Sigala, T012-796 3653.
Gorgeous home-made Italian ice cream, plus coffee that's the real-deal, this cute corner café never disappoints. They also have a new place at the Marina Blvd, Gelateria Due Soli. It is more about the gelati than the coffee.

Miramar
Mohamady Hwedak St, T065-345 0920.
An upmarket coffee shop frequented more by wealthy Egyptians than package tourists. Dark red interiors with striped Moorish arches, Orientalist prints on the walls, and comfy indoor and terrace seating, you soon forget the ugly main road outside when puffing on one of the best *sheeshas* in town.

Safaga

Most restaurants are confined to the hotels, as are the bars and

Listings

discos. The Menaville's is at present the most popular. There are some cheap cafeterias selling standard grilled fare along the main drag, Sharia Al-Gomhuriyya.

El-Quseir

Stall food like *fuul* and *taamiyya* can be found around the seafront and the main market street. Any of the coffee shops lining the beach are cheap, fun places to hang out in the evenings with a *sheesha*.

Al Quseir Hotel €€€
Has a good chef who (with advance warning, T065-333 2301) can put on a great spread with your choice of meat/fish/veggies for around E£70. The price goes down the bigger the group.

Marianne Restaurant €€
On the Corniche, T065-333 4386.
Open 0800-2400.
The upstairs balcony laden with bougainvillea and pottery urns is the place to dine – choose from Italian dishes, kebabs, fish, calamari and more. Rice and salad included. Vegetarians are catered for and drinks are moderately priced. The toilets leave a lot to be desired.

Rocky Valley Beach Camp €€
T065-333 5247, T010-6532964, rockyvalleydivers camp.com.
Call in the morning and you can state your preference for dinner,

eaten under the stars. **Mazenar Tours** are an associated business (see page 223).

Marsa Alam

Outside of the hotels, there's really only one local café that's clean enough to warrant a recommendation. It's at the entrance to town on the right side of the main road, across from the port. There is no name, but you'll see it. Order whatever's on the stove.

Sharm El-Sheikh

El-Fanar €€€
At Ras Um Sidd lighthouse, T069-366 2218, elfanar.net.
Under Italian management, serves excellent, albeit pricey, food with a variety of wines. The atmosphere is majestic, open-aired, with a stunning view of the sea and mountains of Ras Mohammed. There is live music most evenings. A fantastic place for sunset.

El Masrien €€
Market area, T069-366 2904 (home deliveries).
Always packed with Egyptian families feasting, this institution has plenty for vegetarians alongside its famed skewered meats. Noisy indoor seating as well as plenty of outdoor table space.

Fisherman's €€
Also confusingly signed Al Sayad, market area.
Primarily another seafood dive, but in addition serves up some Western and Russian dishes. Enjoy a beer amidst fabulous fairy lighting.

Terrazzina Beach €€
Next to Iberotel Palace, T069-366 5046.
Enjoy fresh and excellent seafood with your toes in the sand, then chill in the Dahab-style area with a *sheesha*. Avoid Friday unless you want to be part of the 'beach party' from noon until sunset. It costs E£50 if you wish to lounge on their patch of beach for the day.

Koshary Shihk Elbalad €
Market area.
Head up the stairs to eat tasty, reliable *koshary*. Has a good vantage point of the market from behind glass – great when the wind's whipping across the bay, though a bit hot in summer.

Koshary el Sheik €
Near the microbus stand opposite the Tiran Centre.
Cheap and tasty.

Na'ama Bay

Hard Rock Café €€€
Next door to Abou El Sid, T069-360 2664, hardrock.com/sharm.
Map: Na'ama Bay, p220.
Regular Hard Rock offerings

and atmosphere, good nachos, children's menu, the bar gets kicking after midnight.

Little Buddha €€€
Na'ama Bay Hotel, T069-360 1030.
Map: Na'ama Bay, p220.
Sushi and Asian fusion cuisine in sophisticated surroundings, worth a splash.

Rangol €€€
At the Sofitel, T069-360 0081.
Map: Na'ama Bay, p220.
Excellent Indian in a splendid setting with a stunning view out to sea. But arrive early (open 1900) as after 2100 the entertainment team gets loud and ruins any chance of romance.

Inuka-Ya €€
King of Bahrain St.
Map: Na'ama Bay, p220.
The best of the new wave of Japanese restaurants in Na'ama. Sushi starts at E£20 and tepanyaki is around E£60. The low-lit terrace and leather seating make for a classier dining experience.

Tam Tam €€
At the Ghazala Hotel.
Map: Na'ama Bay, p220.
Long known for excellent Egyptian food and has a large selection of salads in a pleasant beachfront location. An Oriental dance show welcomes non-guests on Sunday, Wednesday, Thursday at 2030, and costs E£120 (including dinner).

Al Capone €€€
Masbat, next to the bridge.
The food is tasty and plentiful, but what makes this place a hit with Egyptians and tourists is the belly- and sufi-dancing performances in the evenings. It invariably attracts a horde of locals, who hang off the bridge straining to see, and the atmosphere can get excitable.

Blue Beach €€€
Masbat, above Seven Heaven.
This relatively new Thai place might look un-prepossessing, but the dishes are wonderfully authentic as the owner comes from Thailand. Chicken forms the core of the menu and makes a refreshing change from fish.

Carm Inn €€€
Masbat, T069-364 1300.
This chi-chi place lives up to its name, Bedouin Arabic for 'small oasis and place of bounty'. Delectable dishes from all over the globe, including India and Indonesia, with inventive vegetarian options, are served in a softly lit grotto among palm trees.

Dolphin Café €€€
Next to Dolphin camp in Mashraba.
In addition to solid breakfast fare, the dinner menu includes Indian and vegetarian dishes for under US$4, Bedouin-style seating, good samosas and curries.

Lakhbatita €€€
On the promenade in Mashraba, T069-364 1306.
Offering the freshest seafood and a wide array of authentic Italian dishes and world cuisines. Romantic atmosphere interestingly decorated with doors and dusty oddments from the Delta. Indoor and outdoor seating area a metre from the sea.

Leila's German Bakery €€,
Attached to Alf Leila B&B, El Fanar St, Masbat, T069-364 0594.
This is a really comfortable place to indulge any cravings for

What the locals say

For a romantic dinner in the middle of the desert, I recommend booking a wadi candlelight dinner. You will be picked up from your hotel and taken to a setting against the mountains, looking to the sunset. It costs €30 for fresh chicken or fish served with salad and potatoes or rice, and Egyptian wine. Always book one day before.

Karin Coolen, long-term guest,
Alf Leila Boutique Hotel, Dahab.

Entertainment

Western sandwiches and delights such as black-forest gateau, apple strudel and pastries. An attractive and shady enclosed terrace with wicker furniture gives respite from the heat.

Nuweiba to Taba

Castle Zaman €€€
Just north of Basata Ecolodge (see page 214), T069-350 1234, castlezaman.com.
The owner has spent years perfecting every detail of this exquisite venue, which provides a dream setting for true culinary delights. A minimum charge of E£50 per person allows use of the pool and private beach, and is enough for a sunset drink as the lights start twinkling across the water in the villages of Saudi Arabia. There are a couple of rooms, available only when booking the entire castle for an event; you'd need to contact them direct to negotiate prices.

Habiba €€
T012-217 6624, sinai4you.com/habiba.
Open until midnight.
Beachside restaurant that cooks up fresh Bedouin bread, can get busy from midday as it caters to tourists on day trips from Sharm enjoying the buffet (E£50), there's an à la carte menu in the evenings.

El-Gouna

Bars & clubs
Barten
At the end of the marina is an intimate bar with modern decor highlighted by red lights and minimal furniture. Popular with young trendy Cairenes.

Mangroovy Beach Bar
Special seafood dinners with dancing round the bonfire on Sunday and Wednesday. Access by shuttle bus.

Sand Bar, Kafr El-Gouna
Small in size but with a lively atmosphere, cheap draught beer, good selection of wine and tasty bar snacks, cold beer and loud music, very popular with divers.

Hurghada

Bars & clubs
The Blackout
At the southern part of the resort strip on the way out of town.
A bit of a haul from the city centre. it's worth the trek on Tuesdays, though, when a popular foam party has the place jumping.

Calypso
On the hill (Sharia Hadaba) at the southern end of Sigala, toward the resort strip.
A bonafide disco with a like-it-or-not Russian show every night at 0130.

Head Candy
On Marina Boulevard.
A chilled-out vibe by the sea, during the day it's a pleasant spot to relax on the beach then it transforms at night-time into a full on club. They have excellent full-moon parties.

Little Buddha
Next to Sindbad Resort, Village Road, Resort Strip, T065-345 0120, littlebuddha-hurghada.com.
Open 2330-0400.
The coolest place to go out; many now rate it as the best in town.

Ministry of Sound
El Sakia, Sigala, T012-774 3801.
Resident and guest DJs from Europe, as you'd expect from the MoS the music gets everyone going seven nights a week.

Papas I
On Marina Boulevard.
Great for a drink, then, of course, the dancing gets started later, they often have bands playing.

Papas II
Sharia Mustashfa, Dahar.
Dark decor, frequent live music and always buzzing. The most popular venue in Dahar.

Na'ama Bay

Bars & clubs
Camel Bar/The Roof
Camel Hotel, T069-360 0700.
Open 1700-0200.
Typical bar fare, good music and reasonably priced drinks. Very

popular with divers and beer enthusiasts, young and old. The Roof bar is a bit more chilled.

Echo Temple
pachasharm.com.
A venue in the middle of the desert beneath the stars. As well as club nights, hosts special events from concerts to movies, organized through Sanafir.

Hard Rock Café
In front of the Naama Centre, T069-360 2664, hardrock.com/sharm.
With a family-friendly atmosphere in the early evening, dance music kicks in later on.

Little Buddha
In the Na'ama Bay Hotel, T069-360 1030.
Where the cooler crowd sprawl on comfy seats. The party gets started around 2330 and entry is free.

Pacha
pachasharm.com.
Now have a vast venue at the Sanafir, with Ministry of Sound nights at weekends, House Nation on Thursday, and pumping tunes every other night.

Pirates Bar
In Fayrouz Hilton.
Favoured by the expat divers community. Standard pub fare with guaranteed cold brew. Evening happy hour starts at

1800 and daily live music (of the romantic variety) from 2000.

Na'ama Bay
Bus Stop, at Sanafir Hotel.
Where it's at for dancing. E£20 entry includes a drink and is open until the wee hours with lots of noise, dancing and billiards downstairs.

Bars & clubs
Furry Cup
North of the lighthouse in Blue Beach Club, T069-364 0411.
Indoors is probably the closest thing to a pub in Dahab, equipped with TV airing football. An offshoot beach-bar across the boardwalk swings from being very chilled to party central.

Rush
Masbat.
Has a more refined air at a cool new location near the bridge, playing a mix of decent tunes.

Tree Bar
Off the promenade in Mashraba.
Larger than it looks from the outside, this bar with a flashing dance floor throws a couple of parties a week. Has a pool table.

Yallah bar
Next door Nirvana, at the northern end of Masbat.
Always attracts a fair few drinkers of an evening and a good spot to watch the world go by.

Shopping

Books
Aboudi Bookshop
Near Three Corners Empire.
Good selection of European books, maps and guides.

Al Ahram
Esplanada Mall, south of Sigala.
Open 0900-2200.

Pyramid Bookshop
Jasmine Village.
With international newspapers.

Red Sea Bookshop
In the Zabargad Mall.
The best selection of books in Hurghada.

The Tiran Centre, Sharm El-Maya bay offers upscale shops and chain restaurants. In Hadaba, the monstrous edifice of the Il Mercato complex is saturated with all things Western. The nearby **Alf Leila** centre attempts a more rustic feel and sells all the standard souvenirs.

Most shops in Na'ama Bay are linked to the hotels and are well stocked with provisions for beach lounging or diving and snorkelling accessories. Tourist shops abound, selling T-shirts, perfume bottles, sheesha pipes, Bedouin jewellery and the rest.

Activities & tours

There are also duty-free shops. The Na'ama Centre, on the northern side of Na'ama Bay, overflows with fashion and jewellery shops as well as chain restaurants.

Maison de la Mer
On the Promenade, opposite the Kanabesh's beach, T069-3601445. Open daily 1000-1500, 1800-2200.
Stocks beach clothes and water-sports kit from well-known brands, Seven Tenths and the like. It's staffed by young, helpful guys who aren't there to give you the hard sell.

Dahab

There are several supermarkets, which are open 0730-2400. They stock most of the basics including bottled water and toilet paper. **Ghazala** supermarket, near the police station, is well equipped with most of the essentials. As you'd expect there's a good scattering of dive shops, although prices for kit aren't must cheaper here than at home.

For more information on the best dive spots in the Red Sea, see page 64.

El-Gouna

Diving
This resort town (see page 189) boasts flora and fauna not normally found any further north and allows day boats to reach dives normally accessed only by live-aboards. Dives may include the two wreck sites as well as the coral gardens and pinnacles. Diving Clubs are all top-notch in terms of safety and eco-consciousness, but are some of the most expensive in Egypt. Snorkelling day trips are offered, mainly to the Dolphin House, Gobal Island or Tawila Island.
    Among many are: **Blue Brothers Diving Centre**, Divers' Lodge, T065-545161; **The Dive Tribe**, Movenpick; **TGI Diving** (tgidiving.com) T012-741 1336, centres at The Club House and Sheraton Miramar Hotel.

Water sports
Most dive schools will offer snorkelling day trips, mainly to the Dolphin House, Gobal Island or Tawila Island.

Orange Concept
Abu Tig Marina, Ocean View Hotel, T065-354 9702, or 77976 from anywhere in El-Gouna, theorangeconcept.com.
This high-standard Dutch venture offer kiteboarding,

Red Sea conditions

Conditions vary little from top to bottom of both Red Sea coastlines. Visibility along the Gulf of Suez is almost always good, and there are currents on deeper open dives and calm dives closer to shore. The reefs themselves are a healthy mix of hard and soft coral that support creatures of all sizes, although to see the larger ones you do need to head away from the shore. Water temperatures vary from a tropical 28-29°C in the summer to a more temperate 20°C in the middle of winter. In south Sinai the reefs off the headland and along the Gulf of Aqaba are some of the best in the world with incomparable coral reefs and colourful marine life. The waters are warm year round, currents are relatively benign and visibility is consistently good.

wakeboarding, waterskiing, parasailing, etc, for all ages and levels of experience. Dinghy and catamaran sailing lessons should also be available from late 2009. Look for their agents at the following hotels: Three Corners Ocean View; Three Corners Rihana Resort & Hotel; Sheraton Miramar; Movenpick Resort and Abydos Marina.

Hurghada

Boat trips
Ask at your hotel or with local tour operators (see page 222).

Venomous Lion Fish.

All-day boat/snorkelling excursions go to Giftun Island, in the bay (E25), E£10-15 for a couple of hours or E£400 to rent a private boat from the port or the athletic marine club for a day. Also possible are glass-bottomed boats (E£40 per hour per person); trips to Tobia Island with its sandy lagoons and untouched corals surrounded by turquoise water; and sea cruises via Shadwan Island, the Gulf of Suez, and even Ras Mohammed (at least 6 hours, E£100).

The Aquascope
Book through Hor Palace,
T065-344 3350.
Submerges up to nine people in a sci-fi bubble for around one hour. Reservations are necessary.

Sindbad Submarine
T065-344 4688.
This Finnish-built air-conditioned 44-seater submarine offers a three-hour round trip including an hour underwater. Transfer by boat 30 minutes, out to submarine, which goes down to 22 m with diver in front attracting fish with food (not a recommended procedure). Daily trips, book at least a day in advance. Price US$50 for adults and US$25 for children under 12.

Diving
Opposite Sharm El Sheikh, on the other side of the Straits of Gubal, Hurghada is ideally located for divers who want to access the wrecks of Gubal and/or join live-aboard trips to sites including The Brothers and Elephinstone (see page 65).

Local dive sites include
Um Gamar, 1½ hours north, a plateau of beautiful soft and hard corals with a good drop-off and cave. Also has a kingdom of poisonous snakes. Dives are made onto a slope that drops gradually from 15 m to 76 m.

Sha'ab Al-Erg, is 1½ hours north. There's a coral plateau including table coral and, if you are lucky, manta rays and dolphins.

Careless Reef is one place that you may well see shark. There is a spectacular drop-off and ergs (sand dunes). This site is for advanced divers only, due to the currents.

The Giftun Islands are close to Hurghada and thus very popular, and fast deteriorating. Fortunately they do possess a number of reefs still teeming with plenty of fish including moray eels.

El-Fanadir, is a popular site close to Hurghada with a pretty reef wall and drop-off with nice soft corals.

Sha'ab Abu Ramada, 40 minutes south, is usually a drift dive. It has a good drop-off, lots of fish and coral, most notably the unique, round, brain-like variety.

Nearby **Gota Abu Ramada**, is nicknamed the 'Aquarium' due to the abundance of marine life among the mountainous coral

Listings

garden, including butterfly fish, snappers, and banner fish.

Further afield are a series of islands including **Shadwan, Tawlah** and **Gubal,** around which there are chances of seeing pelagic fish and dolphins. The spectacular **Brothers Islands** (see page 65) are also an overnight sail from Hurghada port.

This selection of diving clubs all teach accredited dive courses and offer live-aboard safaris to nearby sites, daily and extended trips:

Bubbles Diving College
In Andrea's Hotel, Sigala,
T065-344 2057,
bubbles- diving.com.
Also specialize in free-diving.

Easy Divers
Triton Empire Beach Resort,
Dahar, T012-230 5202,
easydivers- redsea.com.
Long established set-up, caters for all levels with instructors speaking numerous languages.

Emperor Divers
Hilton Resort, T065-344 4854.
With branches all over the Red Sea they come highly recommended.

James and Mac
Giftun Beach Resort, T012-3118923, james-mac.com).
Good reputation.

Jasmine Diving Centre
Grand Seas Resort,
T012-244 7897,
info@jasmin-diving.com.
A German-run centre, among the best in the area.

Some tour operators and hotels, including **Flying Dolphin Sea Trips, Nefertiti Diving Centre** and **Sunshine Sea Trips,** organize extended boat trips including three-day trips to Gubal Island, overnight excursions to Giftun, and expeditions to the deeper reefs such as Elephinstone (20 km south) where experienced divers have a chance of seeing hammerheads, tiger sharks and other exotic marine life.

Snorkelling
Three Corners, Shedwan and **Coral Beach** hotels all have house reefs, but the best reefs are offshore. Popular snorkelling sites include Giftun Islands (gets overcrowded and sadly, the coral off the main beach is relatively colour- and life-less), Fanadir and Um Gamar. Book at least a day in advance by enquiring at your hotel or the marina, or contact a local tour operator (see below).

Tour operators
Tours to Luxor depart Hurghada with the morning convoy at 0600 and return in the evening. For boat trips and day-long tours to the Nile Valley:

Eastmar Travel
Behind La Perla Hotel,
El Hadaba, T065-344 4851.

Misr Travel, Sigala
T065-344 2131.

Thomas Cook
3 Sharia El-Nasr, Dahar,
T065-354 1870.

Windsurfing & kitesurfing
The best equipment is found at centres offering specialized holiday packages. Expect to pay about E150 per hour, more for kitesurfing.

Planet Windsurf
planetwindsurf.com.
British-based company; also do kitesurfing.

Happy Surf
happy-surf.de.
Have branches at the Hilton Plaza and **Sofitel** (German-run).

Safaga

Diving
Quieter than Hurghada, the reefs here are in good condition. The best dive sites around Safaga are **Panorama,** where a sloping hill leads to a dramatic drop-off where curious turtles as well and sharks and mantas often linger; and **Abu Qifan,** a remote and pristine site that leaves behind the traffic of Hurghada live-aboards. The prolific marine life is an underwater

photographer's dream with dolphin, ray, barracuda, reef and leopard shark frequently putting in an appearance.

A controversial inclusion on the dive list is the wreck of the **Salem Express**. In 1991, this passenger ferry was heavily overloaded with pilgrims returning from Mecca to Safaga hit a reef at Sha'b Shear, a hour or so short of home. She sank with huge loss of life. Many people feel that she should be left in peace. She is majestic in her demise and should be dived with all due respect.

All dive centres in Safaga organize day trips and half-day to the nearby sites.

Barakuda
At Lotus Bay, T065-325 3911, barakuda-diving.com.
Have several centres around the Red Sea and a live-aboard.

MenaDive
T065-326 0060, mena dive.com.
A well-established eco-conscious operation running out of the Menaville Hotel.

Marsa Alam

Desert safaris
Fustat Wadi El Gemal
T012-240 5132, wadielgemal.com.
Wadi Gemal is a protected area south of Marsa Alam. This eco-conscious set-up provides a rare opportunity to trek into the Valley of the Camels, with a local

Beja guide, for a day or few. Not only does this mean the chance of seeing ibex, gazelle and migratory birds, but the scenery is stunning and savannah-like, and historical sites can be explored on the way.

Mazenar Tours
Sharia Port Said, south of the Corniche, T065-333 5247, rockyvalleydiverscamp.com.
Sat-Thu 1000-1500 and 1800-2400.
Organize a range of short jeep safaris into the Eastern Mountains, some with a geological bent, for around E35 per night including Bedouin BBQ. One-day's hiking, half-day camel safaris to the village of Oum Hamid or trips to the camel market at Shalatein (E80) are also available. Pretty flexible and comparatively cheap.

Red Sea Desert Adventures
Shagra Village, Marsa Alam, redseadesertadventures.com.
Led by an experienced Austrian named Thomas and his Dutch partner, geologist Karen, who have been in the area for more than 12 years living among the local Bedouin tribes. They organize anything from a day trek to a two-week expedition from October-March; longer safaris require a minimum of five people and need to be booked at least a month in advance.

Diving
With the arrival of an international airport at Marsa Alam (page 193), divers can reach reefs, previously only accessible by live-aboard, from the coast's hotels and dive centres. There are coastal mangroves and seagrass areas, and the hard coral systems are the healthiest in Egypt forming splendid formations, mazes and caverns. **Daedelus** and **Zabargad** reefs, **Fury Shoals** and **St John's** were once just daydreams for most; now there are clusters of resorts in Marsa Alam town, on the beautiful bay at Abu Dabab and even near Hamata, nearly as far south as you can go before reaching the Sudanese border.

As well as **Elphinstone Reef** (see page 65), which is 12 km off shore, local site include the **Abu Dabab** dive site, where dugongs are seen on most days in the sea-grass, hence it is very popular. Too popular in fact, as the propellers of boats and hundreds of divers daily are causing stress to the ponderous beasts, who do not necessarily like being followed as they are trying to feed. Turtles, guitar sharks and rays are also frequent visitors.

Daedalus Reef, 60/96 km offshore; Dolphine Reef, 15 km to the northwest of Ras Banas; Zabargad Island, 45km southeast of Berenice.

Sha'ab Samadai, the Dolphin House, 5 km southeast in Marsa

Alam National Park, comes with a 100% guarantee of seeing spinner dolphins. Entrance fees apply to the crescent-shaped reef and numbers are restricted to 100 divers and 100 snorkellers per day. There is also a no-human zone as efforts are made to protect the pod who are unusual in their behaviour by staying at the reef rather than the open ocean as spinners typically do. Divers cannot enter the lagoon but can dive around the outside of the reef, where there are caves and pinnacles of soft and hard coral.

All the big resorts around Marsa Alam have their own dive centres, and there are three smaller outfits and a decompression chamber at Tondoba Bay, 14 km south of Marsa Alam, where there is a house reef.

The following are both reputable and offer open-water courses: **Aquarius**, T010-646 0408, aquariusredsea.com; **South Red Sea Enterprises**, T02-2635 2406, southredsea.net. **Blue Heaven Holidays**, T012-313 1157, blueheavenholidays.com, offer a unique opportunity in Egypt for divers to get involved in reef conservation and monitoring efforts alongside marine scientists. Part of the global Reef Check programme, it's a chance to enhance your own environmental knowledge while collecting valuable data that will aid the protection of the southern reefs. Visit their website to see when the next surveys are being undertaken.

Sharm El-Sheikh

Desert safaris
Most hotels in Na'ama Bay offer a sort of desert safari, but for the most part they're intended for tourists who want to look through the window of an air conditioned bus and the experience can be shared with quite a crowd. A tour to St Catherine's Monastery (10 hours), which may include a trek to the summit of Mount Sinai and a visit to a Bedouin village, costs from US$50-100.

If you're interested in a more extensive, authentic and rugged desert experience, a better plan is to set off with a real Bedouin guide from Dahab or Nuweiba.

Diving
The heartland of diving in Sinai is Sharm El-Sheikh, home to Egypt's first marine park, Ras Mohammed, and the Straits of Tiran, which can be easily reached for a day's diving. In efforts to preserve Ras Mohammed's pristine marine garden, access to some areas is restricted and there are limits on the number of boats that can approach. Try to book ahead, or if you would rather dive from shore, plan to bring a diving guide and your own gear with you.

Other key local dive sites:
Against the odds, **Na'ama Bay** still teems with life and many novices will do their introductory courses here. Another local site

in front of the light tower and within walking distance of Sharm El-Sheikh, is **Ras Umm Sidd**.

Shark Bay dive site is about 10 km north of Na'ama Bay, offering a smooth slope shore entry. It's ideal for beginners and first-time night divers. It also has a reputation for manta rays.

Ras Nasrani is a dramatic reef wall dotted with caves. It has two spots worthy of note: The Light, a 40-m drop-off, with large pelagic fish; and The Point, with hard coral boulders. Be mindful of currents.

The Tower has been so over-dived in recent years that the spot has lost some of its old splendour, but the steep 60 m wall, large caves and colourful fish still impress.

HMS Thistlegorm
Live-aboards charter south towards the Straits of Gubal, the entrance to the Suez Canal, where wreck diving is fantastic. The most famous is the HMS Thistlegorm, a British cargo vessel that was bombed during

Tip...

Most divers will book a package in advance, including diving courses, offshore dive trips to major reefs and live-aboard safaris in combo with accommodation and airfare, but independent travellers are also fine to head to the main dive centres in Na'ama Bay. Also worth checking out are the dive centres at most large hotels.

Diving at HMS Thistlegorm.

the Second World War. Most live-aboard itineraries feature it.

Camel Dive Club
Centrally located in Na'ama Bay, T069-360 0700, cameldive.com.
One of the longest established dive centres in Na'ama, slick and friendly service with a 3.5-m training pool. Popular bar inside the dive club area and internet café. Appeals to young cosmopolitan crowd. There is a hotel with 38 rooms in the dive club – comfortable and convenient if you're here to dive, but not cheap.

Emperor Divers
At the Rosetta Hotel on Peace Rd. T069-360 1734, emperor divers.com.
Highly recommended and known for being sticklers when it comes to safety. A good choice

Diving tips...

❶ Before signing up to any diving course make sure your instructor can speak your mother tongue. You can't be safe if you cannot understand the instructor. 'We all speak the same language underwater', is a sign you should be looking elsewhere. Be careful in choosing your dive centre – safety, environmental impact and price should be on your agenda. Bargain-basement prices could mean that short cuts are being made.

❷ Make sure you are insured to dive.

❸ Fly-by-night operators do exist. Always be on your guard. Go to an approved operator and watch out for scams, eg non-PADI centres flying PADI flags. Often the best options are those centres that have regular guests on dive holidays flying in from abroad. Contact PADI, BSAC, CMAS and SSI while at home for advice.

❹ Common tricks include: cheap deals, making you feel guilty or rude if you refuse, sudden loss of understanding of your language, free desert/ restaurant trips and offers of marriage! Also talk of donations to the decompression chamber, Sinai National Parks and/or Giftun Islands – these are virtually all compulsory and it is the diver that pays. (The government has introduced a US$1 a day charge for the decompression chamber and a US$2 tax for the Giftun Island Reef.)

❺ Membership of the Red Sea Diving and Watersport Association and the Egyptian Underwater Sports Association is not proof of safety either. Membership is a requirement of law.

❻ HEPCA (Hurghada Environmental Protection and Conservation Association), hepca.com, is concerned about environmental destruction. It organizes cleanups at various Red Sea sites. Some dive centres are members, but this is not a guarantee of safety.

❼ Ask whether dive centres will pick you up or if you will have to arrange your own transport.

Sun n Fun
Na'ama Bay, T069-360 1623, sunnfunsinai.com.

Thomas Cook
In Gafy Mall (Peace Rd).

Falcon Hotel
King of Bahrain St),
Na'ama Bay, T069-360 1808.
Helpful with travel arrangements to other cities, also reserves tickets on the ferry to Hurghada.

Travco
Banks Rd, Hadaba,
T069-366 0764, travco.com.
One of Egypt's biggest agents, offering a wide range of day trips throughout Sinai.

Water sports
In addition to snorkelling and diving, there are rental windsurf boards and hobi cats. Jet skis are banned.

The **Movenpick** offers parasailing. Colona watersports, at the **Regency Plaza Resort** in Nabq (colonawatersports.com), offer kiteboarding, and in four days you can become a qualified IKO Level II kiteboarder.

Dahab

Desert safaris
Virtually all of the camps and hotels can either organize short or extended safaris to nearby attractions or point you in the direction of someone who can.

for an open-water course (nursery pool for your confined dives) as well as being hugely popular with experienced divers.

Oonas Dive Club
At the far northern end of Na'ama Bay, T069-360 1501, oonasdiveclub.com.
Mainly European instructors and divers. Pretty much the cheapest for PADI courses, unusual in that first dives are actually in the sea in a buoyed-off area.

Red Sea Diving College
On Na'ama Bay boardwalk.
T069-360 0145, redseacollege.com.
PADI five-star fully equipped IDC centre. Opened 1991, at least 10 multilingual PADI instructors from a good purpose-built facility. Like Oonas, it's one of the cheaper and more reputable places to take a course.

Sinai Dive Club
In Hilton Fayyrouz, Na'ama Bay.
T069-600136.
Offers live-aboards and all PADI courses. Excellent service, kind and knowledgeable dive instructors.

Sinai Divers
In Ghazala Hotel, sinaidivers.com.
Claims to be the largest diving centre in Na'ama Bay, certainly one of the most established. Book in advance in the winter high season. Consistently runs week-long live-aboard boats of a high spec, in addition to lots of daily dive trips and the full range of PADI-certified courses).

Tour operators
Although hectic and exhausting, day trips to Cairo and Luxor can be crammed into your beach experience.

Best Friends Safari

T069-364 1211.
The owner, Ahmed, is a vibrant, friendly man who knows the desert well and has worked with local Bedouin for years. He will help you create the trip you want.

Embah Safari

In the middle of the Masbat, near Tota, T069-364 1690, embah.com.
Co-run by an Irish-Egyptian couple with the intention of bridging Bedouin and Western cultures to build understanding and mutual appreciation, they provide tailor-made excursions for days or weeks at a time. A professional choice. Booking ahead is advisable.

Diving

With numbers on land and in the water being fewer, Dahab is certainly a more relaxing place for learners to pass their Open Water course and qualified divers to discover what Sinai has to offer beyond Ras Mohammad. For starters, this is shore-diving territory where you kit up on stable ground – often a blanket laid on the beach – and then walk or swim out to a break in the coral to make your descent. Doing away with the added expense of a boat keeps the prices down a bit and allows greater flexibility as divers are not tied to any pre-set sailing times.

The main section of Dahab Bay – logged by divers as Bannerfish Bay – has a sandy bottom and only a thin scattering of fish. It is predominantly used by instructors holding Open Water courses who use the shallow, buoyed- off shelf at the top end of the bay for the confined lessons. The Lighthouse, a colourful wall of reef with a satisfying assortment of fish that follows the curve of the coastline, is easily accessible. Dive schools will include transfer by pick up truck or 4WD to sites north, including the Blue Hole (see page 67) or south of the Bay (key sites are included here, dive schools can suggest more), and some lead trips further afield.

North from the lighthouse:
The **Eel Garden**, off Assalah, is a shallow coral reef good for snorkelling and a safe spot for beginner divers. There's a sandy bottom with a garden of eels, swaying like flowers in the currents as they wait for fish.

The **Canyon** is located opposite Canyon Dive Centre a few kilometres north of Dahab. Accessible from the shore, you snorkel along the reef through a narrow break before diving into the canyon. A popular spot for more experienced divers, it bottoms out at 50 m.

A bit further out than the aforementioned sites lies **Ras Abu Gallum** (also see page 202), a majestic and remote protectorate

What the locals say

The best sites aren't necessarily the most famous ones. Try Abu Helal or drifting from Abu Telha to Abu Helal. You need to wait for good conditions (no/low wind and high tide), but the reward is better coral and aquatic life than you'll find anywhere else in Dahab.

Said Khedr, Dahab's first Bedouin dive master and owner of Desert Divers.

Listings

area that shelters some of the richest marine life in Sinai. Beginning about 15 km north of Dahab, this stretch of 30 km is only accessible by camel. There are three main dive sites with virgin reefs and a wide array of marine life. Access to the underwater cave network at **Ras Mamlah** (the nothern corner of Ras Abu Gallum) is strictly forbidden. Many divers have died here.

There are more than 40 diving centres in and around Assalah that rent equipment and run PADI diving courses. Not all are considered to be safe. Ask around before choosing a dive centre and ensure whoever you choose to study or dive with is PADI certified, reputable and experienced.

Big Blue
Assalah, T069-364 0045, bigbluedahab.com.
A well-regarded operation, provides underwater camera for use on last day of the PADI course.

Desert Divers
Masbat, T069-364 0500, desert-divers.com.
The only Bedouin-owned dive operation in Dahab has local Bedouin dive guides. Long-established and friendly. Offers free-diving and diving safaris to isolated dive spots, plus weekly yoga on the roof terrace.

Fantasea
At the northern end of Masbat bay, near the lighthouse, T069-364 1195, fantaseadiving.net.
Also rent out windsurf boards.

Inmo
Inmo Hotel and Dive Centre, T069-364 0370-1, inmodivers.de.
Long established. Recommended.

Poseidon Divers
Camel Resort, Peace Rd, Mashraba, T069-364 0091, poseidon divers.com.
Known for their camel safaris to Ras Abu Ghallum, and all-day trip

with two dives and Bedouin lunch for E110. If you need to hire diving equipment it's E20 extra.

Reef 2000
Bedouin Moon Hotel, between Dahab and Blue Hole, T069-364 0087, reef2000.org.
Catering mainly for the British and German markets. Offers camel safari to Ras Abu Ghallum, includes food and two dives, E100. Also run 'yoga diving' courses, blending the two disciplines to get the best of both worlds.

Sinai Divers
Hilton Resort, Lagoon, sinaidivers.com.
A large operation with branches all around the Red Sea.

Kitesurfing & windsurfing
Several of the high-end hotels, including the **Hilton** and the **Coralia** (see page 212) with its perfect private windsurfing beach, offer surfing schools with introductory classes up to three-day courses. In Assalah, **Fantasea** dive centre rents boards.

Snorkelling
All dive centres in Dahab rent snorkel, mask and fins for around E£30 per day.

Left: Windsurfing in Dahab.
Opposite page: Coloured Canyon, Nuweiba.

Transport

Nuweiba to Taba

Desert safaris
Bedouin Cultural Safaris
Nuweiba, office to the left of Han Kang restaurant, T018-111 7189.
An ethical venture who are part of the Nuweiba Association, a group set up to help the Mazena tribe to sustain themselves through micro-loans and tourism. As well as tailored trips by jeep or camel, they offer cultural experiences under the stars with great Bedouin food.

Farag (from the Mazena tribe)
Based at the Ciao Hotel between the port and the city, T010-188 1852, farag_soliman2003@yahoo.com.
Farag's trips to the mountain plateaux of Gebel El-Guna pass through little-visited *wadis* where the wind has carved the coloured sandstone into supernatural forms and awesome white sand dunes startle the eye (around E£100 per person per day).

Diving
Certainly better known for sandy beaches than diving, but, because its waters are quiet and clear, it makes a suitable spot for beginners. There are a few dive centres around, all of which offer trips to nearby sites that are more impressive than the few reefs off Nuweiba shores.

Dive Point
At the Hilton Coral Resort, T069-352 0327.
Offers beginners' courses and excursions.

SCUBA Divers
At La Sirene, T069-350 0705.
Contact them in advance to check whether an international certified instructor is present on site to teach beginners' courses, as now that Nuweiba is so quiet he/she may not always be in town. However, diving and snorkelling gear are always available to rent.

Sinai Diving Centre
Nuweiba Village, T069-3500 4013, nuweibaresort.com.
Have a well-maintained and efficient centre.

El-Gouna

Air
At just 20 km away, Hurghada airport is close, and flights so frequent, it's easy to just hop on a bus and transfer between towns. Taxis from Hurghada airport cost E£100, depending on your bargaining skills.

Bus
Buses to Hurghada leave every 20 minutes from 0700-2400, E£5. **High Jet Company** buses are cheaper and less luxurious. **El-Gouna Transportation Company** operates several buses between El-Gouna and Cairo each day at 0930, 1400, 1630, 1930 and 0030.

Taxi
A ride between El-Gouna and Hurghada costs E£50-70.

Hurghada

Air
There are two or three daily flights from Hurghada to Cairo, and also direct to Aswan and Sharm El-Sheikh. Times and numbers of flights change frequently so it is best to visit an **EgyptAir** office or go online, as the phones are rarely answered.

EgyptAir, (egyptair.com), in the square with the new mosque and a branch on Sharia Sheraton, T065-346 3034-7, open 0800-2000.

Listings

Bus
Upper Egypt (T065-354 7582), **El-Gouna** (T065-355 6199) and **Superjet** (T065-355 3499) operate here. Those to and from Cairo are genuinely 'lux', with air conditioning and plastic still covering the seats, and therefore more expensive. It's wise to check schedules south to Marsa Alam as they fluctuate seasonally, and a good idea to book a ticket a day in advance if you are going to Luxor or Aswan.

Superjet has four daily buses to Cairo at 1200, 1430, 1700 and 2400 (6 hrs), and El-Gouna has 12 daily buses to Cairo (via El-Gouna), 6 hours.

Upper Egypt run 11 buses each day to Cairo's Turgoman station (6-7 hrs); six per day to Luxor (5 hrs), two of which carry on to Aswan (8 hrs); to El-Quesir (2 hrs) via Safaga at 0100, 0300, 0500 and 2000, carrying on to Marsa Alam (4 hrs).

Car
Most car rental agencies are scattered around Sharia Sheraton.

Ferry
High speed air-conditioned ferry to Sharm El-Sheikh on the Sinai Peninsula (2 hrs). Ferries leave Hurghada for Sharm El-Sheikh at 0930 on Saturday, Monday and Tuesday and at 0430 on Wednesday and 0900 on Thursday. They depart from Sharm El-Sheikh back to Hurghada on the same days at

1700, or 1800 on Wednesday. Booking is essential through **International Fast Ferries** (office on the Sharia Sheraton in front of Pacha resort, T065-344 7571), or through a travel agent such as **Thomas Cook** (Sharia El Nasr, Dahar, T065-354 1870) or Spring Tours (Sharia Sheraton, Sigala, T065-344 2150).

Taxi
For independent travel to the Nile Valley (Luxor 4 hrs; Aswan 6 hrs) in private car or with a contracted service taxi, foreigners are required to travel in police-escorted convoys. One leaves daily from Hurghada's southern-most checkpoint at 0600. When demand is high, there is another later in the morning. For long distances, fares and travel times are less than the bus but it's more dangerous as drivers often speed fearlessly. The service taxi station is across the roundabout from the **Telephone Centrale**. Journey times to other destinations by service taxi (may or may not require a convoy): to Safaga (1 hr), Marsa Alam (3 hrs), Cairo (5-7 hrs).

Safaga

Bus
Suez-bound departures, stopping at Hurghada, leave every 1-2 hours, five of which go on to Cairo (7-8 hrs). Buses to Luxor and Aswan four-five times a day; to El-Quesir (2 hrs) and Marsa Alam (3 hrs) leave at 0600, 1600, 1900, 2100, 0200.

Taxi
Service taxis follow all the bus routes – change at Suez for Cairo. Prices are comparable to bus costs. Journeys tend to be a bit faster, hence more unnerving.

El-Quseir

Bus
Daily to Cairo (10 hrs) via Safaga and Hurghada (2 hrs) at 0500, 1230, 1730, 2000, 2030, 2230 and 2330. There is at least one daily bus to Qift that presently departs at 0500. From there, you can bus or train it to Luxor (1 hr) and Aswan (4 hrs). As with other cities on the coast, independent travellers bound for the Nile Valley on public buses generally won't get kicked off if there are only four or less on board. There are also supposedly four buses per day to Marsa Alam (2 hrs) and beyond at 0500, 0900, 1900 and 2000.

Taxi
Service taxis and microbuses that congregate next to the bus terminal go to all these destinations throughout the day. Change at Suez for Cairo. These are a more flexible option and tend to be quicker.

Marsa Alam

Bus
To get out of Marsa Alam, ask the locals about the latest schedules once you get to town, as things change with the winds. At

present, from Marsa Alam to Cairo, there are buses that stop in Safaga and Hurghada at 1030, 1530, 1830 and 2030; otherwise head to Hurghada and transfer. Crossing to Edfu from Marsa Alam is supposedly difficult for tourists, as many get kicked off the public buses or service taxis at one of the three checkpoints, but if you want to try and trust the unspoken four tourists or less rule, the public bus heads west around 0700 from the T-junction and takes five hours. Buses run every few hours to El- Quseir (2 hrs), where more northbound and westbound buses depart from.

Sharm El-Sheikh

Bus
From the East Delta bus station, T069-366 0600, halfway between Sharm and Na'ama, there are at least 12 trips daily to Cairo, from 0730 in the morning until 0100 (6-8 hrs). To Dahab, six buses a day, from 0600-0100 (1½ hrs), of which the early morning bus goes on to St Catherine's (4 hrs), and of which two go on to Nuweiba (2½ hrs) and one of these to Taba (3½ hrs). **East Delta** run one bus daily to Luxor at 1800 (12-14 hrs). **Superjet**, next to East Delta bus station, T069-366 1622, have slightly more comfortable buses with toilets, five per day to Cairo between 1000 and 2300. **Superjet** buses also call at El Gouna Transport on Peace Road opposite Delta Sharm Hotel.

Ferry
Sinai to Hurghada, T069-360 0936, five per week on Saturday, Monday, Tuesday and Thursday at 1700 and Wednesday at 1800 (from Hurghada to Sharm, same days at 0930, or 0430 on Wednesday), takes two hours. To secure a spot, make reservations a day in advance at a hotel or private travel agent like **Thomas Cook**, T069-360 1808. Ferry leaves from the Sharm Marina, T069-366 0313.

Dahab

Bus
Daily buses to Cairo depart at 0830, 1230, 1430 and 2200 (8-9 hrs) via Sharm El-Sheikh (1½ hrs), plus a further eight buses to Sharm, the last one leaving at 2230. Three buses go north to Nuweiba at 1030, 1600 and 1830 (1 hr) of which the 1030 carries on to Taba (3 hrs). There's a sporadic service to St Catherine's 0930 daily (1½ hrs). There's a gruelling bus to Luxor every day at 1600 (13-14 hrs) which also stops at Hurghada. Bus schedules are posted around most camps.

Service taxis
Faster than the bus, another way to get around from city to city is to hire a service (pronounced *servees*) taxi. If you are travelling en masse or can team up with some other wanderers, you can bargain with a driver to take you almost anywhere.

Nuweiba

Bus
Departures for Cairo at 0900 and 1500 (7 hrs); for Sharm El-Sheikh (3 hrs) via Dahab (1 hr) leave at 0630, 0815, 1030 and 1600. All depart from the terminal at the port. Departure times frequently change so ask at any hotel or camp to confirm times, or call T069-520 3701. For St Catherine's, go to Dahab and change there. **Microbuses**, cheaper and sometimes quicker, have a leave-when-full policy and travel north and south along the main highway as well as to Cairo. Negotiate prices before setting off, but you shouldn't pay more than E£100 to go to Cairo.

Service taxis
Available from Nuweiba port to Taba and other towns in the region.

Taba

Bus
East Delta Bus Company to Cairo, daily at 1030 and 1630 (6-7 hrs); Sharm El-Sheikh (4 hrs) via Dahab (3 hrs) and Nuweiba (1 hr) at 0900 and 1500. For St Catherine's, change at Dahab.

Service taxis
More frequent, more comfortable, and quicker than buses, they regularly transport visitors to Nuweiba, Dahab and Sharm.

Contents

Practicalities

Two girls ride camels.

Getting there

Air

From UK and Ireland

Take advantage of charter flights to Hurghada, Marsa Allam, Luxor, Taba and Sharm El-Sheikh. Good deals can be found at thomsonfly.com, firstchoice.co.uk and fly thomascook.com. From London, BMI, British Airways and EgyptAir fly to Cairo International. British Airways also fly to Sharm El-Sheikh; EgyptAir to Luxor. There are no direct flights from Ireland so most people fly via London.

From North America

From New York EgyptAir has an 11-hour daily direct flight to Cairo. Most European carriers fly from major North American cities to Cairo via their European hubs. British Airways and KLM serve the bigger cities on the west coast. From Canada, there are direct flights with EgyptAir from Montreal two or three times a week, taking about 11 hours. Some European airlines also have connecting services from Montreal and Toronto that do not necessitate overnight stays in Europe.

From rest of Europe

Air France offers direct flights to Cairo via Paris. From Germany, Lufthansa, via Frankfurt, and TUIfly are a good budget choice from Berlin, Munich and Cologne. KLM, fly to Cairo from Amsterdam. Austrian Airlines, Czech Airlines, Malev and Olympic Airways have services too, often at competitive prices.

Airport information

Cairo airport (cairo-airport.com) is 22 km (30-45 mins) northeast of the city. Terminal 1

(T02-2265 5000/1) and Terminal 2 are mainly used by international airlines. Terminal 2 (T02-2265 2222, departure information; T02-2265 2077, arrival information) is 3 km away from Terminal 1, transit between them by free airport shuttle bus. Terminal 3 is EgyptAir's hub for domestic and international flights, connected to T2 by a bridge. All have tourist information, ATM machines and banks that remain open through the night. Visas are sold just before passport control (US$15 or equivalent in euro or sterling).

Taxi drivers will descend on you, asking for E£80 to the centre. They get cheaper the further you head out of the car park, cheaper still outside the airport precincts. Another option is the **Shuttle Bus** (T19970, from the limousine counter on arrival or you pre-booked) whose seven-seater minibuses drop at various districts for set prices (for example, Downtown E£55, Zamalek E£66).

International and domestic flights pass through **Luxor airport** (T095-237 4655), 7 km east of the town centre. Visas are on sale just before passport control. It isn't well connected by public transport so taxis to town are unquestionably best (£30-40). Domestic flights connect airports at Aswan and Abu Simbel to the rest of Egypt.

Hurghada's airport is the gateway used by the majority of domestic and international flights to and from the mainland Red Sea coast. It is 6 km southwest of the town centre, taxis to/from town cost E£25, or E£100 to neighbouring El-Gouna. An international airport 60 km north of Marsa Alam serves the coast south of Hurghada although it is small and flights are relatively infrequent.

Some 10 km north of Na'ama Bay and 17 km from Sharm, **Sharm El-Sheikh International Airport** is the gateway to the southern Sinai coast. Most European charter flights and British Airways leave from Terminal 1 while British charter flights leave from Terminal 2, but check as it's a five-10 minute walk between. A handful of charter flights from Europe fly to and from **Taba International Airport**, 35 km from the resort centre. Also an option is **Eilat airport** (15 km from Taba) which has direct daily flights to major European cities.

Road & Sea

If you are already travelling in the region, the main overland and sea entry points are from Israel, Eilat–Taba (best time to cross through the checkpoints 0700-2100), from Jordan via Israel overland, or Aqaba–Nuweiba by ferry or motorboat. A slow ferry travels between Aquaba in Jordan and Nuweiba Port, taking three hours (barring potential obstacles). Times are erratic. There is also a more comfortable and reliable speedboat, taking one hour. Cancellations are frequent due to bad weather. Potentially risky are Egyptian border areas near Libya (Al-Bardia–Sollum) and Sudan. The Gaza–Rafah border crossing was closed at the time of writing.

Getting around

From camel to plane to *felucca*, Egypt is equipped with numerous transport options. Congestion and chaos can be a bit anxiety-provoking on long road ventures, but with a bit of courage and flexibility, you can access most areas without too much effort. As for timetables and infrastructure, the country seems to run on magic. There are few regulations and little consistency, but somehow, people always seem to get where they want to go.

Tip...

Hitchhiking has a measure of risk attached to it so is not recommended, and is only really a consideration in outlying places not well-served by public transport. Rides are often available on lorries and in small open trucks but payment is expected. Women travelling alone or without a male escort are strongly advised not to hitchhike, as they may be mistaken for prostitutes.

Air

EgyptAir connects Cairo, Luxor, Aswan, Abu Simbel, Sharm El-Sheikh and Hurghada (example flight times: Cairo to Luxor 1 hr; Cairo to Aswan 2 hrs; Aswan to Abu Simbel 40 mins; Cairo to Hurghada, 1 hr). In peak seasons, demand can be high and booking ahead is essential. E-tickets can be booked at egyptair.com, at EgyptAir offices, by travel agents or ask if your hotel arranges onward travel.

Rail

Rail networks are limited, but travel by train can be delightful, especially to a few key destinations along the Nile. First class is most comfortable, but second class is very similar and almost half the price. Third class never has air conditioning and can be quite cramped and dirty, and a foreigner travelling on main routes would not be sold a ticket anyway.

Train travel does have restrictions. Although dozens of trains travel south from Cairo to Middle and Upper Egypt, foreigners are technically only permitted to ride on three, those guarded by policemen. For train travel once in Upper Egypt, the tickets visitors can purchase are still restricted, but it's sometimes possible to board the train and pay the conductor once in motion. It's highly unlikely you will be kicked off.

For detailed train information, contact the **Cairo information office**, T02-2575 3555, or visit egyptrail.gov.eg.

Approximate journey times from Cairo: Luxor 9 hrs; Aswan 12 hrs. Example fares: Cairo to Luxor, E£90 1st class, E£55 2nd class; Cairo to Aswan, E£110 1st class, E£60 2nd class. Families can buy four seats (E£90/each) in a Nefertiti Cabin (which seats six privately) and the other two won't be sold. Privately run sleeper trains to Cairo (Abela Egypt, T02-3574 9474) cost US$80 per person single, or US$60 per person double, US$45 children 4-9 years, payable in US$ or euro only.

Road

Car

Vehicles drive on the right in Egypt. An international driving licence is required. Petrol (super) is E£2-3 per litre. Road signs are in Arabic, with most offering the English transliteration. Cairo does have street signs in Arabic and English on all the major thoroughfares, but driving there can be nightmarish all the same with no margin for error and constant undertaking.

Road conditions vary from new dual carriageways to rural tracks only one-vehicle wide to far-flung roads that are a rough and unsurfaced. Problems include encroaching sand, roads that end with no warning and lunatic drivers. Driving at night is especially hazardous as people only put their headlights on to flash at oncoming vehicles. If you are going to give driving a shot, make sure that you are well insured as the road accident rate is one of the highest in the world.

Car hire

The main car hire firms are **Avis** (avis.com), **Hertz** (hertz.com) and **Budget** (budget.com). Costs vary greatly relative to the quality of the vehicle and the location of the rental agency, and a large deposit is generally required. Some companies place restrictions on areas that can be visited. Be aware that there are many police checkpoints for cars in Egypt and they often request to see your papers. To avoid a hefty fine keep them to hand (approximate journey times from Cairo by road: Sharm El-Sheikh 6 hrs; Aswan 16 hrs; Luxor 10 hrs).

Bus/coach

The main mode and cheapest means of transport, link nearly all towns in Egypt. It's advisable to book tickets 24 hours in advance, though this is not possible in some oases towns or from Aswan.

Tip...

Buses in Upper Egypt, if carrying more than four foreigners, are required to be in a convoy, so it is essential that you purchase your ticket in advance (where possible) to ensure a seat. Because of these restrictions, travel by train offers the most flexibility and reliability in the region. It's also generally faster, more consistent and comfortable.

Upper Egypt, East Delta and West Delta are the three main operators covering the whole country and are cheapest, usually with air conditioning and assigned seats. **Superjet** and **El-Gouna Transport** also offer buses to/from most towns to Cairo, with more luxurious buses that are about 30% more expensive. The downside is they play videos half the night. There are usually night buses that can save you losing a day on long journeys, and drivers

always make a couple of tea-and-toilet stops at
roadside coffee shops. Later buses tend to cost
a bit more than early morning ones.

Approximate fares:
Cairo to: Luxor E£100; Aswan E£100; Hurghada E£65
-75; El-Gouna E£85-100; Marsa Alam E£91; Sharm
El-Sheikh E£60-85; Dahab E£85. Luxor to: Aswan
E£10 via Kom Ombo (E£2), Edfu (E£4) and Esna
(E£6); to Dahab E£130 via Sharm El-Sheikh E£120;
Hurghada E£35. Aswan to Abu Simbel E£25.
Hurghada to: El-Quesir E£25, via Safaga E£5-7; to
Marsa Alam E£35. Sharm El-Sheikh to: Dahab E£11;
St Catherine's E£25; Nuweiba E£20-25; Taba E£35;
Luxor E£100. Dahab to: Nuweiba £11; Taba E£22;
St Catherine's E£16.

Taxis & service taxis
Smaller private vehicles (called microbuses or
service taxis, pronounced *servees*) cover the same
routes as buses and usually cost the same, or
perhaps 25% more. Service taxis in Upper Egypt
generally do not accept foreigners when travelling
between towns so they can avoid the confines of
the convoys. If a foreigner is found unescorted at a
checkpoint, the drivers may be severely fined.
   Example costs from Luxor: direct to Aswan
E£275; with stops in Esna, Edfu and Kom Ombo
E£300; Dendara and Abydos E£250.

Sea & river

Ferry
Ferries connect Hurghada on the Red Sea coast to
Sharm El-Sheikh in the Sinai five times a week. One-way
fare costs E£250, E£450 return, takes two hours.

Nile cruises, *felucca* & *dahabiyas*
Cruise boats travel from Luxor to Aswan (see
page 156), while *dahabiyas* chart between Esna and
Aswan, and on Lake Nasser (page 181). *Feluccas* go
downstream from Aswan to finish at Kom Ombo
(one night) or Edfu (two nights) (page 181).

Tip...

If you want to take a service taxi from Hurghada to Luxor or Aswan, get a group together and work it out privately, as the service taxi drivers will have to join a convoy to transport foreigners in order to avoid having their licenses taken away. Don't listen to drivers who insist there is a 'convoy charge', and expect to pay about E£300.

Directory

Customs & immigration

You may be asked to declare if you have more than one of any electrical item with you on a D form. In case of theft, report to police or they will assume you have sold them and will charge you duty. Goods may be imported as follows: 200 cigarettes or 250 g of tobacco, 2 litres of alcohol, 1 litre of perfume, gifts up to the value of E£500. Foreigners are also permitted 48 hrs from arrival to buy a further 3 litres of alcohol at duty-free shops.

Passports should be valid for at least 6 months beyond the period of your stay. Visas are required by all except nationals of the following countries: Bahrain, Jordan, Kuwait, Libya, Oman, Saudi Arabia and the UAE. Most Western tourists buy a renewable 30-day tourist visa (US$15 or equivalent in euro or sterling) on arrival at all international airports – but this is not possible when you are entering via an overland border crossing or a port.

If you are restricting your travel to south Sinai, including St Catherine's Monastery, a Sinai-only visa permits a stay of up to 14 days. They are free of charge at the entry points of Taba, Sharm el-Sheikh airport, Nuweiba and Sharm el-Sheikh seaports. They are not valid for Ras Mohammed or trekking in Central Sinai.

Disabled travellers

Although there is access to the Sound and Light show at the Sphinx, and the Giza Pyramids plateau is being made more user-friendly, few provisions are made for disabled travellers.

Cairo's high and frequent kerbs make hiring a taxi for the day to take you around the most sensible option. In the Sinai, some dive companies accept students with disabilities and disabled people have been known to camel ride up Mt Sinai. Consider booking a tour with a company that caters to the needs of disabled travellers. Contact the **Society for the Accessible Travel & Hospitality** (sath.org); egyptforall.net and access-able.com.

Drugs

The penalties for drug use and possession (even of small amounts) can be severe – lengthy prison sentences (25 years), life imprisonment or the death penalty. Smoking pot is essentially a thing of the past in Dahab where the tourist police maintain a subtle but persistent presence. Growing marijuana is not illegal for Bedouins, but selling and using it is.

Emergencies

Ambulance T123; Fire T125; Police T122 (from any city); Tourist Police T126.

Etiquette

A few considerations are worthy of note for non-Muslims. Dress respectfully, conforming to the broad lines of the practice of the house – except on the beach or 'at home' in the hotel (assuming it is a tourist rather than local establishment), this means trousers for men rather than shorts and covering the greater part of the legs and arms for women. If swimming outside a touristy area, wear shorts and an opaque T-shirt. If visiting during Ramadan, dress particularly conservatively and avoid eating, drinking and smoking in public. If offering a gift to a Muslim friend, be aware that pork and alcohol are forbidden. If you choose to offer other meat, ensure it is hallal.

If dining in a traditional Bedouin context, do not use your left hand for eating since it is ritually unclean (when knives and forks are provided, both hands is fine). Do not accept or ask for alcohol unless your host clearly intends to imbibe. Keep your feet tucked under your body away from food.

Additionally, be conservative in greeting and appreciating people of the opposite sex. Do not show the bottom of your feet or rest them on tables or chairs as this is considered extremely rude. As a single woman in Egypt, always sit in the back seat, at a diagonal to the driver.

Taking photographs of any person without permission is unwise, of women is taboo. Photographs of police, soldiers, docks, bridges, military areas, airports, radio stations and other public utilities, are prohibited.

Families

Egyptian's are incredibly receptive to children (though only restaurants in higher-end hotels will have high-chairs to hand). Sensible precautions that you would take in any hot place all apply, as does exercising extra prudence when choosing a place to eat. Pushchairs are not really feasible in the big cities and the noise and filth make walking around with children a fraught experience. Hazards include the traffic, pollution and dust, and lack of safety barriers in high monuments (particularly in Islamic Cairo).

Health

There are many excellent private and government clinics/hospitals. But as with all medical care, first impressions count. If a facility looks grubby then be wary of the general standard of medicine and hygiene.

Ideally, see your GP or travel clinic at least 6 weeks before your departure for general advice on travel risks in the region, malaria and vaccinations. For further information visit **The Health Protection Agency**, hpa.org.uk, or **The Foreign and Commonwealth Office** (UK),fco.gov.uk; **Travel Screening Services** (UK) travelscreening.co.uk.

Health underwater

If you plan to dive make sure that you are fit to do so. The **British Sub-Aqua Club** (BSAC), T01513-506200, bsac.com, can put you in touch with doctors who will carry out medical examinations. For your own safety, don't take risks and always stay within the limits of your qualification.

Insurance

Comprehensive travel insurance is recommended and, if necessary, extend the policy to cover activities such as scuba-diving, kitesurfing, wind surfing, hiking etc, which may not be included as standard.

Money

The Egyptian pound is divided into 100 piastres. Notes are in denominations of E£1, E£5, E£10, E£20, E£50, E£100, E£200 and 25 and 50 piastres. New E£1 coins are coming into circulation, and other denominations (which are almost not worth carrying) are 5, 10, 20, 25, and 50 piastres. Many tourist centres and hotels quote their prices in euro, however, Egyptian pounds are used for the vast majority of everyday transactions and hotels are generally happy to accept the equivalent value in E£. Carry a small amount of foreign cash, US$, sterling or euro, in case of an emergency.

Police

Dial T122 from any city.
If involvement with the police is serious (more so than obtaining papers to substantiate an insurance claim for lost or stolen property), for example, as a result of a driving accident, contact the nearest consular office without delay. Some embassies advise leaving the scene of an accident immediately and heading straight to your embassy.

Travelling around Egypt in private cars is often accompanied by the bear hug of the police (mainly the tourist police) from which little can be done to gain liberty – the government being determined that no further tourist lives will be lost to terrorism. The best way to handle this is to create a *cordon sanitaire* around your vehicle; keep out of sight line of their weapons and keep a great a distance between your own car and that of your escort so as to avoid a collision.

Post

Post offices are open daily (0800-2000) except Fri. Airmail letters take about 5-10 days to get to Europe, 2 weeks to North America, New Zealand and Australia. Postage stamps can be purchased from post offices, cigarette kiosks or hotels (from where mail can be posted too). Take parcels, unsealed, to main post offices for sending.

Safety

Confidence tricksters are the most common 'threat' to tourists. They are found where people are on the move – at airports, railway and bus stations – offering extremely favourable currency exchange rates, selling tours or 'antiques' and spinning hard-luck stories.

It is very unlikely that you will be robbed but take sensible precautions, such as storing valuables in a hotel deposit box or keeping them on your person, but well concealed. Avoid carrying excess money or wearing obviously valuable jewellery when sightseeing and stick to the main thoroughfares if walking around at night. Keep clear of all political activities.

9/11, the war on Iraq and the attacks on foreigners in the Sinai in 2004/5 brought about a new set of challenges for the tourist industry and reinforced the government's attempts at ensuring safety for foreign visitors. Part of the system requires most Western tourists travelling in private cars, hired taxis and tourist buses to travel in police-escorted convoys when journeying between towns, particularly in Upper Egypt. Scheduled convoys travel between significant tourist destinations: Luxor and Aswan; Luxor and Hurghada; Aswan and Abu Simbel; Luxor to Dendara and Abydos.

A general warning applicable to all desert-border areas and deserts around Safaga and Hurghada, but especially pertinent to Sinai, is to never allow your driver to stray off the tracks – many areas still have landmines.

Telephone

The country code is 20. Dialling codes for the main cities and resorts are: Aswan 097; Cairo 02; Hurghada 065; Luxor 095; Sharm El Sheikh 069.

Time difference

The time in Egypt is GMT plus 2 hrs.

Tipping

Baksheesh is a word you will fast learn. It's a way of life – everyone except high officials expects a reward for services actually rendered or imagined. Rather than make a fuss, have some small bills handy. Alms-giving is also a personal duty in Muslim countries. It is unlikely that beggars will be too persistent.

Voltage

Egypt's power is 220V, 50Hz, sockets are 2-pin round plugs.

Language

It is impossible to indicate precisely in the Latin script how Arabic should be pronounced so we have opted for a very simplified transliteration that will give the user a sporting chance of uttering something that can be understood by an Egyptian.

Where? *Fein?*
Where's the bathroom? *Fein el hamam?*
Who? *Meen?*
Why? *Leih?*
How? *Izay?*
How much? *Bikam?*

Greetings & farewells

Hello *ahlan wasahlan/assalamu aleikum*
Goodbye *ma'a el salama*
How are you? *Izayak?* (m); *Izayik?* (f)
Fine *kwayis* (m); *kwayissa* (f)
See you tomorrow *Ashoofak bokra* (m);
 Ashoofik bokra (f)
Thank God *il hamdullil'allah*

Basics

Excuse me *law samaht*
Can you help me? *Mumkin tisa'idny?* (m);
Mumkin tisa'ideeny (f)
Do you speak English? *Bitikalim ingleezy?* (m);
 Bitikalimy ingleezy? (f)
I don't speak Arabic *Ma bakalimsh 'araby*
Do you have a problem? *Fee mushkilla?*
Good *kweyyis*
Bad *mish kweyyis, wahish*
I/you *ana/inta* (m); *inty* (f)
He/she *howwa/heyya*
Yes *aiwa/na'am*
No *ia'a*
No problem *mafeesh mushkilla*
Please *min fadlak* (m); *min fadlik* (f)
Thank you *shukran*
You're welcome *'afwan*
God willing *Insha'allah*
What? *Eih?*

Numbers

zero	*sifr*	16	*sittashar*
one	*wahad*	17	*sabatashar*
two	*etneen*	18	*tamantashar*
three	*talaata*	19	*tissatashar*
four	*arba*	20	*'ayshreen*
five	*khamsa*	30	*talaateen*
six	*sitta*	40	*arba'een*
seven	*saba'a*	50	*khamseen*
eight	*tamenia*	60	*sitteen*
nine	*tissa*	70	*saba'een*
10	*ashra*	80	*tmaneen*
11	*hidashar*	90	*tissa'een*
12	*itnashar*	100	*mia*
13	*talatashar*	200	*miteen*
14	*arbatashar*	300	*tolto mia*
15	*khamstashar*	1000	*alf*

Dates & time

Morning *el sobh*
Afternoon *ba'd el dohr*
Evening *masa'*
Hour *sa'a*
Day *yom*
Night *bil leil*
Month *shahr*
Year *sana*
Early *badry*
Late *mit'akhar*

Today *inaharda*
Tomorrow *bokra*
Yesterday *imbarah*
Everyday *kol yom*
What time is it? *E'sa'a kam?*
When? *Imta?*

Days of week

Monday *el itnein*
Tuesday *el talaat*
Wednesday *el arba'*
Thursday *el khamees*
Friday *el goma'*
Saturday *el sapt*
Sunday *el had*

Travel & transport

Airport *el matar*
Plane *tayara*
Boat *markib*
Ferry *'abara*
Bus *otobees*
Bus station *mahatit otobees*
Bus stop *maw'if otobees*
Car *'arabiya*
Petrol *benzeen*
Tyre *'agala*
Train *atr*
Train station *mahatit atr*
Carriage *karetta; calesh*
Camel *gamal*
Donkey *homar*
Horse *hosan*
Ticket office *maktab e'tazakir*
Tourist office *makta e'siyaha*

Dodging touts

You'll get hassled less and respected more if you learn a bit of Arabic.

La'a shocrun   *no thank you!*

U'Itilak la'a   *I told you no!*

Mish ay-yez (m) mish ay-zza (f)
I don't want; I'm not interested

Bess   *enough*

Khalas   *finished, that's it*

F'il mish mish   *'when the apricots bloom'*
(ie *'in your dreams'*)

I want to go... *a'yiz arooh* (m); *a'yiza arooh* (f)
Does this go to... *da beerooh*
City   *madeena*
Village   *kareeya*
Street   *shari'*
Map   *khareeta*
Passport   *gawaz safar*
Police   *bolice*

Half a pound   *nos gineih*
How many?   *kem?*
How much?   *bikem?*
Jewellery   *seegha*
Market   *souk*
Newspaper in English   *gareeda ingleeziya*
One pound   *gineih*
Silver   *fada*
That's too much   *kiteer awy*
Where can I buy...   *fin ashtiry...*

Directions

Where is the...   *fein el ...*
How many kilometres is...   *kem kilometers el...*
Left   *shimal*
Right   *yimeen*
After   *ba'ad*
Before   *'abl*
Straight   *doghry; ala tool*
Near   *gamb*
Far   *bi'eed*
Slow down   *bishweish*
Speed up   *bisora'*
There   *hinak*
Here is fine   *hina kwayis*

Food & drink

Beer   *beera*
Bread   *'aysh*
Chicken   *firakh*
Coffee   *'ahwa*
Coffee shop   *'Ahwa*
Dessert   *helw*
Drink   *ishrab*
Eggs   *beid*
Fava beans   *fu'ul*

Money & shopping

25 piasters/a quarter pound   *robe' gineih*
Bank   *benk*
Bookstore   *maktaba*
Carpet   *sigada*
Cheap   *rikhees*
Do you accept visa?   *Mumkin visa?*
Do you have...   *'andak...* (m); *andik...* (f)
Exchange   *sirafa*
Expensive   *ghaly*
Gold   *dahab*

Felafel *ta'ameyya*
Fish *samak*
Food *akul*
Fruit *fak ha*
I would like... *a'yiz...* (m); *a'yza...* (f)
Juice *'aseer*
Meat *lahma*
Milk *laban*
Pepper *filfil*
Restaurant *mata'am*
Rice *roz*
Salad *salata*
Salt *malh*
Soup *shorba*
Sugar *sucar*
The check please *el hisab law samaht* (m); *samahty* (f)
Tea *shay*
Tip *baksheesh*
Vegetables *khodar*
Vegetarian *nabaty*
Water *maya*
Water pipe *shisha/sheesha*
Wine *nibeet*

Accommodation

Air conditioning *takeef*
Can I see a room? *Mumkin ashoof owda?*
Fan *marwaha*
Hotel *fondoq*
How much is a room? *Bikam el owda?*
Is breakfast included? *Fi iftar?*
Is there a bathroom? *Fi hamam?*
Room *oda*
Shower *doush*

Health

Aspirin *aspireen*
Diarrhea *is hal*
Doctor *dok-tor*
Fever *sokhoniya*
Hospital *mostashfa*
I feel sick *ana 'ayan* (m); *ana 'ayanna* (f)
I have a headache *'andy sod'a*
I have a stomache ache *andy maghas*
I'm allergic to *'andy hasasiya*
Medicine *dawa*
Pharmacy *saydaliya*

Useful words

Church *kineesa*
Clean *nadeef*
Cold *bard*
Desert *sahara*
Dirty *wisikh*
Hot *har*
Less *a'al*
More *aktar*
Mosque *gami'*
Mountain *gabal*
Museum *el mathaf*
River *nahr*
Sandstorm *khamaseen*
Sea *bahr*
Summer *seif*
Valley *wadi*
Winter *shita*

Who's who in Ancient Egypt

Kings and queens

Akhenaten

Amenhotep IV, who later took the name of Akhenaten, ruled for 15 years around 1379-1352 BC. He is remembered for the religious revolution he effected.

The authority of the priests of Amun-Re, the Sun God, the chief god of the Egyptians, had grown so great it almost rivalled that of the pharaohs. The pharaoh was regarded as the son of Amun-Re and was bound by strict religious ritual, part of a theological system understood clearly only by the priests, wherein lay their power.

Meanwhile a small religious cult was developing with the god Aten (a manifestation of the old sun-god Re of Memphis) at the centre, the sole god. This new cult appealed to the young prince and after he succeeded his father he changed his name to Akhenaten meaning 'it is well with the Aten' and moved his capital from Thebes to an entirely new city identified with the modern Tell El-Amarna, though no trace remains (see page XXX).

This idea of the sole god was new in Egypt, new in the world, and Akhenaten is known as the first real monotheist. There is no evidence that the new religion appealed to the mass of the people for while the king was deeply involved in his worship his empire fell into decay.

The new religious ideas were expressed in carvings. While the pharaoh as the son of god could not be portrayed and the queen rarely appeared at all in reliefs and statues, Akhenaten changed all the conventions and his artists represented him, and his wife and family, as they were, riding in chariots, bestowing gifts to his followers, even kissing.

When Akhenaten died at the age of 41, his half brother, Tutankhaton, a young boy, succeeded him. The Court returned to Thebes, the priests of Amen returned to power, the king changed his name to Tutankhamen (see page XXX) and everything possible was done to wipe out Akhenaten's 'heretical' religion.

Cheops

Cheops or Khufu was an Old Kingdom pharaoh, the second king of the fourth Dynasty succeeding his father Snefru. His mother was Queen Hetepheres. He reigned between 2549 BC and 2526 BC. He is well known as the builder of the Great Pyramid of Giza (see page XXX). He is recorded as having had four wives. Three names are given – Merityetes, Hen-utsen and Nefert-kau, one of whom was his sister/half-sister, and one queen is unnamed. For Merityetes and Hen-utsen there are smaller pyramids built beside his own.

Herodotus records his reign and that of his son Chephren (Khafre) as a century of misery and oppression under wicked and tyrannical kings but in Egyptian history he is considered to have been a wise ruler. Nevertheless, there certainly was misery. He shut all the temples and forbade the people to make sacrifices. At the same time he forced them to give up their livelihoods and assist in the construction of the pyramid being part of the team of a hundred thousand men who worked a three month shift. The preliminaries and actual construction took over 20 years. Part of the preparation was the construction of the oldest known paved road. Its purpose was to allow the huge granite facing blocks for his pyramid to be dragged and rolled to the site. Small fragments of the road exist today.

Cleopatra 69-30 BC

In 51 BC at the death of her father Ptolemy XIII she became joint ruler of Egypt with her younger brother. Three years later she was ousted from the throne but reinstated by Julius Caesar. It is related that while Julius Caesar was seated in a room in the citadel in Alexandria two slaves entered bearing a magnificent carpet. 'Cleopatra,

Queen of Egypt, begs you to accept this gift' said one and as the carpet unrolls out sprang the 19-year-old Cleopatra. Dazzled at the sight of such loveliness, so the tale goes, the stern warrior fell in with all her plans, helping her subdue her enemies and permanently dispose of her brother.

When the daggers of the conspirators at Rome removed Caesar's protection she turned her charms on Mark Antony. Called to his presence to answer charges of assisting his enemies she came, not as a penitent but in a barge of beaten gold, lying under a gold embroidered canopy and fanned by 'pretty dimpled boys'. This certainly caught his attention and conveniently forgetting his wife and duties in Rome he became her willing slave. While Cleopatra had visions of ruling in Rome as Antony's consort his enemies at Rome prevailed on the Senate to declare war on such a dangerous woman. The battle was fought at Actium in 31 BC but Cleopatra slipped away with her ships at the first opportunity leaving Antony to follow her as a hunted fugitive.

Cleopatra attempted to charm Octavian, Antony's conqueror, but he was made of sterner stuff and proof against her wiles. Antony killed himself and Cleopatra, proud and queenly to the last chose to die by the bite of a poisonous asp (an unsubstantiated fact), rather than be taken to Rome in chains. Certainly an eventful life for a woman who never reached her 40th birthday.

Hatshepsut

She was the first great woman in history living about 1503-1482 BC in the 18th Dynasty. She had immense power, adopted the full title of a pharaoh and was dressed in the full regalia down to the kilt and the false beard. She ruled for about 21 years.

She was the daughter of Tuthmosis I and Queen Ahmose and was married to her half brother Tuthmosis II who came to rule Egypt in 1512 at the death of his father. He was not very strong and at his death Hatshepsut, who had had no sons of her own, became the regent of his young son Tuthmosis III, son of a minor wife/woman in the harem. She took effective control of the government while pretending to be only the prince's regent and Tuthmosis III was made a priest of the god Amun.

Around 1503 she gave up all pretence of being subservient to her stepson and had herself crowned as pharaoh. To have reached this position and to retain it indicates the support of a number of faithful and influential officials in her government. Her steward Senenmut was well known and may have been the father of her daughter Neferure.

Determined to expand commercially she despatched (with Amun's blessing, she said) an impressive expedition to Punt on the African coast (now part of Somalia) from which were brought gold, ebony, animal skins, live baboons, processed myrrh and live myrrh trees to decorate her temple and that of Amun in Karnak. Tributes also flooded in from Libya, Nubia and the nearer parts of Asia.

In the name of/to honour the god Amun-Re (the main god of the region and her adopted 'father') she set about a huge reconstruction programme repairing damage caused to earlier temples and building new ones. The chapels to the Thebian Triad behind the Great Pylon of Ramses II at Luxor were built by Hatshepsut and Tuthmosis III. She renovated The Great Temple of Amun, at Karnak where she introduced four huge (30 m+) obelisks made of Aswan granite. At Beni Hasan she built a rock cut temple known as Speos Artemidos but her finest

achievement was her own beautiful temple on Luxor's West Bank cut into the rock at three different levels.

The wall reliefs in the temple fortified her position of importance, her divine birth which is a very complicated set of scenes involving the god Amun, her mother and herself as a baby; her selection as pharaoh by Hathor; her coronation by Hathor and Seth watched over by her real father, Tuthmosis I.

Her expedition to the exotic land of Punt is depicted in very great detail with pictures of the scenery (stilt houses) and selected incidents from the voyages (some baboons escaping on the rigging). Items brought back are offered to Amun in another relief. She even had depicted the huge barges used to transport the four obelisks she had erected for her adopted father (Amun) in Karnak.

To continue her position as a pharaoh even after her death she had her tomb cut in the Valley of the Kings. It was the longest and deepest in the valley.

Late in his reign Tuthmosis III turned against the memory of Hatshepsut and had all her images in the reliefs erased and replaced with figures of himself or the two preceding male pharaohs. In many places her cartouches have been rewritten too. Unfortunately he had all her statues destroyed.

Ramses III

Ramses III reigned from 1198-66 BC, in the 20th Dynasty, which was noted for the beginning of the great decline of Egypt. He was not part of the decline, however, and was considered a worthy monarch. He excelled himself in the earlier part of his reign with victories on land and victories at sea vanquishing the Cretans and the Carians. On land he used the military colonies established by previous rulers such as Ramses II and Seti I to conduct his missions further into Asia. He had little trouble subduing the tribes far into Asia but had problems nearer at home – having to fight to hold his position as pharaoh. A group of invaders made up of Libyans, Sardinians and Italians managed to advance as far as Memphis in the eighth year of his reign but their defeat put him in a much stronger position internally.

Having had his fill of expeditions to foreign parts, and no doubt having returned with sufficient booty to have made the trips worthwhile and make him a very wealthy monarch, he paid off his troops and set about adding to and constructing temples and other monumental works. Of particular note are the buildings at Medinet Habu (see page XXX). Here there is a magnificent temple with the walls covered in reliefs depicting the engagements on land and sea in which he had been so successful. Even the gate is inscribed with reliefs showing the despatch of prisoners and where a neat design on the pylons shows a cartouche of each vanquished country surmounted by a human head and with bound arms. This is a valuable historical record of Egypt and the surrounding lands at this time.

In brief he restored law and order within Egypt and provided some security from outside aggression. He revived commercial prosperity. His attentions to the temples of Thebes, Memphis and Heliopolis certainly enriched Egyptian architecture. He was, however, unable to turn the slow ebb of his country's grandeur that was said to be suffering from 'fundamental decadence'.

He was assassinated. Four sons, all bearing the his name, succeeded him but their reigns were not distinguished and the decline of Egypt was hastened.

Tutankhamen

Pharaoh of the New Kingdom, 18th Dynasty, Tutankhamen reigned from 1361-1352 BC. He was the son of Amenhotep III and probably his chief queen Tiy and was married to Akhenaten's daughter. He was too young to rule without a regent. He died in the ninth year of his reign at about 18 years of age, leaving no surviving children, his regent Ay succeeded him by marrying his widow.

He was originally called Tutankhaton but changed his name to Tutankhamen to distance himself from Atun and the cult of Atun worship of his half brother Amenhotep IV (Akhenaten). He moved his capital back to Memphis and to eradicate the effects of the rule of his predecessor he restored the temples and the status of the old gods and their priests. His greatest claim to fame was his intact tomb discovered by Howard Carter in 1922, details of which are given on page XXX.

Tuthmosis I – the trend setter

He was an 18th-Dynasty pharaoh who ruled from around 1525-1512 BC. He is noted for his expansion of the Egyptian Empire south into Nubia and east into present day Syria. He led a river-bourne expedition into Nubia to beyond the fourth Cataract (he was after the gold there) and set up a number of defensive forts along the route. His foray across the Euphrates was part of his campaign against the Hyksos who caused many problems for the Egyptians. Tuthmosis I used the Euphrates as the border over which he did not intend these enemies to cross.

He is also noted for the building and renovation works he contracted at Karnak. Much of the inner temple of Amun at Karnak is attributed to him. In particular the sandstone fourth Pylon in front of which one of his obelisks still stands, and the limestone fifth Pylon that marked the centre of the temple at the time, and behind which was the original position of the sanctuary of Tuthmosis I.

He was born in the era when burial in a pyramid was 'out of vogue' and being buried in a secret tomb in the rocks of the surrounding hillside was just coming 'in'. It is suggested that his tomb was the first in the Valley of the Kings and he certainly set a trend. His red quartzite sarcophagus was found in the tomb of his daughter Queen Hatshepsut and is now in the museum in Cairo.

Zoser

This was a king of the Old Kingdom, the second king of the 3rd Dynasty. It is hard to piece together his history. He succeeded his brother and perhaps reigned for 19 years between 2667-2648 BC. Two of his daughters were called Intkaes and Hetephernebti, their names taken from steales in the complex.

His funerary complex at Saqqara (see page XXX) is an example of some of the world's most ancient architecture and it was all, not only the Step Pyramid, but also the huge enclosure wall and the subsidiary temples and structures, designed by Zoser, under the charge of his talented architect/chancellor/physician Imhotep. This building was important being the first large scale building to be made completely of stone. In addition it was of an unusual stepped design. Many of the buildings in the surrounding complex were never intended for use but were replicas of the buildings used by the pharaoh on earth so that he could use them in eternity. Eventually hè was buried under his Step Pyramid. So what was the other tomb for in the complex? Perhaps it was for his entrails as it was too small for a royal person?

He made Memphis his capital, giving impetus to the growth in importance of this town, which eventually became the political and cultural centre.

Travellers interested in seeing his likeness must visit room 48 in the museum in Cairo. It has the huge seated figure of King Zoser taken from the complex.

Deities

There were hundreds of gods and goddesses worshipped by the ancient Egyptians. Over time some grew in favour and others became less important. In addition each district of the country had its own deities. It is useful to have an idea of their role in ancient Egypt and to recognize them on the wall paintings and carvings. They could be represented in more than one way, being different aspects of the same god.

Aker

An earth god often shown with the head of a lion, Aker guarded the east and west gates of the afterlife.

Amun

He was first worshipped as a local deity in Khmun in Middle Egypt in Hermopolis and later when his cult reached Thebes his importance spread to all of Egypt. He was believed to be the creator of all things, to order time and the seasons. When he sailed over the heavens he controlled the wind and the direction of the clouds. His name means 'the hidden' or 'unseen one'. At times he was identified with the sun-god Re, hence Amun-Re, and as Amun-Min was the god of fertility. He was often drawn as a human form with twisted ram horns

and two tall feathers as a headdress, a sceptre/crook in one hand and a ceremonial flail in the other, an erect phallus and a black pointed beard.

The sacred animals with which he was identified were the ram and the goose (the Great Cackler). As the ram-headed god he renewed the life in the souls of the departed. He was part of the Thebian Triad with Mut, his wife, and Khonsu, his adopted son.

Anubis

This god was responsible for the ritual of embalming and looking after the place where the mummification was done. Indeed he was reputed to have invented embalming, his first attempt of this art being on the corpse of Osiris. When Anubis was drawn on the wall on either side of a tomb's entrance the mummy would be protected. He helped Isis to restore life to Osiris. He was also included in scenes weighing the dead person's heart/soul against the 'feather of truth', which was the only way to enter the next world. In the earlier dynasties of the Old Kingdom he held an important position as lord of the dead but was later overshadowed by Osiris. Later he was better known simply as a conductor of souls. He was closely associated with Middle Egypt and bits of Upper Egypt. He was depicted as a recumbent black dog/fox/jackal or a jackal-headed god. On any illustration the ears of the creature were alertly pricked up and slightly forward. The association with a fox/jackal was the number of jackals that were to found in the cemeteries. Sometimes he was shown seated on a pylon.

Anukis

This was the wife of Khnum and the mother of Sartis, the third member of the Elephantine Triad. She was the goddess of the first cataract area and was depicted wearing a high crown of feathers and carrying a sceptre of papyrus plant.

Apis Bulls

The sacred bulls of Memphis were black bulls with a white triangle on the forehead and a crescent shape on the flank. A sacred bull was believed to contain the spirit of Ptah, lived in a palace and was guest of honour at state functions. When it died it was mummified and buried at the tomb of the Serapeum at Saqqara and a new younger bull, its reincarnation, took its place. It was sometimes represented with a sun disc between its horns.

Apophis

This was a symbol of unrest and chaos in the form of a large serpent. It was kept under control by the stronger powers of good, in particular the cat-goddess Bastet and by Sekhmet the fierce lioness god.

Aten

He was the sun-god depicted as the solar disc emitting bright rays that often terminated in human hands. For a time, under Akhenaton, worship of Aten was the state religion. He was considered the one true god. After the demise of Akhenaton he disappeared into obscurity.

Atum

This was one of the first forms of the sun-creator god. He was originally just a local deity of Heliopolis but joined with Re, as Atum-Re, he became more popular. Re took the part of the sun at the zenith and Atum that of the setting sun when it goes to the underworld. As this he was represented as a man, sometimes an old man, indicating the dying of the day.

Bastet

The famous cat goddess of the Delta region was the daughter of Re. She represented the power of the sun to ripen crops and was considered to be virile, strong and agile. Her home city was Bubastis (see page XXX) but her fame spread widely. She was initially a goddess of the home but in the religion of the New Kingdom she became associated with the lioness war goddess. She was regarded as a friendly deity – the goddess of joy.

She was represented as a woman with a cat's head, carried an ancient percussion instrument, the sistrum, in her right hand, a breast plate in her left hand and had a small bag hung over her left arm. Numerous small cat

figures were used in the home for worship or as amulets. Mummified cats (votive offerings) were buried in a vast cemetery at Bubastis. She was loosely connected with Mut and Sekhmet.

Bes

This was a strange creature, the god of dancing, merriment and music, and capable of playing many musical instruments. He was always portrayed as a jolly dwarf with a large head, a round face, round ears, goggle eyes, protruding tongue, sprouting lion's whiskers, which later became stylized as a fancy collar, under a tall headdress of feathers. He had short bow legs and a bushy tail. He was one of the few gods drawn front face on rather than in profile.

It is suggested his hideousness

was to drive away evil spirits and hence pain and sorrow. As the guardian of women and children he kept the house free from snakes and evil spirits. He was portrayed on vases, mirrors, perfume jars and other toilet articles and even on the pillows of mummies. He was frequently represented in birth houses as the guardian of women in childbirth.

Buto

This deity, also known as Wadjet, was a cobra goddess whose fame spread from the Delta to all of Lower Egypt. She was known as the green goddess (the colour of papyrus) and was said to be responsible for the burning heat of the sun.

Geb/Shu/Nut

These members of the Heliopolitan ennead are frequently depicted together. Geb (god of the earth), son of Shu (god of the air or emptiness), was married to his sister Nut (goddess of the sky). The sun-god Re was displeased with this association, although most gods seem to marry their sisters, and ordered Shu to keep the two apart. Hence all three are represented together with Shu between Geb's green recumbent form and Nut arching in the sky.

Geb

As explained, this was the god of the earth, the physical support of the world. Along with his sister/wife Nut he was part of the second generation ennead of Heliopolis. He was usually drawn as a man without any

distinguishing characteristics though he sometimes had the head of a goose which was distinguishing enough. He could be also be depicted as a bull in contrast to Nut's cow. His recumbent form mentioned above represented the hills and valleys and the green colour the plants growing there.

He was the cause of the bitter quarrel between Osiris and his brother Seth for at his retirement he left them both to rule the world. Hence the famous myth.

Hapi/Hapy

He was the god who lived next to the river because he controlled the level of Nile and was responsible for the floods. He was even responsible for the dew that fell at night. He was represented as a bearded man with a female breast wearing a bunch of papyrus on his head and carrying offerings or leading a sacrifice. There was an association here with Apis.

There was another god Hapi who was one of the sons of Horus, the baboon headed guardian of the Canopic jar of the lungs.

Harpokrates

This was the name given to Horus as a child. In illustrations he was a naked child with a finger in his mouth. The side lock of hair he wore is an indication of youth.

Hathor

This was the goddess of the sky who was also known as the golden one. Her name means 'castle of the sky-god Horus'. She was a goddess of festivity, love and dance. The original centre of her cult was Dendara and her importance spread to Thebes and Memphis. With the increase in her fame and contrary to her earlier nature she became known as a goddess of the dead and the region of the dead. She was believed to have

been responsible for nearly destroying all mankind. On illustrations she was represented as a cow, a cow-headed woman or a woman with a headdress of a disc between two horns and large cow-like ears.

Heh

This lesser known god can be seen kneeling holding a palm branch notched with the number of the years in a king's life.

Heqet

This was a frog goddess who sometimes assisted at childbirth.

Horus

Horus was a very important god, the falcon-headed sky god. Horus means 'he who is far above' and the hawk fits this image. Hence he was depicted as hawk-headed or even a full hawk often wearing the double crown of Egypt. The hawk's eyes are thought of as the sun and the moon. Horus' left eye was damaged in his conflict with Seth and this was thought to indicate the waxing and waning of the moon. He probably originated in the Delta region and the cult spread to all of Egypt. It was only later that he became associated with Isis and Osiris as their son.

Imhotep

He was a man, one of two mortals (the other was Amenhotep) who were totally deified. He was recorded as the designer of the first temple at Edfu and the official architect of Zoser's step pyramid. When he was later deified it was as a god of healing and made the honorary son of Ptah. He was known, not as a temple builder, but, as a patron of scribes, a healer, a sage and a magician, and was worshipped as a god of medicine. He was considered to have been a physician of considerable skill.

At the time of the Persian conquest he was elevated to the position of a deity. His cult reached its peak in Greaco-Roman times where his temples at Memphis and on the island of Philae in the Nile were often crowded with unhealthy people who slept there hoping that a cure for their problems would be revealed to them in their dreams. He was depicted on wall illustrations as a seated man holding an open papyrus.

Isis

She was one of the most important ancient Egyptian goddesses, the most popular goddess in Egypt from around AD 650 right up to the introduction of Christianity. Originally the cult was in Lower Egypt but it spread to embrace eventually the whole of Egypt and parts of Nubia. Her name means 'throne' and because the word throne is feminine it was depicted by a woman's figure. This made her the mother of the king who sat on the throne. She receives a number of mentions as the grieving widow of Osiris. She was also the sister of Osiris, Seth and Nephthys.

She was held in high esteem as the perfect wife and mother and became the goddess of protection. She was also an enchantress, using

her power to bring Osiris back to life again. She was represented as a woman with the hieroglyph sign for a throne on her head, an orb or sun between two horns, and was generally sitting nursing her son Horus, or seen also kneeling at a coffin of Osiris. Her ability to give life to the dead meant she was the chief deity at all funerals.

There are temples to her at Dendara, on Philae and in the Nile Delta. Several temples were dedicated to her in Alexandria where she was the patroness of seafarers. She was guardian of the Canopic jar that held the viscera.

Khepri

He was the sun-god represented as a scarab beetle with a sun disc. As the scarab beetle rolls a ball of dung around so the Egyptians thought this was how the sun was moved. They thought the scarab possessed remarkable powers and used it as an amulet.

Khnum

He was represented on wall drawings as a man with a ram's head with long twisted horns. The Egyptians believed he made the first man by moulding him in clay from the Nile on a potter's wheel. Over time his area of responsibility changed. He lived at the first cataract on the Nile where he presided over all the cataracts of the Nile. He had the authority to decide whether or not the god Hapi 'rose' and the Nile flooded. He was associated with temples at Elephantine and Esna.

Khonsu

He was regarded as the son of Amun and Mut. The three made up the Thebian Triad. He had the ability to cast a range of spells, dispel demons and act as an oracle. He travelled through the sky at night and sometimes assisted the scribe of the gods. As the moon god he was usually represented as a man wearing a disc of the full moon and horns on his head or the head of a falcon. He had a single lock of hair to show his youth.

Ma'at

This well loved deity was the goddess of order, truth and justice. She was the daughter of the sun-god Re and Thoth the goddess of wisdom. She can be seen at the ceremony of judgement, the balancing of the heart of the deceased against a feather. The scale was balanced by Ma'at or her ideogram, the single ostrich feather as a test of truthfulness. The priests with her were judges. She often appears, confusingly, as two identical goddesses, a case of double judgement. She was very popular with the other gods. She was also depicted on wall paintings in the solar barque.

Mertseger

This was the goddess of the west, a cobra goddess from Thebes. She was said to punish those who did not come up to scratch with illness or even death.

Min

This was the god of sexual prowess, of fertility and of good harvests. He was depicted bearded, wearing a crown of two feathers, phallus erect, a ceremonial flail in his raised right hand and a ribbon from his headdress reaching down to the ground at the back. He was worshipped at Luxor. His feast day was an important festival often associated with wild orgies. He was worshipped too as the guardian of travellers as he protected the routes to the Red Sea and in the Eastern Desert. The lettuce was his sacred plant.

Montu

The war god Montu who rose to importance in the 11th Dynasty protected the king in battle. He has a temple to the north of the main temple in Karnak. His image was hawk-headed with a sun disc between two plumes.

Mut

She was originally a very ancient vulture goddess of Thebes but during the 18th Dynasty was married to the god Amun and with their adopted son Khonsu made up the Thebian Triad. The marriage of Amun and Mut was a reason for great annual celebrations in Thebes. Her role as mistress of the heavens or as sky goddess often had her appearing as a cow, standing behind her husband as he rose from the primeval sea Nu to his place in the heavens. More often she was represented with a double crown of Egypt on her head, a vulture's head or lioness' head on her forehead. Another role was as a great divine mother. She has a temple south of the main temple at Karnak.

Nefertum

He was one of the Memphis deities most often associated with perfumes. He was represented as a man with a lotus flower on his head.

Neith

The goddess of weaving, war and hunting, among other things. She was also protector of the dead and the Canopic jars. She wore a red crown of Lower Egypt and a shield on her head (sometimes held in her hand), held two crossed arrows and an ankh in her hand. She was connected with Sobek and was worshipped at Memphis, Esna and Fayoum.

Nekhbet

In her more important guise she was the vulture or serpent goddess, protectress of Upper Egypt and especially of its rulers. She was generally depicted with spreading wings held over the pharaoh while grasping in her claw the royal ring or other emblems. She always appeared as a woman, sometimes with a vulture's head and always wearing a white crown. Her special colour was white, in contrast to her counterpart Buto (red) who was the goddess of Lower Egypt. In another aspect she was worshipped as goddess of the Nile and consort of the river god. She was associated too with Mut.

Nephthys

Her name was translated as 'lady of the house'. She was the sister of Seth, Osiris and Isis. She was married to Seth. She had no children by her husband but a son, Anubis, by Osiris. She wears the hieroglyphs of her name on her head. She was one of the protector guardians of the Canopic jars and a goddess of the dead.

Nut

She was goddess of the sky, the vault of the heavens. She was wife/sister of Geb. The Egyptians believed that on five special days preceding the new year she gave birth on successive days to the deities Osiris, Horus, Seth, Isis and Nephthys. This was cause for great celebrations. She was usually depicted as a naked woman arched over Shu who supported her with upraised arms. She was also represented wearing a water pot or pear shaped vessel on her head, this being the hieroglyph of her name. Sometimes she was depicted as a cow, so that she could carry the sun-god Re on her back to the sky. The cow was usually spangled with stars to represent the night sky. It was supposed that the cow swallowed the sun that journeyed through her body during the night to emerge at sunrise. This was also considered a symbol of resurrection.

Osiris

This was one of the most important gods in ancient Egypt, the god of the dead, the god of the underworld and the god of plenty. He had the power to control the vegetation (particularly cereals because he began his career as a corn deity) that sprouted after the annual flooding of the Nile. He originated in the Delta at Busiris and it is suggested that he was once a real ruler. His importance spread to the whole of Egypt.

Annual celebrations included the moulding of a clay body in the shape of Osiris, filled with soil and containing seeds. This was moistened with water from the Nile and the sprouting grain symbolized the strength of Osiris. One of the main celebrations in the Temple at Abydos was associated with Osiris

and it was fashionable to be buried or have a memorial on the processional road to Abydos and so absorb the blessing of Osiris. There are temples dedicated to Osiris at Edfu and on Bigah Island opposite Philae.

According to ancient Egyptian custom when a king and later any person died he became Osiris and thus through him mankind had some hope of resurrection. The Apis bull at Memphis also represented Osiris. The names Osiris-apis and Sarapis are derived from this.

He was shown as a mummy with his arm crossed over his breast, one hand holding a royal crook the other a ceremonial flail. These crook and flail sceptres on his portraits and statues showed he was god of the underworld. He wore a narrow plaited beard and the white crown of Upper Egypt and two red feathers.

Ptah

He was originally the local deity of the capital Memphis and his importance eventually spread over the whole of Egypt. He was very popular at Thebes and Abydos. He was worshipped as the creator of the gods of the Memphite theology. Ptah was the husband of Sekhmet and father of Nefertum. Only later was he associated with Osiris. He was the patron of craftsmen, especially sculptors. He was renowned for his skill as an engineer, stonemason, metal worker and artist.

He was always shown in human form, mummified or swathed in a winding sheet, with a clean shaven human head. He would be holding a staff and wearing an amulet. The Apis bull had its stall in the great temple of Ptah in Memphis.

Qebehsenuf

The falcon headed guardian of the Canopic jar of the intestines was the son of Horus.

Re

This was the sun-god of Heliopolis and the supreme judge. He was the main god at the time of the New Kingdom. His importance was great. His cult centre was Heliopolis and the cult reached the zenith in the fifth Dynasty when he had become the official god of the pharaohs and every king was both the son of Re and Re incarnate.

Re was the god who symbolized the sun. He appeared in many aspects and was portrayed in many different ways. He was found in conjunction with other gods Re-Horakhte, Amun-Re, Min-Re etc. As Amun-Re (Amun was the god from Thebes) he was king of the gods and responsible for the pharaoh on military campaigns where he handed the scimitar of conquest to the great warriors. Re was king and father of the gods and the creator of mankind. It was believed that after death, the pharaoh in his barge joined Re in the heavens.

He was thought to travel across the sky each day in his solar boat and during the night make his passage in the underworld in another boat. He was represented as man with a hawk or falcon's head wearing a sun disc or if dead with a ram's head.

Sekhmet

This was another aspect of the goddess Hathor. Sekhmet the consort of Ptah was a fierce goddess of war and the destroyer of the enemies of her father the sun-god

Re. She was usually depicted as a lioness or as a woman with a lion's head on which was placed the solar disc and the uraeus. She was also

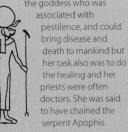

the goddess who was associated with pestilence, and could bring disease and death to mankind but her task also was to do the healing and her priests were often doctors. She was said to have chained the serpent Apophis.

Selket

This was one of the four goddesses who protected the sources of the Nile. As the guardian of the dead she was portrayed often with a scorpion on her head. She was put in charge of the bound serpent Apophis in the underworld.

Seshat

Seshat was shown as a woman with a seven-point star on her head, and dressed in a panther skin. She was the goddess of writing and of recording the years. She carried a palm leaf on which she wrote her records.

Seth

Seth did not begin with such bad press. He was in favour in the 19th Dynasty especially in the Eastern Delta around Tanis but by the Late Period he was considered evil and on some monuments his image was effaced. By the Christian era he was firmly in place as the devil. The Egyptians thought Seth, who was the brother of Osiris, Isis and Nephthys, tried to prevent the sun from rising each dawn. As such an enemy of

mankind they represented him as a huge serpent-dragon. He was sometimes depicted as a hippopotamus and sometimes took the form of a crocodile as he did to avoid the avenging Horus. More often he was depicted as an unidentified animal, a greyhound, dog, pig, ass, okapi, anteater or a man with the head of an animal. The head had an unusual long down curved snout and the ears were upstanding and square-tipped. The eyes were slanting and the tail long and forked. He was also seen in drawings standing at the prow of the sun-god's boat.

Shu

He and his twin sister and wife Tefnut were created by the sun-god Re by his own power without the aid of a woman. They were the first couple of the ennead of Heliopolis. He was father of Geb the earth god and Nut the sky goddess. He was the representation of air and emptiness, of light and space, the supporter of the sky.

He was portrayed in human form with the hieroglyph of his name, an ostrich feather on his head. Often he was drawn separating Geb and Nut, for their union was not approved of by Re.

Sobek

He was known as the crocodile god, protector of reptiles and of kings. Crocodile gods were common in Fayoum, mainly at the time of the Middle Kingdom and also at Esna and Kom Ombo. Live crocodiles at the temples were believed to be this god incarnate and accordingly were treated very well.

These sacred crocodiles were pampered and bejewelled and kept in a lake before the temples. After death they were mummified. Confusingly he was usually depicted with Amun's crown of rams' horns and feathers.

Taweret

This upright pregnant hippopotamus had pendant human breasts, lion's paws and a crocodile's tail.

Sometimes she wore the horns of Hathor with a solar disc. She was also known as Apet/Opet. She was the goddess of childbirth and attended both royal births and the daily rebirth of the sun. She was a goddess at Esna.

Tefnut

She was the wife/sister of Shu, the lion-headed goddess of moisture and dew, one of the Heliopolitan ennead.

Thoth

His cult originated in the Nile Delta and was then mainly centred in Upper Egypt. He was held to be the inventor of writing, founder of social order, creator of languages, patron of scribes, interpreter and adviser to the gods, and representative of the sun-god Re on earth. He gave the Egyptians knowledge of medicine and mathematics. He possessed a book in which all the wisdom of the world was recorded. In another aspect he was known as the moon god. He was also associated with the birth of the earth.

Thoth protected Isis during her pregnancy and healed the injury to

Horus inflicted by Seth. He too was depicted in the feather/heart weighing judgement ceremonies of the diseased and as the scribe reported the results to Osiris. His sacred animals were the ibis and the baboon. Numerous mummified bodies of these two animals were found in cemeteries in Hermopolis and Thebes. He was usually represented as a human with an ibis' head. The curved beak of the ibis was like the crescent moon so the two were connected and the ibis became the symbol of the moon god Thoth.

Wepwawet
He was the jackal-headed god of Middle Egypt, especially popular in the Assiut region. He was know as 'the opener of the ways'.

Glossary

A

Abbasids Muslim Dynasty ruled from Baghdad 750-1258
Agora Market/meeting place
Aïd/Eïd Festival
Aïn Spring
Almohads Islamic Empire in North Africa 1130-1269
Amir Mamluk military officer
Amulet Object with magical power of protection
Ankh Symbol of life
Apis bull A sacred bull worshipped as the living image of Ptah
Arabesque Geometric pattern with flowers and foliage used in Islamic designs

B

Bab City gate
Bahri North/northern
Baladiyah Municipality
Baksheesh Money as alms, tip or bribe
Baraka Blessing
Barbary Name of North Africa 16th-19th centuries
Basha See Pasha
Basilica Imposing Roman building, with aisles, later used for worship
Bazaar Market
Bedouin Nomadic desert Arab
Beni Sons of (tribe)
Berber Indigenous tribe of North Africa
Bey Governor (Ottoman)
Borj Fort
Burnous Man's cloak with hood – tradional wear

C

Caid Official
Calèche Horse-drawn carriage
Canopic jars Four jars for storing the organs of the mummified deceased
Capital Top section of a column
Caravanserai Lodgings for travellers and animals around a courtyard
Cartouche Oval ring containing a king's name in hieroglyphics
Chechia Man's small red felt hat
Chotts Low-lying salt lakes
Colossus Gigantic statue

D

Dar House
Darj w ktaf Carved geometric motif of intersecting arcs with super-imposed rectangles
Deglet Nur High quality translucent date
Delu Water-lifting device at top of well
Dey Commander (of janissaries)
Dikka Raised platform in mosque for Koramic readings
Djemma Main or Friday mosque
Djin Spirit
Dólmenes Prehistoric cave
Dour Village settlement

E

Eïd See Aïd
Eïn See Aïn
Erg Sand dune desert

F

Faqirs Muslim committed to a vow of poverty
Fatimids Muslim dynasty AD 909-1171 claiming descent from Mohammed's daughter Fatimah
Fatwa Islamic district
Fellaheen Peasants
Felucca Sailing boat on Nile
Fondouk/Funduq Lodgings for goods and animals around a courtyard
Forum Central open space in Roman town
Fuul Fava beans

G

Gallabiyya Outer garment with sleeves and a hood – often striped
Garrigue Poor quality Mediterranean scrubland
Gymnasium Roman school for mind and body

H

Haikal Altar area
Hallal Meat from animals killed in accordance with Islamic law
Hamada Stone desert
Hammam Bath house

Harem Women's quarters
Harira Soup
Hypogeum The part of the building below ground, underground chamber

I

Iconostasis Wooden screen supporting icons
Imam Muslim religious leader

J

Jabal See Jebel
Jami' Mosque
Janissaries Elite Ottoman soldiery
Jarapas Rough cloth made with rags
Jebel Mountain
Jihad Holy war by Muslims against non-believers

K

Ka Spirit
Khedivate The realm of Mohammed Ali and his successors
Kilim Woven carpet
Kif Hashish
Kissaria Covered market
Koubba Dome on tomb of holy man
Kufic Earliest style of Arabic script
Kuttab Korami school for young boys or orphans

L

Lintel Piece of stone over a doorway
Liwan Vaulted arcade
Loculus Small compartment or cell, recess

M

Mahboub Coins worn as jewellery
Malekite Section of Sunni Islam
Malqaf Wind vent
Maquis Mediterranean scrubland – often aromatic
Marabout Muslim holy man/his tomb
Maristan Hospital
Mashrabiyya Wooden screen
Mastaba Tomb
Mausoleum Large tomb building

Medresa School usually attached to a mosque
Médina Old walled town, residential quarter
Mellah Jewish quarter of old town
Menzel House
Mihrab Recess in wall of mosque indicating direction of Mecca
Minaret Tower of mosque from which the muezzin calls the faithful to prayer
Minbar Pulpit in a mosque
Mosque Muslim place of worship
Moulid Religious festival
Moussem Religious gathering
Muezzin Priest who calls the faithful to prayer
Mullah Muslim religious teacher
Murabtin Dependent tribe

N

Necropolis Cemetery
Noas Shrine or chapel
Nome District or province

O

Oasis Watered desert gardens
Obelisk Tapering monolithic shaft of stone with pyramidal apex
Ostraca Inscribed rock flakes and potsherds
Ottoman Muslim Empire based in Turkey 13th-20th centuries
Ouled Tribe
Outrepassé Horse-shoe shaped arch

P

Papyrus (papyri) Papers used by Ancient Egyptians
Pasha Governor
Phoenicians Important trading nation based in eastern Mediterranean from 1100 BC
Pilaster Square column partly built into, partly projecting from, the wall
Pisé Sun-baked clay used for building
Piste Unsurfaced road
Pylon Gateway of Egyptian temple
Pyramidion A small pyramid shaped cap stone for the apex of a pyramid

Q

Qarafah Graveyard
Qibla Mosque wall in direction of Mecca

R

Rabbi Head of Jewish community
Ramadan Muslim month of fasting
Reg Rock desert
Ribat Fortified monastery
Riwaq Arcaded aisle

S

Sabil Public water fountain
Sabkha Dry salt lake
Saggia Water canal
Sahel Coast/coastal plain
Sahn Courtyard
Salat Worship
Saqiya Water wheel
Sarcophagus Decorated stone coffin
Sebkha See Sabkha
Semi-columnar Flat on one side and rounded on the other
Serais Lodging for men and animals
Serir Sand desert
Shadoof Water lifting device
Shahada Profession of faith
Shawabti Statuette buried with deceased, designed to work in the hereafter for its owner
Shergui Hot, dry desert wind
Sidi Saint
Souk Traditional market
Stalactite An ornamental arrangement of multi-tiered niches, like a honeycomb, found in domes and portrals
Stele Inscribed pillar used as gravestone
Suani Small, walled irrigated traditional garden
Sufi Muslim mystic
Sunni Orthodox Muslims

T

Tagine/tajine Meat stew
Taifa Sub-tribe
Tariqa Brotherhood/Order
Thòlos Round building, dome, cupola

Triclinium A room with benches on three sides
Troglodyte Underground/cave dweller

U

Uraeus Rearing cobra symbol, sign of kingship

V

Vandals Ruling empire in North Africa 429-534 AD
Vizier Governor

W

Wadi Water course, usually dry
Waqf Endowed land
Wikala Merchants' hostel
Wilaya/wilayat Governorate/district

Z

Zaouia/zawia/zawiya Shrine/ Sennusi centre
Zellij Geometrical mosaic pattern made from pieces of glazed tiles
Zeriba House of straw/grass

Index

A

B

C

Index

Tread your

Footprint Lifestyle guides

Books to inspire and plan some of the world's most compelling travel experiences. Written by experts and presented to appeal to popular travel themes and pursuits.

A great book to have on your shelves when planning your next European escapade
Sunday Telegraph

Footprint Activity guides

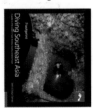   

These acclaimed guides have broken new ground, bringing together adventure sports and activities with relevant travel content, stunningly presented to help enthusiasts get the most from their pastimes.

This guide is as vital as a mask and fins.
David Espinosa, Editor of Scuba Diver Australasia

own path

Footprint Travel guides

For travellers seeking out off-the-beaten-track adventures. Rich with places and sights and packed with expertly researched travel information, activities and cultural insight.

Footprint can be depended on for accurate travel information and for imparting a deep sense of respect for the lands and people they cover
World News

Available from all good bookshops or online

 footprintbooks.com